LIFE – SPAN
DEVELOPMENTAL PSYCHOLOGY

Intergenerational Relations

LIFE – SPAN
DEVELOPMENTAL PSYCHOLOGY.

Intergenerational Relations

Edited by

Nancy Datan
University of Wisconsin – Green Bay

Anita L. Greene
West Virginia University

Hayne W. Reese
West Virginia University

LEA LAWRENCE ERLBAUM ASSOCIATES, PUBLISHERS
1986   Hillsdale, New Jersey   London

Lawrence Erlbaum Associates, Inc., Publishers
365 Broadway
Hillsdale, New Jersey 07642

Library of Congress Cataloging-in-Publication Data
Main entry under title:

Life-span developmental psychology.

Proceedings of the Ninth West Virginia University
Conference on Life-Span Developmental Psychology held
in Morgantown on May 10–12, 1984.
Includes bibliographies and index.
1. Developmental psychology — Congresses. 2. Intergenerational relations — Congresses. I. Datan, Nancy.
II. Greene, Anita L. III. Reese, Hayne, Waring,
1931–   . IV. West Virginia University Conference
on Life-Span Developmental Psychology (9th : 1984)
[DNLM: 1. Family — congresses. 2. Human Development —
congresses. 3. Interpersonal Relations — congresses.
4. Psychology — congresses. WS 105.5.F2 L722 1984]
BF712.5.L52 1986   155   85-16172
ISBN 0-89859-536-3

Printed in the United States of America
10   9   8   7   6   5   4   3   2   1

Contents

Salutogenic and Pathogenic Processes

List of Contributors

Aaron Antonovsky Ph.D., Ben-Gurion University of the Negev, Beer Sheva, Israel

Vern Bengston Ph.D., Andrus Gerontology Center, University of Southern California

Andrew M. Boxer Ph.D., Michael Reese Hospital, Chicago, IL

Bertram Cohler Ph.D., Committee on Human Development, University of Chicago; and Michael Reese Hospital

Judith Cook Ph.D., Committee on Human Development, University of Chicago

Catherine E. Cross Ph.D., Carolina Population Center, University of North Carolina, Chapel Hill

Nancy Datan Ph.D., Human Development Program, University of Wisconsin – Green Bay

Geraldine Downey Ph.D., Department of Human Development and Family Studies, Cornell University

Charlotte Dunham Ph.D., Andrus Gerontology Center, University of North Carolina, Chapel Hill

Anita L. Greene Ph.D., Department of Psychology, West Virginia University

Shirley J. Hatchett Ph.D., Institute for Social Research, University of Michigan

Marjorie P. Honzik Ph.D., Institute of Human Development, University of California, Berkeley

James Jackson Ph.D., Institute for Social Research, University of Michigan

Corinne N. Nydegger Ph.D., Medical Anthropology Program, University of California School of Medicine, San Francisco

Eloise Rathbone-McCuan Ph.D., Department of Special Education, University of Vermont

Dean Rodeheaver Ph.D., Human Development Program, University of Wisconsin – Green Bay

Jeanne Thomas Ph.D., Behavioral Science Division, University of Wisconsin – Parkside, Kenosha

Preface

This volume contains the papers presented at the ninth biennial West Virginia University conference on life-span development. The conference was held in Morgantown on May 10–12, 1984, and the topic was designated as "Intergenerational Networks: Families in Context."

One of the themes discernible in the present volume is illustrated fictionally in Samuel Butler's (1902) novel, *The Way of All Flesh*. In this novel, the character Theobold Pontifex had been raised by a harsh father but believed he would be more lenient toward his own son than his father had been toward him. However, he also believed, as had his father, that he must be on guard against being too indulgent, "for no duty could be more important than that of teaching a child to obey its parents in all things" (p. 87). Theobold was unable to break the mold imposed on him by his father. In one incident in the novel, Theobold thrashed his son, Ernest, for deliberately — as Theobold thought — mispronouncing "come" as "tum."

The theme of intergenerational similarity in Butler's novel is confirmed by evidence contained in the chapters herein by Dunham and Bengtson and by Honzik. The six-generation family mentioned by Dunham and Bengtson is a striking example. (A point that is perhaps historically noteworthy but is not otherwise relevant here is that Butler believed intergenerational similarity has an hereditary basis — the inheritance of acquired characteristics as proposed by Charles Darwin's grandfather Erasmus Darwin and, later, by Lamarck.)

Another theme in the conference is exemplified by a tribe of African pygmies, The Mbuti (Turnbull, 1978). Among the Mbuti, the transitions from childhood to youth and from youth to adulthood are *ekimi* (quiet). However, adulthood is not *ekimi*. It is a prolonged transition to elderhood and as such it is *akami* (disturbed). If too much *akami* occurs, the adult becomes *wazi-wazi* (disoriented and unpredictable); but the youth are accorded the power to revise the values of society, to shape the future, in order to deal with *akami*. This role reversal — sought so violently by the American youth of the 1960s — is all the more striking because of the ages involved among the Mbuti. Among the Mbuti, a person leaves childhood and enters youth between 8 or 9 to 11 years of age and leaves youth and enters adulthood at marriage 6 to 7 years later. Elderhood begins when fertility ends. The youth, who control society's values and future, are adolescents 14 to 18 years old. In the 1960s in America, the youth who sought this power were college-aged, about 18 to 22 years old, but an intriguing implication of the cross-cultural similarity should not be overlooked: The American youth of the 1960s were reacting against the *akami* of middle-aged, middle-class America and its elected government.

Although cross-cultural research of the sort implied in this comparison was not represented at the ninth life-span conference, the conference participants represented an interdisciplinary range. The conference and its proceedings thereby reflected a trend evident within the series of West Virginia University conferences on life-span development: The early conferences brought together psychologists and professionals from closely related disciplines, and the later conferences brought together psychologists, anthropologists, gerontologists, historians, psychiatrists, social workers, sociologists, and others. This trend — initiated at the fourth life-span conference (Datan & Ginsberg, 1975) and reintroduced at the eighth conference (McCluskey & Reese, 1984) — was paralleled by another trend: The early conferences in the series were mostly theoretical, the later ones mostly empirical. The earliest contributors represented the fields of child development and gerontology rather than the life-span; later contributors more often represented the life-span. The field of life-span development, in other words, is no longer merely a blueprint for the development of interdisciplinary knowledge; it has become a *domain* of interdisciplinary knowledge, an empirical realization of the definition of life-span developmental science as interdisciplinary.

One bit of evidence on the importance of the topic of intergenerational relations — the specific topic of the ninth conference — is that among the 355 life events examined by Reese and Smyer (1983) in a paper presented at the seventh conference (Callahan & McCluskey, 1983), 24.6% referred to inter-generational relations, all intrafamilial and exclusive of spousal relations. Thus, these relations constitute a significant proportion of events that have been considered sufficiently important to warrant study. Many of the relevant studies have been done outside the discipline of psychology, and these disciplines were represented at the conference — and are represented in these conference proceedings.

The 11 papers presented at the ninth conference are organized into three groups: "Theoretical and Methodological Issues," "Intergenerational Relations and Change," and "Salutogenic and Pathogenic Processes." The first group contains papers on general theoretical issues, their roots in Greek mythology and tragedy, and methodological issues; the second group contains papers on familial and societal roles in individual development; and the third group contains papers on the transmission of order and disorder in individual development.

REFERENCES

Butler, S. (1902). *The way of all flesh.* In *The works of Samuel Butler* (Shrewsbury Edition, Vol. 17). New York: AMS Press.

Callahan, E. J., & McCluskey, K. A. (Eds.). (1983). *Life-span developmental psychology: Nonnormative life events.* New York: Academic Press.

Datan, N., & Ginsberg, L. H. (Eds.). (1975). *Life-span developmental psychology: Normative life crises.* New York: Academic Press.

McCluskey, K. A., & Reese, H. W. (Eds.). (1984). *Life-span developmental psychology: Historical and generational effects.* New York: Academic Press.

Reese, H. W., & Smyer, M. (1983). The dimensionalization of life events. In E. C. Callahan & K. A. McCluskey (Eds.), *Life-span developmental psychology: Nonnormative life events* (pp. 1–33). New York: Academic Press.

Turnbull, C. M. (1978). The politics of non-aggression. In A. Montagu (Ed.), *Learning non-aggression* (pp. 161–221). New York: Oxford University Press.

Acknowledgments

The success of the ninth West Virginia University Conference on Life-Span Developmental Psychology was facilitated by many persons. Thomas J. Knight, Dean of the College of Arts and Sciences, helped in providing university funds. Kathleen A. McCluskey, Chair of the Department of Psychology, generously provided departmental funds and resources and was involved in the early planning stages. Carrie M. Koeturius, Manager of the West Virginia University Conference Services, skillfully managed the production details of the conference. E. Gordon Gee, President of West Virginia University, warmly welcomed the conference participants. Special thanks are due the graduate students in developmental psychology at West Virginia University, who worked with the co-chairs from the beginning of the planning to well past the end of the conference: Carolyn Adams, Donna Barre, Joan Beard, Jodene Brooks, Jeffrey Coldren, Nancy Meck, Rosellen Rosich, and Pamela Kochanevich-Wallace. Our secretaries, Ann Davis and Michelle Nichols, devoted much skill and many hours to every phase of the project, and we gratefully acknowledge their assistance.

THEORETICAL AND METHODOLOGICAL ISSUES

1 Conceptual and Theoretical Perspectives on Generational Relations

Charlotte Chorn Dunham
Vern L. Bengtson
University of Southern California

INTRODUCTION

The problem of generations, particularly for behavioral scientists, involves a complex and multifaceted intellectual agenda. The central issue concerns "social consequences of the succession of age groups – through birth, aging, death, and replacement – upon social organization and behavior" (Bengtson, Cutler, Mangen, & Marshall, 1985, p. 304). Concern about the problem is certainly not new; nor are attempts to disentangle the causes and consequences of change and continuity in the context of generational succession. What may be new are the tools contemporary social scientists have begun to utilize in examining the problem of generations.

In 1971, at one of the very first West Virginia University Conferences on Life-Span Development, the general theme addressed personality and socialization (see Baltes & Schaie, 1973). In one of the presentations, the second author of this chapter (at that time a very junior professor and very happy to have been invited) attempted to consolidate the available research evidence concerning generations, intergenerational relations, and socialization. That paper (Bengtson & Black, 1973) was built around two central themes. First, a major agenda of socialization concerns the creation of family continuity: an ongoing reciprocal process involving negotiations between parents and children. Socialization involves "an interactional confrontation between developing individuals, in which those factors leading to continuity and those leading to change are negotiated" (Bengtson & Black, 1973 p. 103). Second, it was argued that to adequately characterize variables involved in such intergenerational negotiation, two levels of time (developmental and historical) and two levels of social structure (the microstructure of the family and the macrolevel of the broader society) must be considered. The concept of "generation" can be decomposed into its constituent elements to take into account the multiple levels of time and social structure involved in problems of succession.

Since that time, over a decade ago, a number of empirical and conceptual analyses have focused on the problem of generations from a variety of perspectives (Bengtson, 1975; Bengtson & Troll, 1978; Berger, 1984; Elder, 1984; Garms-Holmova, Hoerning & Schaffer, 1984; Hagestad, 1981, 1984; Kertzer, 1983; Marshall, 1984). As a result of such analyses, we are coming to a much broader appreciation of the manner in which age groups relate to other elements of social structure, and the manner in which generations negotiate with each other in the ongoing process of socialization. In this chapter we review some relevant conceptual and theoretical perspectives that should be considered when examining issues of generations and intergenerational relations. Much has changed since the 1971 West Virginia University Conference on Life Span Development, yet many of the central concerns and issues discussed then have remained salient.

The central argument of this chapter can be summarized as follows: (a) we need to employ multiple concepts, each clearly defined in order to adequately characterize relations between generations; (b) we need to link the study of intergenerational relations in the family with broader theoretical perspectives in psychology and sociology.

In the first section, we discuss key concepts in the analysis of generations and review various ways in which the term generation has been used. From antiquity to today, the term generation has been employed frequently to describe relations among age groups; but often its usage has been so casual as to create uncomfortably imprecise distinctions among groups. In this regard, we examine ways in which the concepts of cohort, lineage, and generation help us to understand similarities and differences among age groups and to understand the process of social change.

The second section discusses the contribution of five theoretical perspectives (functionalism, social conflict, interactionism, psychoanalytic theory, and social learning) to the study of generations. We illustrate the manner in which these perspectives provide a useful framework for studying generations and intergenerational relations. More specifically, we explore how these perspectives help to answer the questions: Why are generations similar? And why are they different?

KEY CONCEPTS: THE SEVERAL FACES OF
GENERATIONAL RELATIONS

The problem of generations is as old as mankind's earliest writings and as contemporary as today's newspaper. As Chapters 4, 6, and 7 in this volume suggest, life events and life crises frequently revolve around intergenerational relations and family events. The study of intergenerational relations can have practical significance in that knowledge from research is used by policymakers and practitioners in formulating policy and plans.

An analysis of the literature since 1971 on intergenerational relations indicates many important findings, but little in the way of explicit theory development. Specific findings from empirical studies can be made more useful in the context of theory. Theory, it should be remembered, provides a framework in which knowledge is ordered and classified, and in which both explanation and prediction result. In this way, theory provides a cognitive map in which the world is described. This cognitive map transforms knowledge from a mere description of reality to a device that can be used for prediction and explanation. Theory is necessary in order to go beyond simple statements of *what* to answer questions of *why* and *how* (Dubin, 1978).

The development of precise concepts is the first step toward theory building. Concepts are the descriptions of what is being studied and form units out of which theory is built. To build adequate theory, we need to delineate and define precisely the key conceptual elements of all the units of analysis.

There are seven key concepts that relate to the analysis of intergenerational relations; each presents some intellectual challenge for observers. Alfred North Whitehead noted that the history of any science is the biography of its concepts. One of the problems of researchers and practitioners in life-span developmental psychology and in life course analysis in sociology is that we are the inheritors of some imprecise concepts. Most of the terms used are taken from everyday discourse and thus are in need of considerable definition and refinement before they are useful in scientific analog or in the development and testing of theory.

In an attempt to create greater refinement of terms we will discuss the following concepts: (a) generation; (b) cohort; (c) generation units, seen as forerunners and keynoters and cohort-based social movements; and (d) lineage. These may be considered primary concepts in the analysis of generational relations. Three addititional concepts that appear crucial to further analysis are related primarily to the lineage level of intergenerational interaction: (e) norms; (f) socialization; and (g) solidarity.

Generation

The term generation has multiple meanings — a problem that can be traced to the Greek root of the word *genos* (Bengtson, Cutler, Mangen, & Marshall, 1985). Its general meaning is reflected in the verb *genesthai,* which means "to come into existence." But, as Nash (1978) noted in describing Hellenistic usage of the term, there are many social realities that come into existence. These were described as generations by the earliest social historians such as Homer. Examples of such generations were: a new lineage (the birth of a child to Nestor's family), a new social category (peers who joined Nestor in the sacking of Troy), and even a phase of life (those mature enough to speak to the assembly in Athens). Thus, the ancient Greek term for generation carries a wide scope of meaning.

Modern usage of the term generation continues to have the problem of multiple meanings. *Generation* has been used to describe a population living at a certain point in time, such as Roosevelt's oft-quoted pronouncement during the Great Depression: "This generation of Americans has a rendezvous with history." It has also been used to describe subgroups within a population who share a common experience (the "Vietnam Generation"). In yet another usage — perhaps the most precise — the term generation has described the rank of descent within the family. In spite of the different precise meanings, all the usages of the term generation have one central theme — sameness with one group and distinctiveness from others. When a distinct group comes into existence within a particular social, historical, and temporal context — that group can, in popular usage at least lay some claim to being a generation.

This view of generations — as groups coming into being within a particular context — illustrates the point that the concept of generation is relative, much like the verb "to be." The term generation has meaning only when placed within a broader context of reference. A child forms a generation only with respect to her parents or when children are born to her. "The Depression Generation" exists only because there are other generations who lived during more prosperous times. In each case, generations emerge from a specific context — a child within a family, or a cohort within a population of multiple cohorts. The term generation needs a referent that explains its distinctiveness; one needs to know the context from which it emerges.

There are two general contexts within which generations emerge. First, generations emerge at the macrolevel of society in the form of cohorts: groups of age-related individuals who experience similar historical and developmental events and who are in some observable sense distinctive from other cohorts. As is discussed later, in the service of conceptual clarity it is preferable to use the term *cohort* in this context, rather than *generation*. Second, generations come into being at the microlevel of society. Specifically, generations arise in the context of the family lineage.

In short, generation is a generic term that applies to a general class of groups or individuals who share a common experience; that is, their emergence in a unique period of biological, social, developmental, or historical time. The different classes or categories within that concept describe the societal level (micro or macro) and the temporal context (a number of years or period of history) of that generation. Consequently, a cohort comes into being at the macro level of society within the context of historical time. And, by contrast, a lineage generation exists at the microlevel within biological and developmental time. To state that the use of the term generation is a "liability to science" (Kertzer, 1983) is analogous to saying that the use of the term primary group instead of family is too precise. One needs to recognize the differences between the generic and more specific usages of the concepts involved. In order to achieve greater clarity, in most usages of the term generation it is important to specify the type of generation being discussed.

Cohort

Like *generation,* the term *cohort* has an old and distinguished history with Greek and Latin ethnographic roots. During the first "world war" in 331–323 B.C., cohorts were divisions in Alexander's Roman legions. From Roman times to the present, *cohort* has referred to a group of individuals who share a common experience. In the more specialized context of life course research, a cohort refers to a group of individuals who were born at approximately the same time (generally, within a 5- to 10-year period) and who therefore share some similar characteristics or experiences (Ryder, 1965). When the term cohort is used to refer to individuals born within a specific time period, it is analogous to some usages of the term generation. However, by using the term cohort instead of generation, one is able to avoid some confusion of meanings.

When considering the similarities and differences between cohorts as well as their role in the process of social change, three important factors should be mentioned. These factors – the impact of historical events, demographics, and the process of cohort flow – provide important insights into interactions among age aggregates.

First, cohorts come into being within particular historical settings. As cohort members age, they carry with them the impact of earlier historical influences. Among other things, historical influences affect cohort members' orientation toward social issues (Bengtson *et al*; 1985; Marshall, 1984). However, historical influences have a more pervasive effect than merely shaping opinion and values. History also shapes the way in which individuals follow the course of their lives. For example, Elder and Liker (1980), in their study of women who lived during the Great Depression, demonstrated the lasting influence of financial adversity on the ability of women to cope with events 30–40 years later.

Another important insight Elder and Liker conveyed in this study was that historical events do not influence all cohort members equally. Influence from history is mediated by such factors as personality, family circumstances, social class, gender, and psychological resources. These factors influence how individuals perceive events and how they respond to those events. The differential impact of common social-historical events on the members of a birth cohort reflects, by analogy, the contrast between the terms "touch" and "saturation." Some individuals are barely touched by events around them while others are saturated by the same influences. Moreover, certain historical events have more potential to touch or saturate cohort members than have other events. The Vietnam War, for example, had a more pervasive influence on those individuals of draft age than on other Americans in the 1960s.

Historical periods also have dominant ideologies and belief systems that shape a cohort member's life course. George Herbert Mead (1938) stated that each generation reinterprets history according to its own needs. Ideologies shape the way in which persons interpret reality and the events to which they are subsequently exposed as well as, how individuals respond to events. In this manner, cohorts born during different historical periods will have different interpretations of their environment and, consequently, different responses to it. Gillis (1979), in his analysis of the history of adolescence, found that dominant ideologies concerning the nature of age groups themselves have changed over time. For example, according to his analysis, adolescence as a distinct period of life has been recognized only in modern times. How generations relate to one another is vastly influenced by beliefs concerning developmental stages.

A second set of factors involves demographic processes. External historical factors are not the only forces that impinge on the lives of cohort members. Cohort members are also influenced by the internal structure of the cohorts to which they belong. More specifically, demographic factors play a key role in cohort influences. For example, Ryder (1965) noted that fertility differentials, producing birth cohorts of various sizes, could set the potential for social change. Much of the research in this area has focused on the experiences of the Baby Boom cohort (Easterlin, 1980; Russell, 1981) — an unusually large number of persons who occupy a similar position in the life course, having entered the social system at the same time. Added pressure was placed on society to accommodate these individuals. Schools were built — and were subsequently closed — as the Baby Boom cohort entered and left the school system. As the Baby Boom generation began establishing families, pressure was put on the housing market as Baby Boomers tried to realize the American ideal of a single family dwelling (Russell, 1981). These kinds of influences affect not only members of the particular cohort that has an unusual size or structure but also members of adjacent cohorts. This applies especially to individuals who are off-timers, for example, those who start their families or buy homes earlier or later than is typical for their cohort.

The experience of the Baby Boom generation also illustrates a third issue: cohort flow (Riley, 1976). Society continually adapts and changes as the members of the Baby Boom cohort age and move through the life course. As the Baby Boom cohort experienced successive developmental events, society changed to meet its changing needs. Schools and homes were built to accommodate the increased demands of the Baby Boom. The notion of cohort flow fits the perspective on age stratification advanced by Riley and her associates (Riley, 1976; Riley, Hess, & Bond, 1983; Riley, Johnson, & Foner, 1972). According to this perspective, society is composed of numerous strata of individuals of particular age groups. Social roles and positions are allocated on the basis of age. Consequently, individuals move from one stratum to another as they age. However, because roles are allocated by age, and age by its very nature is transitory, roles are continually occupied and reoccupied by individuals throughout time. Successive cohorts of individuals have experienced different life events and historical influences, and therefore they are likely to be carriers of social change.

Forerunners and Keynoters: Generation Units and Social Change

As cohort members move into new social positions, they may create changes in the social structure by yet another mechanism: their role as forerunners, the innovators of social change (Bengtson & Troll, 1978). (*Forerunner* is used here in place of the less intuitively obvious term *generation unit* proposed by Mannheim, 1936). By forerunners, we mean the members of a birth cohort who become self-conscious agents of social change. Mannheim labeled these individuals as members of generation units, rather than members of "actual" generations. His analysis of 18th and 19th century European social history suggested that social movements, led by visible groups of youths who questioned the existing social order and challenged the *ancien regime,* arose quite regularly. These groups of youths brought forward a protest, a revolt, that received considerable support, especially among their contemporaries. Those youths reflected an elite in Mannheim's analysis. They were forerunners of artistic styles that can be seen to relate to their phenomenological expression and to their philosophical orientation. They occurred as keynoters of social change. It should be acknowledged that Mannheim's analysis appeared more salient a few years ago, during and after the "Decade of Protest," than it does today among the relatively quiescent youth of the 1980s. But future historians will turn again and again to that time in history; indeed four recently published books provide sociological analyses of specific movements during that period (Breines, 1982; Leventman, 1982; Surrey, 1982; Yinger, 1982).

It has been argued that forerunners have effects on social history through a feedback process that occurs in three steps (Bengtson & Black, 1973). Step 1 occurs with the creation of cultural alternatives via new ideals that have emerged due to the phenomenon of fresh contact (Mannheim, 1936). Fresh contact occurs because young people share a similar location in developmental time. Mannheim suggested that as each birth cohort comes into adulthood it experiences fresh contact with the values of the surrounding milieu. Because of their freshness, new adults question the status quo more readily and can criticize more directly the discrepancies between the ideal and the actual in the social system. Ideals have yet another function: they provide an alternative to the cultural status quo. The keynoters of the 1960s argued that if equality is our mandate in the United States political system, then equality should be our practice in daily events. Thus, the protests of youth in the 1960s were in response to the discrepancies they observed between the real and the ideal in our political and social system.

The 1960s debate about the status of conventional marriage provides a case in point. As youth approached the culturally recommended age for marriage, they observed at least half the American marriages terminating in divorce and separation. The high rate of tension and failure that young people saw made them reluctant to accept the existing patterns. Their reluctance led to increasing experimentation with viable options. Living together, trial marriages, childless couples, and compound and communal unions became more common as young people explored various alternatives for the family and for human relationships. Exploration of options is the first step in the emergence of social movements based upon generational lines.

The second step is the testing of cultural options. The young not only become theory builders, they form their own experimental group. Young people inherit their ideals as outsiders and as nonmembers of the very world they want to change. They then test these ideas as they become participants in adult social institutions.

The third stage is the selection of cultural options. Some of the options tested do not prove to be useful or to be any more practicable than the status quo. Other options endure and become the status quo. It may appear quaint to those who are today below the age of 30 to think about the selection, the production, and the testing of cultural alternatives as being the promise of youth. But in the late 1960s such rhetoric was commonplace. There was such a diversity of styles on college campuses that Mannheim's notion of fresh contact appeared valid, and the place of youth as forerunners in cultural options appeared obvious.

Forerunners can also operate in the context of the lineage. Adolescents bring innovative ideals into their position as lineage members, as well as to society as a whole. Some families are more amenable to experimentation than others and are more influenced by fresh contact. These lineages adopt patterns that are different from the cultural norms. They then convey these patterns to the other forerunners, and finally, to other members of the culture (Bengtson & Troll, 1978).

Lineage

Lineage generations are composed of individuals who occupy particular positions in the rank of descent within the family: grandparents, parents, grandchildren. Here the "coming into being" is a result of the birth of a new individual based on the genetic combination of the previous generation.

Lineage is the more intuitively obvious context of generation because it is the most immediately apparent. Tracing descent within most families is simple. But lineage relationships involve the most intimate and quotidian aspects of our lives. Associated with the notion of lineal relationships between generations are specific social roles and the normative expectations that accompany those roles. The reality of lineage generations is embodied in interpersonal behavior, by roles and by norms that impinge on individuals who occupy different positions within lineage structures.

Several concepts can be identified that describe key elements of within-family relations between generations. These include norms, socialization, and solidarity. Each describes an important aspect of the relations between generations by providing conceptual categories for classifying the manner in which generations interact and relate to one another.

Norms: Expectation and Obligation. One of the influences that shape the developing individual is the constellation of norms associated with lineage membership. Each lineage member occupies a particular social role within the lineage that has accompanying proscriptions and prescriptions for behavior. Each role is a position in the ranked descent and is defined by one's relative position in the reproductive cycle. To be a parent, a child, or a grandparent is a reflection of biological events; but, it is the social events pertaining to occupancy of these positions that require considerable analysis (Rossi, 1980). Expectations for behavior range from the obligation to nurture small children as parents to the norm of noninterference between grandparents and grandchildren (Cherlin & Furstenburg, 1985). The nature of these expectations changes throughout the life cycle; for example, parents are not expected to nurture and provide full economic support for adult children.

Norms within the lineage are derived from two sources: (a) from other societal institutions outside the family; and (b) from the internal negotiation process that occurs between lineage members. Societal institutions, such as religion and the state, have expectations regarding the manner in which lineage members relate to one another. For example, in the Judeo-Christian heritage, the Ten Commandments dictate that "Thou Shalt Honor Thy Father and Thy Mother" and the Bible admonishes parents that to spare the rod will spoil the child. At times, these institutions may seek to impose these ideals within the context of a particular lineage.

In both the state and religion, parameters are established for appropriate behavior among lineage members. The state also provides a set of proscriptions and sanctions for enforcing its rules through legal statutes. Child welfare laws assume that parents have certain obligations to nurture and protect their minor children. Not to do so is defined as child abuse, and the state will intervene within the lineage in order to assure that children's needs are met. However, these institutions do not specifically regulate the day-to-day interactions that occur among lineage members nor do they prohibit variation in behavior among lineage members. Despite the prospective intervention by the state, parents have considerable leeway in choosing the manner in which they raise their children. The specifics of intergenerational relations emerge in an ongoing, day-to-day process of negotiation among lineage members (Hagestad, 1981).

Socialization: Socialization involves a process of ongoing negotiation between generations representing complementary roles. This process can be viewed both within and outside the family. Relations between parents and children at each stage of the life course reflect influence processes that are bilateral and continually changing. The patterns of such influences are altered directly and indirectly by societal processes that themselves can be viewed along generational themes; these societal processes derive from period and cohort themes on the one hand and from family themes on the other.

More specifically, socialization is defined as "the teaching and learning of new behaviors that enable an individual to successfully negotiate role transitions" (Bengtson & Black, 1973; p. 208). Socialization occurs throughout life within the context of solidarity, in the tension of distinctiveness, and in the matrix of reciprocal influence.

The outcome of the socialization process is shaped by forces of power and authority within the family. Lineage members have unequal ability to influence one another. Even though the negotiation process may be bilateral and ongoing, the process of influence flows more from some lineage members than from others. In the case of young families, there is the direct issue of the dependence of children on their parents. According to the conceptualization of Jones and Gerard (1967), two types of dependence are manifested throughout life: effect dependence and information dependence. Effect dependence occurs when one individual relies on another for direct gratification of needs. A child's information dependence occurs when, s/he relies on another for explanation and interpretation of external events. Information and effect dependence upon his or her parents decreases as the child develops. However, even though the parental monopoly over the regulation of childhood experiences ceases, it is reasonable to assume that the effects of that monopoly, including a perceptual framework within which experiences are interpreted, persist well beyond the period of actual dependency. This generational overlap of perceptual approaches is one of the factors that leads to intergenerational similarity.

Even though the exercise of power creates influences within the lineage (based on the factor of dependence), some generations — that is, some birth cohorts and some lineage members — are different from those who preceded them as well as from those who will come later. There are contrasts in the degree to which different generations replicate one another in a process of social and biological duplication.

Solidarity: A long tradition within social psychology, from Durkeim to Simmel to the present-day analysis of small groups, suggests the importance of cohesion, or integration, within groups and the ways in which groups differ on dimensions of solidarity. As Durkheim (1893/1956) described it, "solidarity occurs when the image of others unites itself with ours" (p. 62). Durkheim's discussion of this solidarity as a crucial property of social groups was elaborated more comprehensively by Homan's (1950) analysis of similarity, interaction and sentiment in groups. Finally, Nisbet and Perrin (1977) described solidarity as the feeling of "we versus they" that exists within the context of a social group. In this sense, solidarity is a measure of the cohesion and integration present among group members.

Drawing from these conceptualizations of solidarity, different types can be identified, depending on the nature of the social relationships present within a group. Solidarity can occur either as a result of bonds of shared affection, meaning, and experience (*mechanical solidarity*) or as a result of functional interdependence (*organic solidarity*). In the special case of the family and intergenerational relations, solidarity reflects cohesiveness founded on a combination of elements, both organic and mechanical. Based on these considerations, family solidarity "is the totality of activity, feeling, expectations and functions that family members share" (Bengtson, 1984, p. 9). More specifically, family solidarity can be described in terms of the six dimensions: consensual solidarity, normative solidarity, associational solidarity, affectual solidarity, functional solidarity, and family structure (Bengtson & Schrader, 1981).

There are certain qualities of family solidarity that reflect shared meaning, shared experience, and emotional involvement. Family members share meaning in the form of beliefs about what is and what ought to be in the world in general and in terms of specific issues concerning the family. Consensual solidarity (agreement or disagreement in beliefs and orientations toward issues external to the family) and normative solidarity (the degree to which family members share values of familism, filial obligation or deference) are both ways in which members of particular lineages and families share these meanings. Family members also share experiences in the form of associational solidarity (mutually shared activities and interactions), and they manifest emotional bonding in the form of affectual solidarity (degree of positive sentiment). All these types of solidarity emerge from the unity of experience and identity that exists between members of a family, much like Durkheim's conceptualization of mechanical solidarity.

There is also a degree of functional solidarity within a family that is also based on division of labor and functional interdependence. Family members share a bond in the degree to which they depend upon and share mutual aid and support. As with other societal groups, families have a division of labor in which tasks are allocated on the basis of age and gender (Parsons, 1942). The specialization of function that occurs as a result of this allocation makes members of a group mutually interdependent. This interdependence is somewhat analogous to Durkheim's notion of organic solidarity, in which people are bonded together by their differences rather than by their similarities, as they are with mechanical solidarity.

Finally, high solidarity can exist only if the structure promotes it. Family structure, the sixth dimension of family solidarity, is a description of the number and proximity of kin available for interaction. This is a description of the opportunity structure, which provides the conditions under which the other aspects of solidarity can manifest themselves or that limit the development of those aspects of solidarity.

Our current research at the University of Southern California on family solidarity has shown that families report exceptionally high levels of solidarity, but that there is variation in perceptions of solidarity between the generations. For example, both parents and children show high levels of affectual solidarity (Bengtson, Mangen, & Landry, 1984), but the older generation perceives more positive sentiment than does the younger generation. Children tend to understate and parents tend to overstate frequency of shared interaction. Adherence to norms of filial responsibility decline as one moves down the generations; grandchildren are less likely than their grandparents to adhere to these norms. Even though there is greater agreement in perceptions of frequency of interaction between the grandparent and parent generation than between the parent and grandchild generations, the reported frequency for the grandchildren and their parents is higher. The attitudes and opinions of parents and children have low to modest correlations, and parents perceive more consensus with their children than actually exists (Bengtson, et al., 1984).

The preceding examples illustrate the variations in perception of the level and nature of solidarity between lineage members. The differences occur as a result of the intersecting lives of lineage members: individuals are at particular points in the life course with different developmental needs and tasks at each point. At a given point in their life course and their position in the lineage, each generation has a stake in being similar or being different. Parents' perception of greater solidarity means that the parents have a developmental stake in similarity while their children have a developmental stake in distinctiveness or differences (Bengtson & Kuypers, 1971). Parents want to believe that their children are like themselves, carrying on the traditions and values that they taught them. At the same time, children want to establish their independence and their own identity as adults, and to start their own families. The intersection of their lives results in different patterns of solidarity, depending on the needs of each individual.

Cohort and Lineage: Microlevel and macrolevel intersections

As discussed in the preceding section, there are seven key concepts that relate to the problem of understanding intergenerational relations. These concepts intersect in very important ways. For example, lineage members' cohort membership influences their experience as family members. As Hagestad (1981, 1985) has emphasized, it is important to note the intersection between the two levels of generations. This was also suggested by Bengtson and Black (1973) in their statement that it is important to recognize the two levels of time and social structure within which generations emerge.

Understanding the relationship between cohort and lineage is complex (Marshall, 1984). Hagestad (1981) captured this complexity in her aphorism that "generations do not file into families by cohort." The child generation in a particular family may be represented by individuals born 10 years apart; the same may be true of the parental or grand-parental generation. When we move from the microsocial level of a particular family to the macrosocial level of large aggregates (i.e., the population of a nation), the situation is even more complex. The term generation is imprecise in terms of social boundaries. We can refer to the generation of American college students today and assume (although this involves a very loose usage of the term) at least that the referent is to a group of individuals most of whom were born 18 to 22 years earlier. If we refer to the parental generation of the same students, we find a group whose ages may be normally distributed, but with quite a large dispersion about the mean. This is because the timing of the birth of children varies to a much greater extent than does the timing of entry into college. This occurs for two reasons: the timing of first births may not be normatively patterned, and the spacing and number of children within a family intersects with parental age.

The considerable variation in the timing of generations is seen in a recent study of grandmotherhood (Burton, 1985; Burton & Bengtson, 1985). The research involved two groups of grandmothers: those who had assumed the grandparental role "on time" (age 42–60) and those who had become grandmothers "early" (age 27–38). The study found greater role satisfaction, and fewer role conflicts, in the "on-time" sample of grandmothers. But it also suggests some intergenerational patterns of the timing of birth. The study included one six-generation family, in which four of the six generations of women gave birth to their first born when they were 11 or 14 years of age. This case demonstrates two points: first, timing of life events, such as first pregnancy, may be transmitted from generation to generation. Second, it illustrates that although families are differentiated by age and by generational membership, differentiation does not necessarily coincide with the normative pattern of events found within a particular cohort (Elder, 1984).

The age at which parents begin childrearing is not the only timing event that influences their cohort membership relative to their children's. Children who are last born in a family with more than one child will have parents who are older than the parents of their age mates who are first born, if the parents in both cases began childrearing at the normatively expected age. This is especially true in the case of families who have only one or two children compared with families who have many children widely spaced. This means that the cohort membership of a child's parents is related to the timing of the first birth of the parents, as well as the birth order of the child.

These illustrations relate to issues in the emergence of individuals or groups within a particular temporal context. Each generation has its own unique pattern of solidarity, influence, and similarity that makes it distinct from others that preceded it and from those that follow. The context may be within a population of a nation (Kohli, 1984), or, in the more specific context, within that of a family. The notion of context locates a generation within the dimension of social and biological time. Emergence also implies process; process implies change (Marshall, 1984). Generations do not exist as static and unchanging entities; rather, they change over time. As Hagestad (1981) so eloquently points out, lineage is the intersection of the developmental careers of the individual family members as well as of the family. The manner in which those careers intersect will have an impact on the way in which generations relate to one another. When adolescence, which is a period of "winding up," intersects with a period of middle age, which is a stage of "winding down," developmental stress is placed on both lineage members (Rossi, 1980). Rossi notes that the age of the mother of an adolescent daughter has an impact on the manner in which the mother and daughter relate to one another. Elder (1984) illustrates the way in which the lives of individuals who live in particular eras differed because of the unique impact of various historical events. He shows that individual developmental patterns intersect with historical time, which manifests itself in unique life patterns for individuals.

As members of particular cohorts, lineage members who have experienced different historical events bring different perspectives to their performances of the roles they occupy within the lineage. Differences within the lineage are also influenced by the structure of the lineage in terms of forces that impinge on the lives of family members. Therefore, the patterns of interaction, power, and obligation within families represent a complex intertwine of ranked descent and birth-cohort membership, and indeed, historical time.

Conclusion

This review of concepts and issues in the study of intergenerational relations suggests two key points. The first is that there are two dimensions of social location – micro and macro – and two dimensions of time – the historical and the individual-developmental. When analyzing intergenerational relations, it is crucial not to lose sight of the potential distinctiveness that arises within this dimension. The outlooks, values, orientations, and personal preoccupations of the old and the young are different in many respects probably because of the differences in location in developmental time. The life events that occur with the passage of time also have a different impact and different implications for the social-psychological orientations of the individual. So too, the historical dimension has a role in influencing the distinctiveness and similarity of generations – birth cohort and family members.

Second, these concepts have implications at the two different levels of social structure – the macrosocial and the microsocial. Those of us who engage in family research are most focused on the microsocial. It is imperative not to omit the larger structural effects on families and intergenerational relations that shape behavior and influence interactions among individuals. These two points should be incorporated into research agendas for the next decade. The several levels of time and social structure that relate to intergenerational relations must be considered in future research designs.

KEY THEORETICAL PERSPECTIVES: SEVERAL EXPLANATIONS OF VARIATIONS IN GENERATIONAL RELATIONS

While there are several meanings of the term generation, each involves the notion of being distinctive because it occupies a special position in social space and in time. In consequence, there are times when the goals and aims of one generation are incompatible with the goals and aims of other generations.

Even though these goals and expectations may be incompatible at times, social organization requires that generations manage the differences among them. That is, during most periods of history generations maintain cohesiveness (within the family and society) in spite of their differences. Generations also reproduce themselves through time. The question is, how? How are family traditions and family cultures, for example, replicated over time and in the context of social change?

The issues of distinctiveness and similarity among generations can be understood more comprehensively by incorporating issues that are explicated within traditional theoretical perspectives in sociology and psychology. We can improve conceptual clarity and the power of our knowledge about intergenerational relations by incorporating these theoretical perspectives into our research agendas. Five theoretical perspectives have been influential in the conduct of research and scholarly thinking regarding relations between cohorts, relations between lineage members, and even relations between self-conscious generation units. These include the conflict, functionalist, psychoanalytic, interactionist, and social learning perspectives. We will comment briefly on the key elements of each of these perspectives and then on the way in which they add to the understanding of phenomena such as distinctiveness and similarity.

Distinctiveness

One way of addressing the issue of differences among generations is to examine the goals and expectations of generation members and the various means they have of attaining these goals. Each generation member occupies a position within a sequence of individual growth and development cycles; consequently each has specific goals and orientations derived from that life-course position. The ability of a generation member to attain specific goals is a function of the resources that person controls. The control of resources provides an individual with the means of exercising power in order to influence other lineage and cohort members. At times, conflict occurs when opposing generation members exercise power in order to achieve incompatible goals. The various theoretical perspectives examined here differ because some emphasize the study of power and its impact on intergenerational conflict whereas other perspectives emphasize conflict emanating from opposing goals that accompany developmental events.

The *social conflict perspective* in sociology provides the intellectual and theoretical roots for studying the conflict between generations at both the cohort and the lineage levels. The classic articulation of this perspective is by Marx (1867/1977) and in the area of the family, by Engels (1884/1972), but more recent theorists have developed and refined the position (Chafetz, 1981; Collins, 1975; Dowd, 1980).

Three key points in conflict theory pertain to generational distinctiveness and interaction. First, groups in society and individuals within families compete for scarce resources. Second, because there is unequal access to resources, conflict occurs. Third, conflict is not only inevitable but essential in the course of social relationships.

The conflict perspective focuses attention on the distribution of resources among generations and the exercise of power for control of resources. Parents have more power than young children; middle-aged adults have more resources than their adolescent offspring. Unequal resource distribution between generations is the result of three factors: (a) time, (b) size and strength, and (c) physical attractiveness (Collins, 1975). Being in a particular position longer provides more time to accumulate advantage. Adults are bigger and stronger than children, which gives them the ability to require compliance. On the other hand, children's physical attractiveness to parents and their ability to bring parents pleasure is in itself a resource. The capacity to be a nuisance is also a resource available to children that is frequently unappreciated by parents (Sprey, 1981). Because children lack material resources, they are not able to fend for themselves in society and are dependent on adults. Total dependency by one party on another in a relationship may lead to exploitation by the powerful individuals (Sprey, 1981).

The way in which parents are motivated to control children depends on three factors: parental resources, social conditions, and the child's resources. In agrarian societies, for example, parents need children as agricultural workers and are motivated to get children to behave in such a way as to provide labor for the family. These goals require that parents use certain control techniques such as physical punishment, shaming and ridicule, deprivation of love, and control of rewards (Collins, 1975; Smith, 1983). The control system used will vary with the needs of the family and the goals of parents for controlling their children.

The type of resources available to parents and children also varies across the life cycle. Young children depend totally on their parents and have little opportunity to use resources to influence parents. Children are dependent on parents for information and effect (Jones & Gerard, 1967); i.e., for ideas and for material support. This dependency undoubtably contributes to similarity between generations because parents control how children learn about the world and how they process symbols. As children grow older, they have a greater capacity for independence and fending for themselves. Because of this they gain a more equal balance of power with parents (Hesse-Biber & Williamson, 1984; Sprey, 1981).

Conflicts between generations can occur at this point because children acquire more resources to challenge parental control. Parents are also less able to control information because children are also becoming more involved with outside sources such as the peer group and the school. The goals of adolescents and parents may also clash. Parents may wish to continue to control their children's behavior while adolescents wish to establish autonomy. Functionalists might contend that this process occurs as a necessary event in order for society to be able to maintain itself. Children must break away from the dependency that they have on the family and become fully functioning adults in order for society to continue through time.

At the other end of the life cycle, the balance of power may be reversed as parents grow old and frail and become dependent on their adult children for support. Time may no longer be an advantage as older people retire from the social system and become less economically and socially active (Cumming & Henry, 1963). They may no longer have the advantage in physical size and strength, as children have grown up and the parent has become frail. Resources for the elderly include the bond of affection and obligation that has built up over the years in the process of caring for their children (Hesse-Biber & Williamson, 1984).

These ideas can be applied not only at the microlevel but at the macrosocial level as well. Members of earlier birth cohorts have the advantage of time and seniority just as older lineage members do. This may explain part of the process of age stratification. As individuals occupy roles for longer and longer periods of time, they accumulate resources and seniority that enable them to attain higher status and move into the next stratum. The unequal distribution of resources among generations at the cohort level may also create conflict among cohort members. This is the basis for proposals from writers such as Bell (1964), who suggests that class consciousness may be evolving into age consciousness. "The bases for conflict lie with the tensions and deprivations of economic and cultural life which in cases of relative scarcity sometimes pit various cohorts of people against each other in generational conflict" (Tindale & Marshall, 1980, p. 47).

Functionalism, in contrast to conflict theory, which focuses on competition for resources, has to do with the conflict over developmental goals that may occur between generations. Functionalism has a long tradition in both psychology and sociology. Its most articulate early exponents were Durkheim (1893/1956) and Herbert Spencer (1862/1907). Talcott Parsons (1942) applied many specifications, especially to the family.

From the standpoint of sociology, there are four key points in functionalism that contribute to the understanding of intergenerational relations (Bengtson & Dowd, 1981). First, organisms are composed of a system of interrelated parts. Each of the parts contributes to the maintenance of the whole system. For Durkheim, society is like an organism because it too is a system of interrelated parts, each of which contributes to the maintenance of the whole. The family, for example, is essential to the functioning of society because it provides for reproduction and socialization of society's members.

A second key element of functionalism is teleology—looking at the end. Nothing exists for which there is no purpose. The purpose of each part is its contribution to the maintenance of the whole. One can see the influence of evolutionary theory in functionalism. That which exists, exists because it fills some purpose. If it does not fill a purpose, that entity will fail to survive. This is a very simple formula reflective of the social darwinism of the late 19th century.

The third proposition of functionalism, especially from the sociological perspective, concerns the contribution of certain social arrangements to the functioning of the entire social system. For Durkheim, this is the key sociological question. With respect to the generations, the crucial question concerns the contribution of certain aspects of intergenerational relations to the maintenance of society. What is the contribution of solidarity between generations to the maintenance of families through time? What is the contribution to social history?

Fourth, even social conflict is functional. In terms of the issue of conflict between generations, functionalism (unlike conflict theory) emphasizes the developmental goals of parents and children and how differences in these goals produce conflict. It also focuses on the contribution of that conflict to the maintenance of the society and of the family.

Parsons (1942) states that during adolescence youth cultures emerge that "repudiate interest in adult things and feel a certain recalcitrance to the pressure of adult expectations and discipline" (p. 284). This process is a necessary stage in the transition from childhood to adult roles both within society and within the lineage. According to Davis (1940), conflict occurs because of the nature of developmental events, that is, because of the deceleration of socialization that occurs as the child grows older. This conflict is made more intense during the periods of rapid social change in which children control knowledge of new ideas within society.

Conflict is functional because it is the mechanism by which adolescents detach from their families of orientation and from their own family units. This process is important because it assures that the family, and society, will persist through time.

Psychoanalysis also entails the concept of conflict between generations, but portrays the locus of intergenerational conflict as being at a much earlier developmental period than adolescence. Freud (1900/1938) suggested that there is first competition between parents and children and then accommodation as children internalize parental statuses and identities. The psychoanalytic perspective suggests that intergenerational relations may be a recapitulation of previous interactions between generations. That is, interaction that occurs in earliest childhood between parents and children will influence interaction between these individuals throughout their lifetime — even into middle and old age (Terman, 1984).

Psychoanalytic theory particularly addresses the conflict that occurs during the psychosexual development of the child, specifically, the resolution of the Oedipal conflict. According to this perspective, the outcome of that struggle influences future intergenerational relations—well into adulthood. Conflict between generations is the result of unresolved issues from earlier developmental periods or from defenses that are developed during those periods (Grumes, 1984). The outcome of psychosexual conflicts also influences the choices one makes in life, especially in terms of parenthood. Individuals will replicate their relationships with their own parents when relating to their children, and those relationships even will influence the decision whether or not to become a parent (Terman, 1984).

Thus, the three theoretical perspectives differ in how they deal with the issue of distinctiveness and conflict between generations. Functionalism and psychoanalytic theory center on developmental issues and the reasons for intergenerational conflict, whereas conflict theory focuses on the uses of power, resources, and authority that occur as generational members try to attain individual goals.

Psychoanalytic perspectives differ from functionalism in that the developmental processes psychoanalytic theory describes involve the internal struggles involved in psychosexual development, whereas functionalism places the center of intergenerational conflict within the process of the transition from the social role of child to the social role of adult. Each of these theoretical perspectives provides useful explanations as to the causes of distinctiveness and conflict between generations.

Similarity

Conflict implies negotiation; it also implies mutual influence. Negotiation and influence lead to similarity. At the lineage level, relations between generations concentrate primarily on socialization, the transmission of values and patterns of behavior to assure some degree of similarity between older and younger generations. How do generations negotiate similarity despite conflict, differences in social location, and differences of interest?

In examining the contributions of various theories to this question, two additional questions arise, the answers to which help to illuminate the negotiation of similarity between generations both at the lineage and the cohort level. First, what are the processes by which generations influence one another? To what extent is similarity the product of direct influence, through teaching, exhortation, or modeling? Or is similarity between generations the result of generations occupying similar positions in the social structure? Does the influence of social class, race, sex, and historical experience create similarity rather than direct influence between generations? Second, what is the direction of influence? Does the more powerful older generation have singular influence on the younger generation, or is the flow of influence bidirectional?

Interactionism, the fourth theoretical orientation considered here, has been referred to as symbolic interactionism, self theory or role theory. Three points are key to this perspective as it applies to the study of intergenerational relations. First, the social world is created in the process of negotiating meanings. Second, negotiations occur between actors, between individuals, in a given unit of the social world, and by means of symbolic communication; interaction of meaning is transacted by the use of symbols on which there is consensus. Third, individuals develop distinctiveness by virtue of their taking the role of the other and differentiating their self from other selves. The interactionist perspective has been highly influential in family sociology (Hill, 1949) and indeed, is the most easily translated to particular problems of parent-child interaction.

Similarity and influence, according to those who follow an interactionist perspective, can be seen as consequences of the basic human ability to symbolize. For example, Cooley's (1964) concept of the looking glass self implies that we imagine the image that others have of us and that we take that image and incorporate it into our own self-image. Self-image is an important determinant of behavior. Influence comes from the process of interaction between individuals, especially significant others, and from our ability to understand symbols within the context of that interaction. Analyses of intergenerational relations from an interactionist perspective may concentrate on the manner in which generations perceive one another in recognition of the fact that perceptions are passed on from one individual to another. Those perceptions are understood and used in order to give meaning to one's actions and to one's self. For example, in Fitzgerald's study (1983) of the perceptions of the elderly that are held by the elderly themselves and by college students, there was an incongruence in the perceptions of the two groups about the elderly. From an interactionist point of view, this is important because those perceptions will exert an influence on the context of social interaction.

Social learning theory is based on one main assumption: that learning occurs in a complex chain of rewarded responses. The simplest application to intergenerational relations focuses on parental behaviors as reinforcers of children's actions. The rewards parents give to children for behaviors that are congruent with parental expectations are very important in shaping behavior and in assuring similarity between generations.

Social learning theorists propose that the locus of influence occurs within day-to-day interactions between individuals, especially in interaction with significant others such as family members. The perspectives of interactionism and social learning differ in the importance ascribed to the human capacity to symbolize. In social learning, symbolizing is an important mediator in the cognitive process that accompanies learning. From this perspective, learning is the mechanism by which others are influenced (Bandura, 1969). Individuals learn behaviors in the course of interaction with and observation of others. This occurs by two processes: (a) first-hand experience and (b) vicarious experience. In first-hand experience, we find an experience rewarding and wish to continue. Learning also occurs when we observe others being rewarded, and consequently we wish to follow their example. How we model others' behavior depends on such factors as attentional processes, retention processes, motive, and incentive. (The more status and prestige a behavior will give us, the more likely we are to adopt it.) Individuals are also influenced by the social-status cues of the modeling situation. Parents also exercise power in order to influence the process of modeling by nurturance, withdrawal, and fear of the aggressor (Bandura, 1969). Finally, peers and the mass media are sources of influence within the social learning perspective.

Psychoanalytic theory places the mechanism of influence within the process of identification. In contrast to the direct stimulus-response mechanisms of social learning, identification from the psychoanalytic perspective is derived from the negotiation of developmental processes and the successful resolution of conflicts within those stages. Individuals become extensions of their parents' self-ideal and derive their own superego from this process (Schwartz, 1984). Again, early childhood influences and the resolution of early childhood conflicts are important for understanding intergenerational conflicts in this perspective.

Most of this discussion implies that the primary flow of influence is from parents to children. However, those who follow the interactionist perspective recognize that the process of socialization is mutual and bidirectional, that influence flows from parents to children and back again (Hagestad, 1981). The flow of influence may vary across the life cycle (Bengtson & Troll, 1978). Young children are probably more influenced by parents than are parents by their children, because parents control the information to which their children have access. But as children grow older, the flow of influence may become more balanced especially in times of rapid social change, when children are the carriers of new ideas into the lineage (Bengtson & Black, 1973; Davis, 1940). When one considers the mechanism of influence within the interactionist perspective—that interaction is the sharing of meaning from one another—mutual influence is a natural assumption to make.

Recent formulations of the social learning perspective (Bandura 1978, 1983) also suggest that influence is mutual rather than flowing exclusively from parent to child. By existing within the same social environment, individuals influence one another in ways that are complex and multidirectional.

Each of the perspectives reviewed contributes important insights toward the understanding of distinctiveness and similarity between generations. These theoretical perspectives are not necessarily mutually exclusive, though each may illuminate a particular aspect of intergenerational relations. For example, three of the perspectives were employed to examine conflict between the generations. However, functionalists see conflict as coming from structural and social conditions, whereas psychoanalysts understand conflict from the individual, internal and psychosexual developmental process. Social conflict theorists focus upon the process of negotiation and managing of conflict—assuming that conflict is normal and inevitable in human relationships.

Moreover, no one perspective is able to explain all of the complexities of intergenerational relations. Each has something to contribute to a particular level of analysis. The synergistic contribution of multiple theoretical perspectives was recently illustrated by Openshaw, Thomas, and Rollins (1983) in an analysis of socialization and adolescent self-esteem. They constructed a model for explaining transmission of values between generations that included variables developed from social learning theory and interactionism and entered them into a regression equation. Results suggested that each type of variable contributed to the explanation of transmission between generations; more important, to remove one variable from the model reduced its ability to explain and predict behavior. This example suggests that any comprehensive analysis of intergenerational relations should include ideas from several perspectives.

CONCLUSION

Our central point has been that future analyses of intergenerational relations require more explicit attention to constructs and theory than has characterized descriptive empirical studies in the past. First, we have argued, there is a need for explicit construct identification and precise definitions of the concepts employed in analyzing intergenerational relations. Second, any theoretical framework that emerges for studying the relations between generations must attempt to incorporate key notions provided by other, more general theoretical perspectives in sociology and psychology. In addition, we have argued that following these principles in the study of intergenerational relations will provide a richer, more cohesive, and more cumulative body of knowledge by adding the power of explanation to description and classification.

Among the seven key concepts that we suggested as most salient to the current study of intergenerational interaction, the term *generation* is primary. This term reflects the concept of emergence and its multiple usages that pertain to different levels of society, to different aspects of time. Two terms that more precisely make the distinction between the different meanings of generation are *cohort* and *lineage*. A cohort is a group of people born within a particular period of time. It is a phenomenon that applies at the macrolevel of society within the context of historical time. A lineage, the second type of generation, applies at the microlevel of society within the specific setting of the family. The lineage operates primarily within the context of developmental time. We suggested that these two terms be substituted for the generic term generation in order to achieve greater clarity of meaning.

A third concept that is useful to the study of intergenerational relations at the macrosocial level can be termed *forerunner,* or generation unit. A forerunner is a person, or a group, that by virtue of fresh contact with society, introduces new ideas and cultural options within the context of the family as well as the broader society. This concept is important because it suggests that the dynamics between generation members and between entire generations operate both micro- and macrosocially and can affect the structure of society and the structure of its particular institutions such as the lineage.

We suggested three additional concepts that should be considered when dealing with issues of generational relations: socialization, norms, and solidarity. Each concept is important because it gives a notion of the structure and patterns of interaction and influence that occur between generations. These concepts provide frameworks for understanding the nature and dynamics of the relations between generation members.

From the identification of key concepts, the scientific method moves to specification of their linkages; this is the construction of theory. Our analysis suggests the importance of integrating conceptual linkages regarding intergenerational interaction with broader theoretical perspectives in sociology and psychology. We considered some of the basic ideas of five major perspectives (social conflict theory, functionalism, interactionism, social learning and psychoanalytic theory) and suggested that each has certain key explanations that can contribute to a richer understanding of relations between generations. These notions are especially important for explaining the processes that account for observed similarity and distinctiveness between generations.

Each of the theoretical perspectives can provide its own particular piece to the puzzle. The notions and ideas provided by each framework do not exclude the possibility of other frameworks also applying to the understanding of intergenerational relations. In this way, the perspectives are not mutually exclusive and each has a particular level of knowledge to contribute to overall understanding.

ACKNOWLEDGMENTS

We wish to thank our colleagues, Dale Dannefer, Mary Martin, Donna Polisar, and John Schneider for their helpful suggestions. Preparation of this chapter was supported by grants from the National Institute of Aging (#AG 04092) and the National Institute of Mental Health (#MH 38244).

REFERENCES

Baltes, P. B., & Schaie, K. W. (Eds.). (1973). *Life-span developmental psychology: Personality and socialization.* New York: Academic Press.

Bandura, A. (1969). Social learning: Theory of identificatory process. In D. A. Goslin (Ed.), *Handbook of socialization theory and research.* Chicago: Rand McNally.

Bandura, A. (1978). The self system in reciprocal determinism. *American Psychologist, 33,* 344–358.

Bandura, A. (1983). Dynamics and decomposition of reciprocal determinism: A reply to Phillips and Orton. *Psychological Review, 90,* 66–170.

Bell, D. (1964). *The cultural contradictions of capitalism.* New York: Basic Books.

Bengtson, V. L. (1975). Generation and family effects in value socialization. *American Sociological Review, 40,* 358–371.

Bengtson, V. L. (1984, December). *Aging parents: Dimensions of intergenerational solidarity.* Report submitted to National Institute on Aging.

Bengtson, V. L., & Black, K. O. (1973). Intergenerational relations and continuities in socialization. In P. B. Baltes & K. W. Schaie (Eds.), *Life-span developmental psychology: Personality and socialization.* New York: Academic Press.

Bengtson, V. L., Cutler, N. E., Mangen, D. J., & Marshall, V. (1985). Generation, cohorts and relations between age groups. In R. Binstock & E. Shanas (Eds.), *Handbook of aging and the social sciences* (2nd ed.). New York: Van Nostrand Reinhold.

Bengtson, V. L., & Dowd, J. J. (1981). Functionalism and exchange perspectives in gerontological theory. *International Journal of Aging and Human Development, 12*(1), 55–74.

Bengtson, V. L., & Kuypers, J. A. (1971). Generational difference and the developmental stake. *Aging and Human Development, 2,* 249–260.

Bengtson, V. L., Mangen, D. J., & Landry, P. H., Jr. (1984). The multigeneration family: Concepts and findings. In V. Garms-Homolova, E. M. Hoering, & D. Schaeffer (Eds.), *Intergenerational relations.* New York: Hagrefe.

Bengtson, V. L., & Schrader, S. S. (1981). Parent-child relations. In D. J. Mangen & W. A. Peterson (Eds.), *Social roles and social participation.* Minneapolis: Unviersity of Minnesota Press.

Bengtson, V. L., & Troll, L. (1978). Youth and their parents: Feedback and intergenerational influence in socialization. In R. M. Lerner & G. B. Spanier (Eds.), *Child influence on marital and family interaction: A life span perspective.* New York: Academic Press.

Breines, W. (1982). *Community and organization in the new left, 1962–1968: The great refusal.* New York: Praeger.

Burton, L. (1985). *Timing and grandmotherhood in multigenerational black families.* Unpublished doctoral dissertation, University of Southern California.

Burton, L., & Bengtson, V. L. (1985). Black grandmothers: Issues of timing and continuity of roles. In V. L. Bengtson & J. Robertson (Eds.), *Grandparenthood* Beverly Hills, CA: Sage.

Chafetz, J. S. (1981). Family conflict: The application of selected theories of social conflict to the understanding of conflict in families. *Youth and Society, 13,* 157–171.

Cherlin, A., & Furstenberg, F., Jr. (1985). Styles and strategies of grandparenting. In V. Bengtson & J. Robertson (Eds.), *Grandparenthood.* Beverly Hills: Sage.

Collins, R. (1975). *Conflict sociology: Toward an explanatory science.* New York: Academic Press.

Cooley, T. H. (1964). *Human nature and the social order.* New York: Schocken.

Cumming, E., & Henry, W. E. (1963). *Growing old: The process of disengagement.* New York: Basic Books.

Davis, K. (1940). The sociology of parent-youth conflict. *American Sociological Review, 5,* 523–535.

Dowd, J. J. (1980). *Stratification among the aged.* Monterey, CA: Brooks/Cole.

Dubin, R. (1978). *Theory building.* New York: Free Press.

Durkheim, E. (1956). *Division of labor in society* (G. Simpson, trans.). New York: Free Press. (Original work published in 1893).

Easterlin, R. (1980). *Birth and fortune: The impact of numbers on personal welfare.* New York: Basic Books.

Elder, G. H., Jr. (1984). Family and kinship in sociological perspective. In R. Parke et al. (Eds.), *The family*. Chicago: University of Chicago Press.

Elder, G. H., Jr., & Liker, J. K. (1980). Hard times in women's lives: Historical influences across 40 years. *American Journal of Sociology, 88*, 241-269.

Engels, F. E. (1972). *The origin of family, private property and the state*. E. B. Leacock (Ed.) New York: International Publishers (Original work published 1884).

Fitzgerald, J. (1983). Actual and perceived sex differences in interpersonal style: Structural and quantitative issues. *Journal of Gerontology, 33*, 344-407.

Freud, S. (1938). The interpretation of dreams. In A. A. Brill (Ed.), *Basic writings of Sigmund Freud*. New York: Modern Library. (Original work published 1900)

Garms-Holmova, V., Hoerning, E. M., & Schaffer, D. (Eds.) (1984). *Intergenerational relations*. New York: Hargrefe.

Gillis, J. R. (1979). *Youth and history*. New York: Academic Press.

Grumes, J. M. (1984). Parenthood issues in the aging process. In B. Cohler & S. Weissmann (Eds.), *Parenthood*. New York: Guilford Press.

Hagestad, G. O. (1981). Problems and promises in the social psychology of intergenerational relations. In R. Fogel, E. Hatfield, S. Kiesler, & E. Shanas (Eds.), *Aging: Stability and change in the family*. New York: Academic Press.

Hagestad, G. O. (1984). The continuous bond: A dynamic, multi-generational perspective on parent-child relations between adults. In M. Perlmutter (Ed.), *Minnesota symposia on child psychology*. New York: Lawrence Erlbaum Associates.

Hagestad, G. O. (1985). Continuity and connections. In V. L. Bengtson & J. Robertson (Eds.), *Grandparenthood*. Beverly Hills, CA: Sage.

Hesse-Biber, S., & Williamson, J. (1984). Resource theory and power in families: Life cycle considerations. *Family Process, 22*, 261-278.

Hill, R. (1949). *Families under stress*. New York: Harper.

Homans, G. C. (1950). *The human group*. New York: Harcourt Brace.

Jones, E., & Gerard, H. B. (1967). *Foundations of social psychology*. New York: Wiley.

Kertzer, D. (1983). Generation as a sociological problem. *Annual Review of Sociology, 9*, 25-49.

Kohli, M. (1984). Political generations. In V. Garms-Holmova, E. M. Hoerning, & D. Schaffer (Eds.) *Intergenerational Relations*. New York: Hargrefe.

Leventman, S. (Ed.). (1982). *Counterculture and social transformation: Essays on negativistic themes in sociological theory*. Springfield, IL: Thomas.

Mannheim, K. (1936). *Essays on the sociology of knowledge*. London: Routledge & Kegan Paul.

Marshall, V. M. (1984). Concepts & generations. In V. Garms-Holmova, E. M. Hoerning, & D. Schaffer (Eds.) *Intergenerational Relations*. New York: Hargrefe.

Marx, K. (1977). *Capital: A critique of political economy* (Vol. 1. B. Fowkes, trans.). New York: Vintage Books. (Original work published 1867)

Mead, G. H. (1938). *The philosophy of the act*. Chicago: University of Chicago Press.

Nash, L. (1978). The concepts of existence: Greek origins of generations thought. *Daedalus, 107*, 1-28.

Nisbet, R., & Perrin, R. G. (1977). *The social bond*. New York: Knopf.

Openshaw, K., Thomas, D., & Rollins, B. (1983). Socialization and adolescent self esteem: Symbolic interaction and social learning explained. *Adolescence, 18*, 317-330.

Parsons, T. (1942). Status and authority: age and sex in the social structure. *American Sociological Review, 7*, 604-616.

Riley, M. W. (1976). Aging and social systems. In R. H. Binstock & E. Shanas (Eds.), *Handbook of aging and social sciences*. New York: Van Nostrand Reinhold.

Riley, M. W., Hess, B. B., & Bond, K. (1983). *Aging in society: Selected reviews of recent research*. Hillsdale, NJ: Lawrence Erlbaum Associates.

Riley, M. W., Johnson, M., & Foner, A. (1972). *Aging and society. Vol. III: A sociology of age stratification*. New York: Russell Sage Foundation.

Rossi, A. (1980). Aging and parenthood in the middle years. In P. Baltes & O. Brim (Eds.), *Life span development and behavior,* Vol. 2. New York: Academic Press.

Russell, L. B. (1981). The cohort as a concept in the study of social change. *American Sociological Review, 30,* 834–861.

Ryder, N. B. (1965). The cohort as a concept in the study of social change. *American Sociological Review, 30,* 834–861.

Schwartz, D. (1984). Psychoanalytic developmental perceptions on parenthood. In R. Cohen, B. Cohler, & S. Weissman (Eds.), *Parenthood.* New York: Guilford Press.

Smith, T. E. (1983). Parental influence: A review of the evidence of influence and a theoretical model of the parental influence process. *Research in Sociology of Education and Socialization, 4,* 13–45.

Spencer, H. (1907). *First principles.* New York: D. Appleton & Co. (Original work published 1862)

Sprey, J. (1981). Conflict and the study of the family. In W. Burr, R. Hill, F. Nye, & I. Reiss. (Eds.), *Contemporary theories about the family.* New York: Free Press.

Surrey, D. S. (1982). *Choice of conscience: Viet Nam era and draft resisters in Canada.* New York: Praeger.

Terman, D. M. (1984). Affect and parenthood: The impact of the past upon the present. In R. Cohen, B. Cohler, & S. Weissman (Eds.), *Parenthood.* New York: Guilford Press.

Tindale, J. A., & Marshall, V. W. (1980). A generation conflict perspective for gerontology. In V. Marshall (Ed.), *Aging in Canada.* Toronto: Fitzhuey & Whiteside.

Yinger, J. M. (1982). *Countercultures: The promise and peril of a world turned upside down.* London: Collier MacMillan.

2 Oedipal Conflict, Platonic Love: Centrifugal Forces in Intergenerational Relations

Nancy Datan
University of Wisconsin - Green Bay

I read Sophocles before I read Freud, and the *Iliad* of Homer before I read either. I have been writing about the universal messages in Greek tragedies for over 10 years (Datan, 1974, 1980, 1982, 1985). Thus it came naturally to me to consider for this conference an examination of the entire canon of Greek tragedy out of which Freud (1966) selected the tragedy of Oedipus and to ask the question, "Who does what, and with which, and to whom?" of this entire network of mythical intergenerational relations. I might then enquire, "What makes Oedipus different from every other tragic hero?" And I already had the answer to that: Of all the protagonists in Greek tragedy, only Oedipus is innocent. He must have caught Freud's eye for some other reason—and I thought I had a very good idea what that reason was. I had some confidence that Freud had read the *Poetics* of Aristotle and that he would have been influenced, consciously or not, by Aristotle's vision of the tragic hero, the man who is basically decent but meets his doom through a fatal flaw. The example Aristotle chose, as I remember it, was Oedipus. Thus I expected to show with relative ease a serious cause of tunnel vision in Freud and to lay the blame at the feet of Aristotle. It only remained to set the stage, and then to allow the thesis to declare and defend itself.

THE SINS OF THE FATHERS
AND OTHER INTERGENERATIONAL LEGACIES

It was my conviction that the tragic flaw in Oedipus was apparent only to a masculine eye: Oedipus fled from the prophecy which foretold that he would murder his father, and fate, in the form of coincidence, caused him to fulfill

29

the prophecy nevertheless. A mother might see the tragic flaw in Oedipus as nothing more serious than the orderly succession of the generations. If a man sits on the throne of Thebes, he will not gladly surrender it to his son; however, the tragedy of Oedipus is set in motion by his own father Laius when Laius tries to murder the infant Oedipus. Thus, it is arguable that the fears of the father are pivotal to the tragedy. Furthermore, Greek myth reveals that the curse of the so-called house of Oedipus has nothing at all to do with Oedipus. It is a curse laid on his father Laius (Vanggaard, 1972). King Laius abducted the young boy Chrysippus as his lover, and King Pelops, the father of Chrysippus, was outraged — not by his son's seduction, but simply because Laius had not asked for his consent. Pelops cursed the house of Laius — an intergenerational curse if ever there was one, but a curse that has taken a very circuitous route to textbooks of developmental psychology. How does it happen that this rich intergenerational pageant of lust and vengeance never found its way to the tragic stage? The answer is that it did. Euripides wrote a tragedy entitled *Chrysippus,* which is lost to us. In 467 B.C.E., Aeschylus staged a teratology of three tragedies: *Laius, Oedipus,* and *The Seven against Thebes,* and the satyric comedy, *The Sphynx.* All but the tragedy of *The Seven against Thebes* are lost to us (Vanggaard, 1972).

Contemporary physics has made great strides through thought experiments, which set in motion events impossible to test except in the imagination. Let us try a small thought experiment with Greek tragedy. Let us suppose that the *Oedipus* of Sophocles was lost but that the teratology of Aeschylus had survived instead. Would we not find our eyes were opened to the sexual energies of parents, instead of the horror awakened by a prophecy which simply declares that our children will take our places? The tragedy of Oedipus is a tragedy of kings and their mortal limits. For this volume, I had planned to set Oedipus into his proper place, innocent heir to his father's sin, a puppet in an intergenerational tragedy in which the sin of the father is truly visited upon the children.

Furthermore, I had already chosen my tragic counterpoint. We know the house of Laius and Oedipus all too well. I thought to introduce the House of Atreus to life-span developmental psychology and to consider violence not across the generations but between husband and wife — violence set in motion through the murder of children. We have an image of Oedipus in the mind's eye, frozen in horror as he realizes his sin, blinding himself with his mother's brooch-pins. Against this image I want to justapose the figure of Clytemnestra, waiting for Agamemnon as he comes home from the Trojan War, waiting to welcome him back to the palace on a carpet of purple.

Here is Clytemnestra waiting, then. She waits for a husband who has sacrificed their daughter Iphigeneia in the harbor at Aulis, when the calm sea and still winds kept his fleet from sailing into battle (Homer: *The Iliad*). And here comes Agamemnon home from the Trojan War, riding onstage in a chariot, bringing Cassandra home with him: "Hi, honey, I'm back from the war. We sacked Troy. I brought Cassandra home. Isn't she pretty? How have you been? Where are the kids? I missed you!"

Clytemnestra answers:

> It is evil and a thing of terror when a wife
> sits in the house forlorn with no man by, and hears
> rumors that like a fever die to break again....
> Had Agamemnon taken all
> the wounds the tale whereof was carried home to me,
> he had been cut full of gashes like a fishing net....
> And therefore is your son, in whom my love and yours
> are sealed and pledged, not here to stand with us today,
> Orestes....
> Strophious of Phocis, comrade in arms and faithful friend
> to you, is keeping him....
> Such my excuse to you, and it is not deceit....
> Now [you are home]...my suffering is past; with griefless heart
> I hail this man....
> Now, my beloved one,
> step from your chariot; yet let not your foot, my lord,
> sacker of Troy, touch the earth. My maidens there!
> Why this delay? Your task has been appointed,
> to strew the ground before his feet with tapestries.
> Let there spring up into the house he never hoped
> to see, where Justice leads him in, a purple carpet.
> [Thus I]...shall act
> with the god's aid to set right what fate ordained.

Agamemnon replies:

> Great your extravagance....
> [But] so much for all this. Take this stranger girl inside
> now, and be kind to her....
> She was my host's gift to me, and a flower exquisite
> from all my many treasures. She will attend me here.
> Now since my will was bent to listen to you in this
> my feet crush purple tapestries as I enter the hall.

Agamemnon enters the house with Clytemnestra. After a while Clytemnestra comes out of the house alone and tells Cassandra:

> Cassandra, you may go inside the house as well....
> Step from this chariot, then....
> From us you shall have all you have the right to ask.

Cassandra is a prophetess, gifted by Apollo with second sight and then cursed to utter prophecies which no one will hear. She replies:

> What house is this?
> ....a house that the gods hate, guilty within
> of kindred blood shed, torture of its own,
> the shambles for men's butchery, the dripping floor....
> Behold the witnesses....
> The small children wail for their own death
> and the flesh roasted that their father fed upon.
> ....I tell you, you shall look on Agamemnon dead....The two of us
> must die, yet our deaths will be avenged by the gods. For there
> shall come one to avenge us also, born to slay
> his mother, and to wreak death for his father's blood....
> So. I am going in, and mourning as I go
> my death and Agamemnon's.

Cassandra enters the house. We hear the voice of Agamemnon from within:

> Ah, I am struck a deadly blow and deep within!....
> Ah me, again, they struck again, I am wounded twice.

Then the doors of the palace open, revealing the bodies of Agamemnon and Cassandra, with Clytemnestra standing over them. She faces the accusations of the Chorus:

> Can you claim I have done this?
> Speak of me never
> more as the wife of Agamemnon.
> In the shadow of this corpse's queen
> the old stark avenger
> of Atreus for his revel of hate
> struck down this man
> last blood for the slaughtered children...
> No shame, I think, in the death given this man. And did he not
> first of all in this house wreak death
> by treachery?
> The flower of this man's love and mine,
> Iphigeneia of the tears
> he dealt with even as he has suffered.
> Let his speech in death's house be not loud.
> With the sword he struck,
> with the sword he paid for his own act.

Clytemnestra's lover Aegisthus enters and reveals the curse of the house of Atreus:

O splendor and exaltation of this day of doom!
Now I can say once more that the gods look down
on mortal crimes to vindicate the right at last....
For Atreus, this man's father...drove my father forth,
Thyestes, his own brother. Yet sad Thyestes came again
to supplicate the hearth, and win some grace...But
Atreus, Agamemnon's godless sire, . . .
then served my father his own children's flesh
to feed on....
that ghastly food whose curse works now before your eyes.
[For] when he knew the terrible thing that he had done,
[Thyestes] spat the dead meat from him with a cry, [and cursed]...
"Thus crash in ruin all the seed of Pleisthenes."
Out of such acts you see this dead man stricken here,
and it was I...who wrought this murder, I
thirdborn to my unhappy father, and...driven,
a helpless baby in arms, to banishment.
Yet I grew up, and justice brought me home...

The horrified Chorus protests to Aegisthus and Clytemnestra; Clytemnestra
speaks the final lines of the tragedy of Agamemnon:

These are howls of impotent rage; forget them, dearest;
you and I have the power; we two shall bring good order
to our house....

As a Greek audience knows, however, this is not the conclusion at all. It is
merely Act I. In the second tragedy of this trilogy, *The Libation Bearers,*
Orestes will avenge his father's death by murdering his mother Clytemnestra
and her lover Aegisthus, and then claim justice in Apollo's name:

I killed my mother not without some right.
My father's murder stained her, and the gods' disgust...
[Apollo] declared that I could do this and not be
charged with wrong.

His innocence is certainly complete so far as psychoanalysis is concerned, for
his sister Elektra, who never touched the murder weapon, gives her name to
the female equivalent of the Oedipus complex.

However, the Greek gods were not as forgiving as contemporary psychoanalysis — at least not immediately. The tragedy of Orestes is not yet over; he
is pursued by the avenging Furies, the Eumenides, in the third tragedy in the
trilogy of *Aeschylus.* In this concluding tragedy, Orestes is brought to trial
and acquitted by Apollo on the basis of a phallocentric vision of conception,

pregnancy, and birth. The Chorus asks how Orestes could ever possibly be cleared of sin:

> See what it means to force acquittal of this man.
> He has spilled his mother's blood upon the ground. Shall he
> then be at home in Argos in his father's house?
> What altars of the community shall he use? Is there
> a brotherhood's purification rite that will let him in?

Apollo declares in favor of Orestes thus:

> I will tell you, and I will answer correctly. Watch.
> The mother is no parent of that which is called
> her child, but only nurse of the new-planted seed
> that grows. The parent is he who mounts. She is a stranger
> who preserves a stranger's seed.

Then the goddess Athene joins forces with Appolo:

> It is my task to render final judgement here.
> This is a ballot for Orestes I shall cast.
> There is no mother anywhere who gave me birth,
> and... I am always for the male
> with all my heart....
> So, in a case where the wife has killed her husband, lord of the house
> her death shall not mean most to me.

Thus the Furies, relics of matriarchy, are defeated by the imposition of patriarchal justice at the hands of Apollo and Athene (Aeschylus: *Agamemnon; The Libation Bearers; The Eumenides*).

Now, how could anybody overlook this tragic trilogy? One would have to believe in one's bones, as Athene declared, that a woman's death did not mean much. It was perfectly clear from his choice of Oedipus that Freud would agree with Athene. I thought I could coax from Aristotle a similar admission. So I went straight for Aristotle with my gun half out of my holster, and I found Oedipus just where I expected him to be: central to the model of Aristotelian tragedy. He was not, however, all alone at the center of the stage. In fact, he was upstaged by Iphigeneia, the daughter of Agamemnon, whose death had set in motion the events of the Oresteia of Aeschylus (Aristotle: *The Poetics*).

Aristotle judges tragic plots on two criteria: the Act itself, which is either done or not done; and knowledge, which the protagonist may possess or may lack. At the most base level of tragedy is the act done knowingly, as is Medea's murder of her sons. At an intermediate level of tragedy is an act done in ignorance, as is Oedipus's accidental murder of his father. At the highest level of tragedy is the complex reversal, in which a tragic act is averted because ignorance ends with a Discovery, revealing new knowledge. Euripides used an alternative version of the myth of the sacrifice of Iphigeneia, in which she was saved from death by the gods and taken to serve as a priestess on the island of Tauris, where her brother Orestes arrived and was about to be sacrificed as *her* victim when she recognized him, spared him, revealed herself, and begged him:

> O brother, come and save me from a life
> as priestess in a loathesome ritual —
> Save me from dying in this lonely land. (Euripides: Iphegeneia in Tauris).

So much for Aristotle, who turned out to be an ally: he supported my view of the tragic value of the house of Arteus. Aristotle says, "Whenever the tragic deed...is done within the family — when murder or the like is done or mediated by brother on brother, by son on father, by mother on son, or son on mother — these are the situations the poet should seek after." The U.S. Justice Department attests to the easy availability of the raw material of tragedy. A 9-year study reported on CBS Nightly News on April 22, 1984, reports 456,000 cases of family violence; the actual incidence is thought to be far higher than the reported incidence. The most common form of violence is seen between spouses. Thus, with the aid of Aristotle and the Department of Justice, I thought my thesis of Freudian tunnel vision might prove even stronger than I had originally hoped. But a funny thing happened to me on the way to this thesis. I tripped on a parenthetical aside.

FROM THEORY TO PRAXIS:
GENERATIONS OF PHILOSOPHY,
GENERATIONS OF GOVERNANCE

Any investigation is a study of the unknown. I cannot know the mind of Freud as he pondered Oedipus and his tragic fate, but I do know that he chose Oedipus over Agamemnon. I know that Freud chose Oedipus from a total of 33 Greek tragedies. The finitude of this population, in fact, is the point of departure of my investigation. So it seemed natural to point out the historical circumstances that permit me to say that Freud chose, as I have done, from a very small surviving body of Greek tragedy. These circumstances are the rise of Islam and the destruction of the library at Alexandria established by Ptolemy, which was thought to contain most of the works of the poets, philosophers, and historians of antiquity. When was the library destroyed? I needed a date. A simple question, one would suppose.

I turned first to *The Cambridge Ancient History* (Bury, Cook & Adcock, 1958), which notes that Aeschylus wrote 90 tragedies, of which seven survive. What happened to the remaining 83? Not a word. Euripides was a popular dramatist—we have more of his work than of Sophocles or of Aeschylus. More by what proportion? Not a word. I turned to Bowra's study of Greek tragedy (1969). He tells us there are two alternatives in writing about Greek tragedy: one can write a history or write about the art. He chose art. Not a word about the lost tragedies. In McNeill's definitive *History of Western Civilization* (1969), there is no mention of the sack of the library at Alexandria. What had begun as an inconvenience was taking on the aura of a mystery. Marshall Hodgson's history of Islam (1974) made no mention of an action taken by devout Moslems. Might Richard Hofstadter's *Anti-Intellectualism in American Life* (1962) describe this first great and terrible act of book-burning? It did not. The introduction to *The Complete Greek Drama* (Oates and O'Neill, 1938), a two-volume set, did not explain why all the Greek drama ever written could be contained in just two volumes, nor admit that the collection was not really complete. The approach of the scholars whose works on tragedy I owned was represented by Bowra's choice, to write about art, not history (Grene & Lattimore, 1942; Kitto, 1950, 1957).

This was a problem for a social scientist. Aaron Antonovsky trained me to prepare a nonresponse report describing the outcome of fieldwork (Datan, Antonovsky & Maoz, 1981). One goes out to interview or sits down with the tragedies of Aeschylus and files a report on the nature of one's sample. Seven tragedies were at home, and of the remaining 83, some had moved, address unknown; some refused; some were ill; some were traveling abroad; some were dead. Something had happened to those tragedies, and they had to be accounted for. Consider my dilemma. I had a parenthetical statement that had grown to the size of a footnote. My footnote became a problem in historiography and was well on its way to turning into a major paradigm shift. A trivial factual note had become a fact-finding mission of major proportions.

In the end, my ignorance was my salvation. I know so little history that if in fact the library at Alexandria was sacked—a point I had come to wonder about by this time—the evidence would be on my own library shelves, if only I could find it. Hofstadter's *Anti-Intellectualism in American Life,* though it was not the source, was a choice made in the right spirit. In that spirit I turned to Gibbon's *Decline and Fall of the Roman Empire* (1962), which contains an account of the sack of the library at Alexandria so full of Gibbon's despair that I shall share it:

> I should deceive the expectation of the reader if I passed in silence the fate of the Alexandrian library....in his leisure hours the Arabian chief [Amrou] was pleased with the conversation of John...who derived the surname of Philoponus from his laborious studies of grammar and philosophy. Emboldened by this familial intercourse [with Amrou], Philoponus presumed to solicit a gift, inestimable in his opinion, contemptible in that of the barbarains—the royal library, which alone among the spoils of Alexandria had not been appropriated by the visit and the seal of the [Moslem] conquerer. Amrou was inclined

to gratify [this] wish...but...[not] without the consent of the caliph, and the well-known answer of Omar was inspired by the ignorance of a fanatic. "If these writings of the Greeks agree with the book of God, they are useless and need not be preserved; if they disagree, they are pernicious and ought to be destroyed." The sentence was executed with blind obedience: the volumes of paper or parchment were distributed to the four thousand baths of the city; and such was their incredible multitude, that six months were barely sufficient for the consumption of this precious fuel...every [modern] scholar, with pious indignation, has deplored the irreparable shipwreck of the learning, the arts, and the genius of antiquity (pp. 884–886).

That is the end of the Library of Alexandria as I remember it. But Gibbon (1962) has not concluded his remarks. He adds:

For my own part, I am strongly tempted to deny both the fact and the consequences....but when I seriously compute the lapse of ages, the waste of ignorance, and the calamities of war, our treasures, rather than our losses, are the object of my surprise. Many curious and interesting facts are buried in oblivion; the three great historians of Rome have been transmitted to our hands in a multilated state; and we are deprived of many pleasing compositions of the lyric, iambic, and dramatic poetry of the Greeks. Yet we should gratefully remember that the mischances of time and accident have spared the classic works to which the suffrage of antiquity had adjusted the first place of genius and glory.... (pp. 884–886)

We have reason to believe that Gibbon's optimism is misplaced. For example, the tragic poet Agathon, of whom you will hear more, wrote the only tragedy whose basis was not myth but creative invention: *The Anthos.* Nothing at all remains of the work of Agathon; only the judgment of Plato, who took the occasion of Agathon's victory in tragic competition as the setting for his dialogue *The Symposium,* shows how terribly wrong Gibbon was when he claimed that "[no] important truth, [no] useful discovery in art or nature, has been snatched away from the curiosity of modern ages" (p. 886).

There is, however, an historical truth behind Gibbon's optimism. That great art perished we have no doubt; that some survived we also know. Archives were lost. Art that survived existed elsewhere. What, then might have favored the preservation of the works of art that have come down to us?

The surviving dramatic art of ancient Greece is the work of a single century. We can ask, therefore, what else was happening in that century, and how those events might have led to the survival of certain tragedies or might have influenced Aristotle in his choice of tragic themes. And we are immediately struck by two interlocking intergenerational networks of this period: a succession of philosophers and a history of conquest, marked by close ties between philosophers and statesmen in each of those generations—the first illustration in history of the dialectic between theory and praxis.

Socrates, first in the succession of philosophers, is beloved by Alcibiades, a brilliant Athenian general and military strategist without peer. The most gifted disciple of Socrates is the philosopher Plato, who is also the lover of Dion, Tyrant of Syracuse; in his lifetime, Plato voyaged three times to Syracuse in efforts to make his dream of the philosopher-king into a reality. Then the military, philosophical, and dramatic stages shift to Macedon, where Plato's student Aristotle becomes the tutor of Alexander the Great, where the dramatist Euripides writes his final tragedy, *The Bacchae,* in exile, in the company of the tragic poet Agathon, his student. Small wonder that a century that sees the fall of Athens and the rise of the empire of Alexander should favor the tragedies of kingship and succession (Bury, Cook & Adcock, 1953; 1958).

But we can go a little further than this into history without making any speculative leaps. Aristotle's sojourn in Macedon might well have disposed him to recognize the Oedipal triangle, for he was engaged by Philip of Macedon not only to educate Alexander to statecraft and governance, but also to wean him from his mother Olympias, a priestess of the bacchic rituals. Philip was assassinated in 336 B.C.E.; his wife Olympias was implicated in his death. Their son Alexander succeeded to the throne and conquered Asia before his death in 323 B.C.E., just one year before the death of Aristotle, who had fled the city of Athens, saying, "I will not give the Athenians a second chance to sin against philosophy" (Bury, Cook, and Adcock, 1953, p. 351). A father dead, a son on the throne, and a mother from whose seductive embraces Aristotle had failed to steal the young Alexander — this is a theme that appears in a slightly different form in *The Bacchae,* which Euripides composed in Macedon. The tragedy of *The Bacchae* tells of the battle between a mother and her son over the bacchic rites sacred to Dionysus and ends as the mother butchers her son out on the mountainside. Olympias survived the death of her son Alexander by many years and was part of the long wars of succession over the throne of Macedon and the dissolution of Alexander's empire. Euripides in the court of Macedon seems to have foreseen the bacchic priestess who was the mother of young Alexander; history would have favored survival of his prescient tragedy *The Bacchae* (Bury, Cook & Adcock, 1953).

NARCISSUS, EROS, AND THE SUCCESSION OF GENERATIONS

What else can be learned from that century of history and tragedy? Athens is called the cradle of Western democracy. Suppose we shake the cradle a little and see what falls out? It is easy to see that I left my own heart in Athens, and it is a constant, terrible shock when I look back to the golden age of

Pericles and Plato and find myself unable to cast a vote in the great Athenian democracy. Only landowning Athenians voted. The vote was denied to women and to slaves. So it turns out that we are quite correct in seeing the blueprint of our own Constitution in the Constitution of Athens, although some of us might be disappointed to see so little progress in more than 2,000 years.

What were they doing in Athens besides making wars and writing tragedies? They were making love — Athens fell, but the Athenians did not become extinct — and they were writing poetry. Freud suggests three ways to go out and meet the world: the narcissistic temperament will be preoccupied with thought; the active temperament will seek to master the world; the erotic temperament will invest in the love of others (Freud, 1961). In the tragedy of Oedipus, strangely enough, no erotic motives bind the generations. Narcissistic Laius fears to lose his throne; active Oedipus kills a stranger where three roads meet; Jocasta, like any other women of her time, has no voice in her own fate and accepts as husband the stranger who killed her husband and claims the throne of Thebes. A peculiar tragedy to give its name to an early erotic tie; indeed, a tragedy altogether without love. Love and rage bind the generations in the Oresteia of Aeschylus; love and loyalty bind the Antigone of Sophocles to her brother; disappointed love brings about the vengeance of the Medea of Euripides. There is plenty of love in the canon of Greek tragedy. But Aristotle, watching the fall of Athens and the rise of Alexander, might be pardoned for seeing the greater human tragedy in the failure of governance.

Then, too, we must take into account the temperament of the philosopher himself. Socrates and Alcibiades were lovers; Plato and Dion were lovers. There is no record of love between Aristotle and the young Alexander. Plato wrote poetry; he also exiled poets from his philosophical utopia, *The Republic*. The extremes of Plato's nature, the poetic and the philosophical, were reconciled by temperate Aristotle in *The Poetics;* who saw tragedy as catharsis, a purging of the soul. Plato's soul, it seems, was not so easily purged.

It is obvious that Plato means more to me than his teacher Socrates or his student Aristotle. There is more than Plato's passion for poetry behind my preference. If I could go back to Plato's Athens, only he would have given me a chance to study. I could never have walked around Athens with Socrates and the guys; there is no record of Aristotle's ever educating a woman, and indeed Aristotle — himself a married man — likened the institution of marriage to that of slavery (*The Nicomachean Ethics; The Politics*). But Plato argued in *The Republic* for equal education for women and practiced what he preached: two women were admitted to study in his Academy (Winspear, 1956). Both in theory and in practice, Plato's radical nature is unremarked by most classical scholars. Edman's (1928) introduction to the standard Modern Library Edition of the dialogues of Plato dismisses the theme of sex equality as one of "a hundred minor themes" (p. xivi) — this in an age when women were illiterate and married in their teens. Since the historical record is lost, we have nothing left but imagination and inference. I propose that Plato's capacity for love, his lyric poetry, and his recognition of women as educable and as potential equals might have some lessons for a contemporary student of intergenerational relations.

I shall now talk for a while about love — the love of women, the love of men, the love of the self. I begin by correcting some monstrous misuses of language that have to do with love: the terms "Lesbian" and "Platonic" love. In contemporary usage, a lesbian is a woman whose sexual preference is other women. That at least is one of its most benign and restricted meanings. It can have pejorative connotations, as in "man-hating lesbian," as though the love of women precluded the love of men. It is sometimes used to discredit a women with feminist views regardless of her sexual preference, as in "lesbian libber." The right of a lesbian to custody of her children can be an issue in 20th century American courtrooms.

The term lesbian, however, has remarkably modest origins. Lesbos is the name of an island, and a Lesbian was someone who lived on Lesbos, as an Athenian lived in Athens or a West Virginian in the state of West Virginia. The marvelous sexual cornucopia that has come forth from the island of Lesbos is a perverse tribute to its most famous inhabitant, Sappho, who was composing lyric poetry in the century before Plato's birth.

It seems only fair to ask Sappho herself what she thought of the love of women, the love of men, and the love of children. Here is Sappho on the love of women:

It was you, Atthis, who said,
Sappho, if you will not get
up and let us look at you
I shall never love you again!

Get up, unleash your suppleness,
lift off your Chian nightdress
and, like a lily leaning into

a spring, bathe in the water.
Cleis is bringing your best
purple frock and the yellow
tunic down from the clothes chest;
you will have a cloak thrown over
you and flowers crowning your hair...

Paraxinoa, my child, will you please
roast nuts for our breakfast? One
of the gods is being good to us:

today we are going at last into
Mitylene, our favorite
city, with Sappho, loveliest

of its women; she will walk
among us like a mother with
all her daughters around her
when she comes home from exile...

But you forget everything. (No. 43)

You may forget but

Let me tell you
this: someone in
some future time
will think of us. (No. 60)

And here is Sappho on the love of men:

It's no use, mother dear.

I can't finish my weaving.
You may blame Aphrodite:
soft as she is,
she has almost killed me
with love of that boy. (No. 12)

Finally, here is Sappho on the love of children — her own daughter Cleis, first
in infancy:

Sleep, darling.
I have a small daughter called Cleis
who is like a golden flower.
I wouldn't take all Croesus' kingdom,
with love thrown in, for her. (No. 17)

And Cleis, as she grows into young womanhood:

Don't ask me what to wear
I have no embroidered
headband from Sardis to
give you, Cleis, such as
I wore
            and my mother
always said that in her
day a purple ribbon

> looped in the hair was thought
> to be high style indeed
> but we were dark:
>   a girl
> whose hair is yellower than
> torchlight should wear no
> headdress but fresh flowers. (No. 83)

Finally, Sappho on her deathbed speaks to her daughter:

> Must I remind you, Cleis,
>
> That sounds of grief
> are unbecoming in
> a poet's household
> and that they are not
> suitable in ours? (No. 99)

Now we come to Platonic love. "It's only platonic" is what you tell your mother when you are bringing a friend home from college and your mother wants to know how many beds to make up. "Platonic" means two beds, one for you and one for the friend, probably in different rooms. If possible, this is an ever more dreadful corruption of history than the abuses to which "Lesbian" has been subjected. The most casual classical scholar knows that the Greeks institutionalized the love of men for boys (Vanggaard, 1972); a student of Plato knows that he was a lover of men (Winspear, 1956). Platonic love, if kept in separate bedrooms, would probably burn the house down. But our own culture, until recently willing to ignore sexual love between women, finds the sexual love of a man for another man profoundly disturbing. To set this into perspective, consider the effect on an American political career of a revelation of homosexual preferences. Until very recently, that was a declaration of political suicide; it would still be a bar from the White House. If the same prohibition existed in Greek culture, Solon would never have been Archon of Athens, and the first great lawgiver in the history of Western civilization; the Athenian democracy might not have had a quorum. It does not tax the imagination to suppose that the fact of Plato's passion, which was everywhere evident in his writing, has been converted in our own culture by a psychological sleight of hand, which Anna Freud terms reaction formation (1966), so that our esteem for the philosophy of Plato is not undermined by disturbing thoughts of what he did with his body. Furthermore the psychiatric mythology of our culture associates male homosexuality with hostility toward women. So it is more than trivially interesting to learn what Plato actually thought of women.

To begin with, Plato held the work of Sappho in very high regard. He wrote of her:

Some say nine Muses. But count again:
Behold the tenth: Sappho of Lesbos. (Barnstone, 1972, p. 65)

This is a measure of both poets: Sappho herself, and Plato's capacity to esteem the work of women, in which he was very nearly unique in his own time
and not at all ordinary in our own time. But even in our culture, it is recognized that "platonic" friendship might exist between homosexual men and
heterosexual women, friendship untroubled by the tides of sexual desires.
What did Plato have to say about women as sexual creatures? It was straightforward and unmistakeably erotic:

I am an apple tossed by one who loves you.
Yield to him therefore, dear Xanthippe:
Both you and I decay. (Fitts, 1956, p. 80)

And what did Plato say about the love of men? Two of the very best expressions of Plato's own erotic passion are embedded in history. The first is his
poetic elegy on the death of his friend Dion, tyrant of Syracuse, assassinated
in the power struggles Plato had failed to temper:

Tears were for Hekabe, friend,
and for the women of Troy
woven into the Dark Web on the day of their birth.
But for you our hopes were great, and great the triumph
Cancelled alike by the gods at the moment of glory.
Now you lie in your own land, now all men honor you:
But I loved you, O Dion! (Fitts, 1956, p. 129)

The second expression of Eros in Plato's writing is found in one of his *Dia-*
logues. I first read Plato when I was 15, and, of all his dialogues, I could take
in only *The Apology* and *The Symposium.* I failed entirely to grasp Plato's
theory of Ideas: I would never have guessed that one day I would know him
as the first of the organismic thinkers, or would propose to students in life-
span developmental psychology that the organismic-mechanistic controversy
traces back to a schism in early Greek philosophy that is itself a reflection of
contrasting personal temperaments.

   The Apology, considered a record of the speech Socrates delivered in his
own defense when he was on trial for his life before the Athenian democracy,
I grasped immediately. The Apology dealt with standing up for oneself and
talking back to fools and would-be tyrants. At 15, I was already good at that.
My other strong suit in my 15th year was sex, and that is what *The Sympo-*
sium is all about. A symposium, then as now, was a drinking party. At
Plato's symposium a group was gathered to celebrate the victory of the tragic
poet Agathon; each man in turn made a speech in praise of love. The

speakers — all historical figures — included Agathon himself; the comic playwright Aristophanes; two students, Phaedrus and Pausanius; a physician, Eryximachus; and Socrates, whose speech on love retold his encounter with the wise woman Diotima, whom Socrates described as his instructress in love. Diotima's definition of love has just been presented to the group as its intellectual and philosophical climax, only to open the door to the dramatic climax. This is an account, with its basis in history, of the love between the young soldier Alcibiades and the philosopher Socrates. The conclusion of *The Symposium* describes Alcibiades' attempt to seduce Socrates into becoming his lover:

> When Socrates had done speaking...suddenly there was a great knocking at the door....A little while afterwards they heard the voice of Alcibiades resounding in the court. He was in a great state of intoxication and kept roaring and shouting, Where is Agathon? Lead me to Agathon, and at length...he found his way to them. Hail, friends, he said....Will you have a very drunken man at your revels? Or shall I crown Agathon, which was my intention in coming, and go away?... [The company begged him to join them], and Alcibiades took the vacant place between Agathon and Socrates...and embraced Agathon and crowned him. Take off his sandals, said Agathon, and let him make a third on the same couch.

> By all means; but who makes the third partner in our revels? said Alcibiades, turning round and starting up as he caught sight of Socrates. By Heracles, he said, what is this? Here is Socrates always lying in wait for me, and always, as his way is, coming out at all sorts of unsuspected places: and now, what have you to say for yourself, and why are you lying here, where I perceive that you have contrived to find a place, not by a joker or lover of jokes, like Aristophanes, but by [Agathon], the fairest of the company.

> Socrates turned to Agathon and said: I must ask you to protect me, Agathon, for the passion of this man has grown quite a serious matter to me. Since I became his admirer I have never been allowed to speak to any other fair one, or so much as to look at them. If I do, he goes wild with envy and jealousy, and not only abuses me but can hardly keep his hands off me, and at this moment he may do me some harm. Please to see to this, and either reconcile me to him, or, if he attempts violence, protect me, as I am in bodily fear of his mad and passionate attempts.

> There can never be reconcilement between you and me, said Alcibiades, "but for the present I will defer your chastisement. And I must beg you, Agathon, to give me back some of the ribands that I may crown the marvellous head of this universal despot — I would not have him complain of me for crowning you and neglecting him, who in conversation is the conquerer of all mankind; and this not only once, as you were the day before yesterday, but always....

> [Eryximachus said to Alcibiades], Before you appeared we had passed a resolution that each one of us in turn should make a speech in praise of love...

That is good, Eryximachus, said Alcibiades, and yet...I should like to know, sweet friend, whether you really believe what Socrates was just now saying; for I can assure you that the very reverse is the fact, and that if I praise any one but himself in his presence, whether God or man, he will hardly keep his hands off me.

For shame, said Socrates.

Hold your tongue, said Alcibiades, for by Poseidon, there is no one else whom I will praise when you are of the company.

Well, then, said Eryximachus, if you like, praise Socrates....

Then I will begin at once, said Alcibiades...and now, my boys, I shall praise Socrates in a figure which will appear to him to be a caricature....You yourself will not deny, Socrates, that your face is like that of a satyr. Aye, and there is a resemblance in other points too. For example, you are a bully, as I can prove by witnesses, if you will not confess. And are you not a flute-player? That you are, and a performer far more wonderful than Marsyas. He indeed with instruments used to charm the souls of men by the power of his breath....but you produce the same effects with your words only, and do not require the flute: that is the difference between you and him....the mere fragments of you and your words, even at second-hand and however imperfectly repeated, amaze and possess the souls of every man, woman, and child who comes within hearing of them. And if I were not afraid that you would think me hopelessly drunk, I would have sworn as well as spoken to the influence which they have always had and still have over me....I am conscious that if I did not shut my ears against him,...my fate would be like that of others, — he would transfix me, and I should grow old sitting at his feet....he is the only person who ever made me ashamed, which you might think not to be in my nature....And therefore I run away and fly from him, and when I see him I am ashamed of what I have confessed to him. Many a time have I wished that he were dead, and yet I know that I should be much more sorry than glad, if he were to die: so that I am at my wit's end....For let me tell you: none of you know him; but I shall reveal him to you....See you how fond he is of the fair? He is always with them and always being smitten by them....Now I fancied that he was seriously enamored of my beauty, and...I had a wonderful opinion of the attractions of my youth...when I next went to him, I sent away the attendant....Well, he and I were alone together, and I thought that when there was nobody with us, I should hear him speak the language which lovers use to their loves when they are by themselves, and I was delighted. Nothing of the sort; he conversed as usual, and spent the day with me, and then went away. Afterwards I challenged him to the palaestra; and he wrestled and closed with me several times when there was no one present; I fancied that I might succeed in this manner. Not a bit; I made no way with him. Lastly, as I had failed hitherto, I thought that I must take stronger measures and attack him boldly...So I invited him to sup with me just as if he were a fair youth, and I a designing lover. He was not easily persuaded to come, and when he came the first time he wanted to go away at once...and I had not the face to detain him. The second time...after we had supped, I went on conversing far into the night, and when he wanted to go away, I pretended that the hour was late and that he had much better remain. So he lay down on the couch next to me...and there was no one but ourselves sleeping in the apartment. All this may be told without shame to anyone. But what follows I could hardly tell you if I were sober....When the lamp was put out and the servants had gone away, I thought that I must be plain with him....So I gave him a shake, and I said, Socrates, are you asleep? No, he said, Do you know what I am thinking? What are you thinking? he said. I think, I replied, that of all the lovers whom I have ever had you are the only one who is worthy of me, and you appear to be too modest to speak. Now I feel that I should be a fool to refuse you this or any other favour, and therefore I come to lay at your feet all that I have....To these words he replied...: O Alcibiades, my friend, truly you must see in me some rare beauty of a kind infinitely higher than any which I see in you. And therefore, if you mean to share with me and to exchange beauty for beauty, you will have greatly the advantage of me; you will gain true beauty in return for appearance....But look again, sweet friend, and see whether you are not deceived in me. The mind begins to grow critical when the bodily eye fails, and it will be a long time before you get old. Hearing this...I fancied that he was smitten...and so without waiting to hear more I got up, and throwing my coat about him crept under his threadbare cloak, as the time of the year was winter, and there I lay during the whole night having this wonderful monster in my arms...but in the morning when I awoke (let all the gods and goddesses be my witnesses) I arose as from the couch of a father or an elder brother....

This, friends, is my praise of Socrates. I have added my blame of him for his ill-treatment of me; and he has illtreated not only me, but...many others in the same way — beginning as their lover he has ended by making them pay their addresses to him. Wherefore I say to you, Agathon, Be not deceived by him; learn from me and take warning, and do not be a fool and learn by experience, as the proverb says.

When Alcibiades had finished, there was a laugh at his outspokenness; for he seemed to be still in love with Socrates. You are sober, Alcibiades, said Socrates, or you would never have gone so far to hide the purpose of your praises, for all this long story is only an ingenious circumlocution, of which the point comes in by the way at the end; you want to get up a quarrel between me and Agathon, and your notion is that I ought to love you and nobody else, and that you and you only ought to love Agathon...you must not allow him, Agathon, to set us at variance....

Alas, said Alcibiades, how I am fooled by this man; he is determined to get the better of me at every turn...The usual way...where Socrates is, no one else has any chance with the fair...suddenly a band of revellers entered, and spoiled the order of the banquet...great confusion ensued....Aristodemus said that...he himself fell asleep...and when he awoke there remained only Socrates, Aristophanes, and Agathon...the chief thing which he remembered was Socrates compelling the other two to acknowledge that the genius of comedy was the same with that of tragedy, and that the true artist in tragedy was an artist in comedy also. (Abridged from *The Symposium,* 212–223)

The lyric beauty of *The Symposium,* of which the foregoing is only a small portion, inspired Shaul Tschernikovsky, a Russian-born Israeli poet, to learn Attic Greek in order to translate it into Hebrew (1946), the only translation from the Greek he ever did, a labor of love in which he employed the idiom of the Mishnah to capture the flavor of the Greek. Tschernikovsky's translation was already out of print when I learned of its existence, and after exhaustive futile searching I stumbled on a battered copy in a used book store. If my house were on fire, this small book is one of a handful of precious things I would grab before I ran outside. The American composer Leonard Bernstein was moved to create a symphonic opera of *The Symposium,* an artistic venture with such a small audience that many who know Bernstein's work do not know this piece of music. Yet there is very little of philosophical value in *The Symposium.* When it seizes the mind, what part does it seize?

The Symposium is a work of imagination. It was written in 389 B.C.E. Plato's Socrates tells Alcibiades, "sweet friend,...it will be a long time before you get old." But Alcibiades would never grow old: he had been assassinated at the age of 33, in 404 B.C.E., 15 years before *The Symposium* was written. And Plato's Alcibiades complains of Socrates: "Many a time have I wished that he were dead, and yet I know that I should be much more sorry than glad, if he were to die." Five years after the death of Alcibiades, Socrates was executed by the Athenian democracy. Alcibiades was not alive to save him or to know him dead in 399 B.C.E., 10 years before Plato created *The Symposium,* which ends with the declaration "that the genius of comedy was the same with that of tragedy, and that the true artist in tragedy was an artist in comedy also." The whole of the conclusion of *The Symposium* is a bawdy comedy. Only when it is over, and the mind allowed to range over the years before and after this dialogue was written, is the full scope of the tragedy made clear to us. That its protagonists should have died unjustly is tragedy enough; that one should die accused of the other's corruption more tragic still. That history would wonder if the hands of Aristophanes were red with the blood of Socrates, about whom he wrote a comic satire, is yet another tragedy, which Plato sought to avert. That nothing at all should come down to us of the work of the poet Agathon is a tragedy that even Plato did not anticipate.

OEDIPAL CONFLICT, PLATONIC LOVE: CENTRIFUGAL FORCES IN INTERGENERATIONAL RELATIONS

I began with a tragedy of the imagination, a failure to see beyond the boundaries of the loveless tragedy of Oedipus. This tragedy was eclipsed by the historical tragedy that in 6 months of the year 638 C.E. destroyed over a thousand years of genius and deprived us of a compeling body of evidence on the complexities of intergenerational networks. I have concluded with a tragedy that links history and the imagination, the tragedy written between the lines of the comedy of *The Symposium,* a tragedy of lovers who brought death to one another: Alcibiades, gifted with an imagination too versatile for the army of Athens, whose tempestuous charm was never tamed by Socrates, dead at the age of 33; Socrates, brought to trial just 5 years later on charges of mpiety and corruption of the youth; most notably Alcibiades, who wasn't there to save him from a sentence of death.

It is a matter of historical record that Plato wrote a tragedy when young and that he burned it after Socrates asked him to explain its meaning, and he could not do it (Winspear, 1956). But his poetic genius survived to find expression in the tragedy of *The Symposium,* when he brought Socrates and Alcibiades together one last time, to bicker, to tease, and to confess their love for all eternity.

How does the tragedy of Oedipus achieve eternal life? Is it, as Freud has said, that each of us sees within ourselves the longing of the small child for the love of one parent and the death of another? Or is it, as I propose, that each of us sees the parent's terror — that, will it or not, the birth of a child is the measure of one's mortality; that, all things being as they should, one has brought into the world one's own successor? It was Freud's genius to see in Oedipus what no one saw before him. It is my task to point out what no one since Freud has troubled to mention: that Oedipus is innocent. It is true that he did the deed with which his name is forever linked; it is also true that he did it all unknowingly. Yet it is this tragedy, and this alone, that has been elevated not merely to the dramatic stage but to a developmental stage.

There is no need to choose my vision of tragedy over Freud's. In psychoanalysis, as in art, one vision of truth does not exclude another. I have a son who once was 5 years old. From that day to this, I have never thought Freud mistaken. But Aristotle is not wrong either, when he claims that tragedy grips us when it grows out of the dark deeds done within families, the networks of rage and lust so much more complicated than the small boy's yearnings. The ties that bind the intergenerational networks of myth and the Greek tragedies are manifold, and the Oedipus complex is only one of these, with more than a single meaning. Oedipal conflict may also signal the younger generation's assertion of its own claim on power: a centrifugal force dividing, rather than binding, the generations. The complementary centripetal force is Platonic love, which drives out the blood curse and binds the generations of chosen relationships: lovers, teachers, healers — creators of ties of affinity rather than keepers of kinship.

With Oedipus, Freud showed us passion in the nursery. But Sappho, Plato, and Aeschylus show us that passion informs the remaining seven decades of the life cycle as well and that whatever small boys dream unconsciously is not of greater importance than what grown women and men do to one another and to their children, consciously and in cold blood.

REFERENCES

Aeschylus: *Agamemnon.*

Aeschylus: *The Eumenides.*

Aeschylus: *The Libation Bearers.*

Aristophanes: *The Frogs.*

Aristotle: *Nicomachean Ethics.*

Aristotle: *Poetics.*

Aristotle: *Politics.*

Barnstone, W. (1972). *Greek lyric poetry.* New York: Schocken.

Bowra, C. M. (1969). *Landmarks in Greek literature.* New York: Meridian Books.

Bury, J. B., Cook, J. A. & Adcock, F. E. (1953). *The Cambridge ancient history,* Volume VI: *Macedon.* Cambridge: Cambridge University Press.

Bury, J. B., Cook, J. A. & Adcock, F. E. (1958). *The Cambridge ancient history,* Volume V: *Athens.* Cambridge: Cambridge University Press.

Datan, N. (1974, August/September). *After Oedipus: An exploration of psychosexual stages of development in adulthood.* Paper presented at the meeting of the American Psychological Association, New Orleans, LA.

Datan, N. (1980). Midas and other mid-life crises. In W. H. Norman & T. J. Scaramella (Eds.), *Mid-life crises: Clinical issues and implications.* New York: Brunner/Mazel.

Datan, N. (1982). After Oedipus: Laius, Medea, and other parental myths. *Journal of Mind and Behavior, 3*(1), 17–26.

Datan, N. (1985). Androgyny and the life cycle: The Bacchae of Euripides. *Journal of Imagination, Cognition, and Personality: The Scientific Study of Consciousness, 4*(4), 407–415.

Datan, N., Antonovsky, A., & Maoz, B. (1981). *A time to reap: The middle age of women in five Israeli sub-cultures.* Baltimore: Johns Hopkins University Press.

Edman, I. (1928). Introduction. In I. Edman (Ed.), *The works of Plato.* New York: Simon & Schuster.

Euripides: *The Bacchae.*

Euripides: *Iphegeneia in Aulis.*

Euripides: *Iphigeneia in Tauris.*

Euripides: *The Medea.*

Fitts, D. (1956). *Poems from the Greek anthology.* New York: New Directions.

Freud, A. (1966). *The writings of Anna Freud,* Volume II. *The Ego and the Mechanisms of Defense.* Revised Edition, New York: International Universities Press.

Freud, S. (1961). Civilization and its discontents. New York: W. W. Norton.

Freud, S. (1966). The development of the libido and the sexual organizations. In *The complete introductory lectures on psychoanalysis.* New York: W. W. Norton.

Gibbon, E. (1962). *The decline and fall of the Roman Empire,* Volume 3. Abridgment by D. M. Low. New York: Washington Square Press.

The Greek anthology (1916). 5 Volumes. The Loeb Classical Library. Cambridge, MA: Harvard University Press.

Grene, D. & Lattimore, R. (1942). *The complete Greek tragedies.* Chicago: University of Chicago Press.

Hodgson, M. G. S. (1974). *The venture of Islam: Conscience and history in a world civilization,* Volume 1: *The classical age of Islam.* Chicago: University of Chicago Press.

Hofstadter, R. (1962). *Anti-intellectualism in American life*. New York: Random House.

Homer: *The Iliad*.

Kitto, H. D. F. (1950). *Greek tragedy: A literary study*. New York: Doubleday.

Kitto, H. D. F. (1957). *The Greeks*. Revised Edition. Middlesex, GB: Penguin Books.

McNeill, W. H. (1969). *History of western civilization*. Revised Edition. Chicago: University of Chicago Press.

Oates, W. J. & O'Neill, Jr. Eugene (Eds), (1938). *The complete Greek drama*. New York: Random House.

Plato: *The Apology*.

Plato: *The Republic*.

Plato: *The Symposium*.

Sappho: A new translation by Mary Barnard (1958). University of California Press.

Sophocles: *The Antigone*.

Sophocles: *Oedipus Rex*.

Tchernikowsky, S. (1946). *Aplaton: Hamishteh*. [The Symposium of Plato.] Hebrew. Tel Aviv: Schocken.

Vanggaard, T. (1972). *Phallos: A symbol and its history in the male world*. New York: International Universities Press.

Winspear, A. D. (1956). *The genesis of Plato's thought*. Revised Edition. New York: S. A. Russell.

3 Intergenerational Research: Methodological Considerations

James S. Jackson
Shirley J. Hatchett
Institute for Social Research
The University of Michigan

INTRODUCTION

The realization that the context of human development and change is needed to understand complex individual behavior (Baltes & Willis, 1977; Nesselroade, 1977) is leading to a greater focus on the family unit as the appropriate level for study and analysis (Aldous & Hill, 1965; Bengtson & Cutler, 1976; Hagestad, 1981; Huston & Robins, 1982; Kitson, et al., 1982; Troll & Bengtson, 1979). Hagestad (1981) suggested that families are cultural units which form and create their own clusters of life patterns. For a full understanding of individuals who are enmeshed in these units, a social psychological approach to family lineage groups is needed.

Consensus exists among the relatively small but growing number of researchers in this area regarding the importance of understanding family lineage bonds and their reciprocal effects (Bengtson, 1975; Beck & Jennings, 1975; Hagestad, 1981; Hill, 1970; Markides, Hoppe, Martin & Timbers, 1983; Thompson & Walker, 1982; Troll & Bengtson, 1979). However, this agreement regarding the need to study family lineages as complex social psychological units has not resulted in accepted methodological approaches, either in data collection or analysis strategies (Bytheway, 1977; Huston & Robins, 1982; Thompson & Walker, 1982). Several recent papers have noted the failure of dyadic lineage research to address adequately the distinction between the individual and relationship properties, management of discrepant reports (the asymmetry problem), and problems of clearly distinguishing interdependence and independence in dyads (Hagestad, 1982; Huston & Robins, 1982; Thompson & Walker, 1982; Thompson & Williams, 1984).

Methodological problems are greatly increased in family lineage research when an attempt is made to simultaneously study three generations (Bengtson, 1975; Bytheway, 1977; Hagestad, 1981; Hill, 1970; Markides et al., 1983). While a great number of these problems have been delineated, four appear to be the most prominent in current research.

Three Generation Triads Are Not a Panel

Very few three generation research efforts have included a true longitudinal component (Hill, 1970). Most longitudinal lineage research has been restricted to two generation lineage comparisons (Clausen, 1972; Jennings & Niemi, 1981). The majority of well-known three generation research efforts have involved interviewing lineages at only one point in time. Thus, the causal orderings of most variables, as with any cross-section data, are open to question.

It is inappropriate, conceptually or analytically, to treat members of the lineage as the same person measured at different points in time. Analyses that assume such measurement are in serious error. The common, cross-section three generation research design cannot be viewed as multiple longitudinal data points in which different generations represent change over time.

Many observations regarding the need for developmental data to permit clear, unambiguous interpretation of change and causal effects are still true (Schaie, 1977). The three generation research design, we believe, has the potential of contributing greater knowledge to an understanding of cohort, aging, and period effects. However, longitudinal designs that include successive generations of family members are needed to assess developmental change and causal ordering (Nesselroade & Baltes, 1979).

Cohort and Age

In much of the three generation research that has been conducted, little attention has been given to the problem that different lineage generation members across families may represent widely varying ages and cohort experiences (Hagestad, 1981). Thus, to treat each lineage as merely cohorts without taking into account the different ages of the lineage members may do great disservice to the meaning of generation comparisons. For example, it is clear that in some families the timing of marriages and births may vary significantly. Thus, a grandmother in one family may be only 45 years of age; in another, the grandmother may be 70. Disregard of these discrepancies in analysis may lead to misspecification and misinterpretation. As Hagestad (1981) pointed out, such age/lineage discrepancies may be the result of significant differences in family lineages, which can be significantly distorted if lineage members are treated as merely separate cohorts (Hill, 1970).

Unit of Analysis

One major methodological deficiency has been the underutilization of the potential of the three generation sample. In some cases lineage samples have been treated as simple cross-sections, and the special relationship among lineage triads has not been considered (Hagestad, 1981; Troll & Bengtson, 1979). Because each triad is linked by a specified family relationship, the members in different lineage generation positions are not independent of others. A particular problem of this overlap is the lack of knowledge regarding generational linkage. This problem is often ignored in analysis (Bengtson, 1975; Hill, 1970).

As indicated earlier, the problems of conducting dyadic lineage studies are magnified in three generation research. What is the appropriate unit of analysis (Huston & Robins, 1982)? How should the interrelationships and noninterrelationships be treated (Thompson & Walker, 1982)? And how do differing frames of references across lineage generations influence the development of relevant measures and indices (Hagestad, 1981)?

The social sciences have been lax in defining and using aggregate units of analysis. This concern of aggregation and disaggregation is a serious problem for three generaton researchers; a problem that is basic to how we define, sample, and analyze interpersonal and group interaction more generally. This problem can be avoided in an individually focused, psychological perspective on human behavior. In order to study three generation triads, however, methods of treating the triad as the unit of analysis must be found (Hagestad, 1981; Troll & Bengtson, 1979).

The basic unit-of-analysis problem underlies much of the difficulty in developing adequate analysis strategies in three generation research. The problem of agreement versus covariation has been widely noted in the literature (Jennings & Niemi, 1981; Troll & Bengtson, 1979). Pairwise treatment of lineage dyads does not address the problem of aggregation across dyadic relationships (Hagestad, 1981). It certainly does not solve the problem of three generation reciprocal influence, and adds another level of analysis.

At present there is no commonly accepted set of procedures for analyzing three generation triads. Regression techniques have long been used for examining dyads (Bielby, Hauser & Featherman, 1977). Analyses of three generation triads, however, have frequently treated the lineages as independent cohorts. A notable exception is Bengtson's (1975) application of regression procedures in the investigation of similarities and differences across generations and families.

It has been suggested that structural equation modeling can be applied to three generation research questions. Several problems exist with this approach including independence of measurement, adequate specification of the latent variables, and unknown reciprocal causation. These problems have prevented widely disseminated applications of structural equation modeling to three generations datasets. Recent reviews (Hagestad, 1981; Troll & Bengtson, 1979) have suggested that if the field is to progress, answers to the unit of analysis and data analysis issues must be solved.

Sampling and Sample Representativeness

Previous three generation studies have not addressed issues of sampling and sample representativeness. Although sampling issues are often treated as problems of external validity, several recent reviews have noted that poor three generation samples may have resulted in serious misinterpretation of substantive concerns (Bytheway, 1977; Kitson et al., 1982; Markides et al., 1983; Troll & Bengtson, 1979). Several problems in the approaches that have been used are noted in the literature. Among these are unclear specification of how the three generation networks were obtained. For example, Bytheway (1977) notes that in Hill's (1970) study, no procedures or controls were introduced to account for the fact that the sampling plan gave greater probability of inclusion to larger size families, underrepresented childless families, and overrepresented families at retirement who had experienced a death of a spouse. Similarly, much of the previous research has depended heavily on self-administered inventories, with college students asking parents and grandparents to complete a questionnaire. The biases in this procedure are impossible to ascertain. It has been claimed that the lack of attention to representative sampling poses a problem primarily of external validity (Hill, 1977). Growing evidence, however, points to the existence of severe internal validity problems when samples are not representative of some known population, either through the failure adequately to specify the population or through poor response rates (Berk, 1983; Bytheway, 1977). Recent works make evident what has been known for many years in some disciplines (Heckman, 1979). It is only now becoming salient to those disciplines most involved in three generation research (Berk, 1983; Berk & Ray, 1983).

Though not formally stated in the past (Bytheway, 1977; Hagestad, 1981; Troll & Bengtson, 1979), lack of attention of the sampling procedures used in nearly all three generation research studies raises serious questions about the representative nature of the three generation triads. Because sampling and selection are conditional, interdependent phenomena, estimates of the nature of the original population have not typically been available. This has been further confounded by restrictions on the age and cohort membership of generations—for example, when the middle generation is constrained to be approximately 45 years of age, or college students are requested to have their parents and grandparents (of their choosing) complete a questionnaire. As Berk (1983) demonstrated, lack of attention to sampling affects both generalizability and the nature of the relationships observed in the resulting data (Bytheway, 1977). Because of selection bias, the very nature of the observed relationships may be compromised by samples that are not representative of the population of interest (Berk, 1983). This is even more confounded in the three generation situation in which the population is not known and, in most cases, not specified (Hagestad, 1982).

Sampling and sample representativeness are serious problems in three generation research. The lack of specification of the population of interest, the fact that the triad as an analysis unit is highly interdependent and the lack of accepted sampling procedures exacerbates important problems, even in individual or household sampling (Berk, 1983). Although many have called for more refined and better sampling procedures to address these issues (Bytheway, 1977; Hagestad, 1981; Kitson et al., 1982; Troll & Bengtson, 1979), specific approaches have not developed.

In the remainder of this chapter we describe the Family Network Sampling Procedure (FNSP) used in obtaining a national probability sample of three generation lineage families in the continental United States. This procedure addresses many of the sampling and sample representativeness problems described above.

The three generation family lineage study described in this chapter was developed as part of a national investigation of the adult Black population (Jackson, Tucker & Bowman, 1981). Because the three generation study was linked to this national cross-section survey, an evaluation of its outcomes is highly dependent on the quality of the parent survey. In the following pages the national cross-section survey is reported in detail as a basis for the description of the Family Network Sampling Procedure (FNSP) and sample results.

THE NATIONAL CROSS SECTION SURVEY OF BLACK AMERICANS

The national cross-section survey was designed to address two major issues regarding previous research on black Americans. The first was the lack of attention to sample representation in research on ethnic minority populations generally, and black Americans specifically (Jackson, Tucker & Bowman, 1982). The second was the lack of attention to the conceptualization and measurement of constructs appropriate for black Americans in the social sciences (Allen, 1978).

A major objective of the National Survey of Black Americans (NSBA) was to develop a sample based upon the distribution of the black population and not upon the distribution of the general population. Two major differences in the distribution of black Americans in comparison to the total population are that blacks are more heavily concentrated in the southern states and in large urban areas of the country. Both of these differences had to be taken into consideration in designing the sample for this national survey. The survey employed a design in which every black American household in the continental United States had the same probability of inclusion.

Sampling Procedure

The sample was drawn according to a multistage area probability procedure designed to ensure that every black household had an equal probability of being selected for the study (Kish, 1965). The sample was based on the 1970 census distribution of the black population. Seventy-six primary areas were selected, stratified by racial composition (number of black households) and region. Then smaller geographical areas (sample places and clusters) were randomly chosen from these strata. Household sampling and interviewing were conducted in these smaller geographical areas, generally representing city blocks or groups of blocks.

Within each selected black household one person was chosen randomly to be interviewed from those residing in the household who were eligible for the study (Kish, 1965). Eligibility was restricted to persons 18 years of age and older, self-identified as black Americans, and United States citizens. If the person selected for interviewing refused, then the household was classified as a nonresponse. All interviewing was conducted by professionally trained black interviewers.

Household Screening Procedures

The major drawback in conducting surveys of this nature prior to this time was the tremendous cost in developing a self weighting sampling frame for the Black population. Because blacks are highly concentrated in many geographical areas but sparsely distributed in others, a sampling frame that gives equal probability to inclusion of blacks from all geographical areas of the country is generally cost prohibitive. Thus, previous surveys with large samples of blacks have not attempted proprotionate inclusion of blacks who lived in areas of the country with low densities of blacks. Blacks from these areas must be included, however, if a sample that is representative of the wide diversity of black American thought and behavior is to be obtained.

Two special screening procedures were developed to address this issue. The first, the Standard Listing and Screening Procedure (SLASP) was designed for use in high density black areas and was conducted by black interviewers. The other, the Wide Area Screening Procedure (WASP), was used in low density black areas. White interviewers were employed for all WASP screening.

SLASP, designed for use in mixed and mostly black areas, provides a unique method for identifying black households through the employment of "reference housing units." These reference housing units are used by the interviewers to identify the housing units that are black or not black within the defined geographical areas. WASP was used in areas with few or no black occupied households. This procedure employed the reference housing unit approach described for SLASP. In the SLASP procedure, the interviewer was told explicitly which houses to contact.[1] In WASP, the number or location of reference housing units depended on the interviewer's assessment of the number and distribution of housing units in the area. Whereas SLASP interviewers were asked to list and classify each housing unit in the cluster as either black or all other, in the WASP procedure interviewers asked the reference housing units only about blacks within the defined area and then listed only the black housing units. This combination of WASP and SLASP procedures minimized the cost of screening in high density black areas and was highly effective in reducing the cost and time for locating and listing black housing units in low density areas.[2]

Summary

The sampling procedures reported here resulted in a final sample of 2,107 completed interviews conducted during 1979 and 1980. The overall response rate was 67%. The black population is disproportionately distributed within urban areas, where response rates have historically been low. An average of 3.4 (the range was from 1 to 22 calls) callbacks per selected household were required to complete the 2,107 interviews.

Overall, the national cross-section sample is fairly representative of the black population as reported in the 1980 census. However, there is a disparity between the proportions of men and women in the sample and a slight tendency to underrepresent younger people of both sexes and to overrepresent older women. Analyses reveal no sex differences between respondents and nonrespondents. Thus, the sex differences are due perhaps to the disproportionate representation of female headed households in the United States. Finally, there is a slight tendency to overrepresent low income groups and for a slightly higher proportion of individuals to come from the South than their distribution in the population would indicate. These differences from ex-

---

[1] In SLASP, every household was listed and reference households selected using random numbers that were concealed until listing was completed.

[2] Systematic Coverage checks were conducted for each procedure to assess their ability to find and accurately classify black and nonblack households. The results of these checks showed that both procedures worked extremely well and accomplished their efficiency and cost objectives.

pected census distributions are relatively slight, particularly in comparison with other large studies of the black population (Jackson, et al., 1982).

THE THREE GENERATION STUDY OF BLACK AMERICANS

The national cross-section survey served as the "parent" study for the Three Generation Family Study. When the respondents in the cross-section survey had living family members from at least two other generations, interviews were attempted with one randomly selected representative from each of those two generations. Also, the cross-section respondent was re-interviewed with a form of the three generation instrument.

Family Network Sampling Procedure

Multiplicity sampling (Frankel & Frankel, 1977; Sirkin, 1970) is a method that has been used primarily to improve the estimation of such events as births and deaths through an increase in the units reporting the event and an anticipated decrease in the sampling errors and biases (Nathan, Schmelz & Kenvin, 1977). It was adapted in the Three Generation Family Study to provide a procedure for generating new national probability samples from our original national cross-section sample (Nathan, Schmelz & Kenvin, 1977). This approach, the Family Network Sampling Procedure (FNSP), allowed us to generate a nationally distributed sample of three generation families.

With the cross-section respondent as informant, questions were asked at the end of the cross-section questionnaire that allowed the interviewer to determine whether or not each respondent was a member of an eligible three generation family; if ineligible, the cross-section interview was terminated. If the respondent was a member of a three generation family, the interviewer used the specially developed FNSP Sampling Booklet to ascertain which two family members were to be selected. Figure 3.1 describes the rules of inclusion used to select relevant family members. To be eligible, family members had to be 14 years old or older.

Having a defined set of inclusion and exclusion rules, we formed clear multiplicities or groupings of family members across generations from which the two family members could be randomly sampled. We also were interested in attaching a specific probability of selection to each of the new three generation respondents. To accomplish this, a special section of the Re-Interview Questionnaire was used to obtain information from the original cross-section respondent/informant regarding household composition and relationships of all possible members of the multiplicity to the original respondent. The probability of inclusion could be determined, through a series of estimation

Rules for Triad Formation

Parent-Original R-Child Triad

1. If the cross-section R has at least one living parent and at least one child 14 years old or older, follow rules for completion of parent-child triad below. The cross-section R becomes G2 (Second Generation).
2. If R has only one parent alive, choose that parent. That parent becomes G1. If R has more than one parent alive, choose parent for G1 as shown on appropriate randomized page of sampling booklet.
3. Follow section procedures in sampling booklet to randomly select one child from all of the original R's children who are 14 years old or older. This child becomes G3 and completes the triad.

Grandparent-Parent Original R Triad

1. If the cross-section R has at least one parent with a living parent and no children 14 years old or older, follow rules for completion of grandparent-parent triad below. The cross-section R becomes G3.
2. If R has only one parent with living parents, choose that parent for G2. If R has more than one parent with at least one living parent, choose parent listed on randomized page of sampling booklet for G2.
3. Follow instructions on appropriate page of sampling booklet to randomly select (if selected parent has more than one living parent) one of R's parent's parents for G1. If R's parent has only one parent, select that parent for G1.

Original R-Child-Grandchild Triad

1. If the cross-section R has no living parents but has at least one child who has children who are 14 years old or older, follow rules for completion of child-grandchild triad below. The cross-section R becomes G1.
2. From among R's children who have children who are 14 years old or older, randomly select one child using selection table on appropriate page of sampling booklet. This child becomes G2.
3. From among all of the selected child's children who are 14 years old or older, randomly select one child using selection table on appropriate page of sampling booklet. This child is R's grandchild and becomes G3.

Definition of Terms

1. Parent is defined as biological or adoptive caretaker of respondent in childhood before 14 years of age.
2. Grandparent is defined as biological or adoptive caretaker of respondent's parents before parent was 14 years of age.
3. Offspring are defined as biological children or children who were adopted before 12 years of age.
4. Grandchildren are defined as biological offspring or adopted offspring of respondents' offspring.

FIG. 3.1   Network rules of inclusion for Three Generation Family Study.

procedures, for each of the two selected three generation respondents. These probabilities could then be assigned to the three generation family members to form new probability samples (e.g., elderly) and to gain more precise population estimates.

There were three possible three generation family types, dependent on the nature of the original cross-section respondent — parent-child, grandparent-parent, and child-grandchild. In each, the original respondent completed the triad. Thus, the original cross-section respondent was a representative of the first generation (G1) in what we call the Child-Grandchild triad, the second generation (G2) in the Parent-Child triad, and the third generation (G3) in the Grandparent-Parent triad. Eligibility of the cross-section respondents was determined as noted earlier by a special series of questions. Respondents were asked to indicate the number of eligible family members in the two adjacent lineage positions. Identification of these individuals, dependent on generation type, formed the basis for the random sampling procedure. As shown in Fig. 3.1, each representative of the two generations needed to complete each type of triad was selected randomly from all eligible family members in that generation using the FNSP Sampling Booklet. No attempt was made to predetermine the type of lineages selected. If there were more than three generations present, however, parent-child triads were favored.

Following the selection of the appropriate family members, respondents were asked to supply names and addresses for family members that did not live in the sample household. A letter, countersigned by the respondent/informant, was then immediately mailed to the potential three generation respondent describing the nature of the study and requesting an interview when he or she was contacted. If the family member lived within a 50-mile radius, the interview was conducted by the original interviewer from the cross-section study. If not, then the coversheet for the three generation respondent containing information on names and addresses was mailed to the study staff and the closest available interviewer was assigned. Finally, the original interviewer re-interviewed the original cross-section respondent with a modified three generation instrument (re-interview).

Although it was planned to take all the three generation interviews face-to-face, as in the cross-section study, many of the potential three generation interviews fell outside of the original 76 primary areas in which the national cross-section survey was being conducted. The expense thus made direct, face-to-face contact with all generation members impossible. Nearly 1,700 three generation interviews were taken face to face, and the remaining 700 were conducted by telephone at the Survey Research Center.

Results of the Family Network Sampling Procedures

As indicated previously, the national cross-section sample of black adults consisted of 2,107 individuals. Of this number, approximately 53% were eli-

gible for the three generation study. The actual proportion of three generation families, disregarding the age criteria (all respondents had to be at least
14 years of age), was in excess of 60%. The 1,122 potential three generation
triads, consisting of the main cross-section study respondent and two family
members (3,366 possible interviews), formed the sample in which interviews
were attempted. Of the possible 2,244 new family member interviews, 1,006
were completed face to face and an additional 369 were conducted over the
telephone for a total of 1,375 interviews. A total of 865 re-interviews were
collected from the original cross-section respondents who generated the triads, (665 face-to-face and 200 telephone interviews). The final response rate
was approximately 61% for the two generated family interviews and 77% for
the re-interviews with the original respondents. These compare with the overall response rate of approximately 67% in the cross-section adult survey. A
total of 510 complete three generation triads were obtained for an approxi-
mate response rate of 46% of the 1,122 possible complete triads.

Some discussion of the response rates obtained is in order. Because the national three generation survey was linked to the national cross-section survey,
the response rates on the cross-section study directly affected the sampling
frame for the national three generation study. as the national cross-section
survey is a fairly representative sample of the adult black population, there is
no reason to believe that the three generation members obtained from approximately 67% of the sample should differ in any radical way from the
members of the 33% of the sample that was not obtained. Analysis of the
nonrespondents in the sample indicates little bias in the sample based on individuals who were not interviewed. For example, nonrespondents were not
disproportionately male or female. Response rates varied most by region.
The highest nonresponse occurred in the Northeast and the West. In keeping
with the fairly stable 53% of the national sample across regions of the country who turned out to be members of eligible three generation families, we expect that the same 53% would hold for the refusals and nonidentified
nonrespondents as well.

The fact that only a 46% response rate was obtained for triads is a little
more worrisome. However, although this response rate appears low, it must
be remembered that it is for the conditional situation of obtaining *all* three
generation members. More than 77% of the eligible family triads resulted in
dyads, one family member interviewed in addition to the original cross-
section respondent. Of these dyads, 81% were contiguous (1 and 2, or 2 and
3) and 19% were noncontiguous. These latter proportions are as high as or
higher than current completion rates in most sample surveys.

All of these response rates were influenced by the availability of respondents — our ability to contact them for an interview attempt. This availability was constrained by several factors, some owing to natural transitions
and others to changes in our methodology during the field period. A number
of family members died before we were able to interview them; others were

sick, hospitalized, or incarcerated. Because the study was intended to be done face to face, a change to telephone mode made a number of respondents inaccessible because they did not have phones or we were unable to find current phone numbers for them. Estimates of the response rates for this study, which take into account these constraints, should be somewhat higher than those reported above.

ASSESSMENT OF THE FAMILY NETWORK SAMPLING PROCEDURE

The remainder of this chapter examines the success of our Family Network Sampling Procedure in generating a fairly representative sample of three generation lineage families. This assessment begins with a comparison of cross-section respondents who generated three generation families for our study and those who did not. Next, we discuss the sampling frames of the three types of family triads and examine our resulting sample in light of the generated sample. These analyses shed light on the possible impact, if any, of our response rate. Finally, we describe our three generation family study respondents in terms of the distribution of selected demographic and socio-economic characteristics within each generation.

Eligible and Ineligible Cross Section Respondents

One method of ascertaining the quality of the generated three generation sample is to examine whether there are significant differences between the characteristics of the cross-section respondents who were eligible and those who were not eligible members of three generation families. Table 3.1 shows selected demographic and socio-economic characteristics of the cross-sectional respondents by eligibility.

Parental status and marital status are two characteristics of cross-section respondents that would likely be associated with eligibility for an intergenerational study of this sort. As shown in Table 3.1, there are only slight effects for marital status. Individuals who had ever been married (separated, divorced or widowed) and never married respondents were only slightly more likely to be ineligible than the currently married. On the other hand, the effect of parental status is somewhat stronger with ineligible respondents, as one would expect, because they are less likely to have living children.

There appears to be little difference in the age distribution of the eligible and ineligible cross-section respondents. There is a slight tendency for older respondents (those in the categories of 55 to 64 and over 65 years of age) not to have generated a three generation family. These differences are relatively small, however. Similarly, very slight differences are also found for gender.

TABLE 3.1
Selected Demographic and Social Characteristics of Cross Section Respondents by
Eligibility for Three Generation Family Study

Selected Demographic/ Social Characteristics	Eligibility of Cross-Section Respondent	
	Eligible	Ineligible
Marital Status		
Married	42.4%	41.2%
Ever Married	33.4	39.0
Never Married	24.3	19.8
	100.0%	100.0%
Parental Status		
Has Living Children	83.2%	69.4%
No Children	16.8	30.6
	100.0%	100.0%
Age		
18 to 34 years	44.4%	36.9%
35 to 54 years	33.0	29.7
55 to 65 years	8.8	14.3
Over 65 years	13.8	19.1
TOTAL	100.0%	100.0%
Gender		
Males	35.7%	40.3%
Females	64.3	59.7
TOTAL	100.0%	100.0%
Region		
North East	18.0%	19.2%
North Central	23.4	20.7
South	52.8	54.1
West	5.8	6.0
TOTAL	100.0%	100.0%
Urbanicity		
Large Urban	46.6%	48.9%
Small Urban	33.6	28.7
Rural	19.8	22.3
TOTAL	100.0%	100.0%
Education		
Zero to six years	11.3%	12.3%
Seven to eleven years	32.0	32.1
Twelve years	32.4	30.0
More than twelve years	24.3	25.6
TOTAL	100.0%	100.0%
Family Income (dollars)		
Under five thousand	25.1%	25.1%
Five to ten thousand	25.1	26.1
Ten to twenty thousand	26.5	27.1
More than twenty thousand	23.2	21.7
TOTAL	100.0%	100.0%

Females are slightly more likely than males to have generated an eligible three generation family. Also, slight differences are found by region. Eligibility for the cross-section respondents across regions follows the same distribution as that found for cross-section interviews. Again, attesting to the quality of the cross-section and the three generation samples is the fact that there were very slight urbanicity differences in eligibility for the three generation family study. Approximately the same proportions of eligible and ineligible cross-section respondents were found in large urban, small urban, and rural areas.

We also examined a number of familial variables to ascertain whether structural or social factors related to families influenced reporting information used in determining eligibility (not shown in Table 3.1). No significant differences in eligibility by family geographical proximity, family availability, or family contact were found. These outcomes suggest that the procedures utilized for random selection from three generation family networks were successful and that no biases, at least those related to these variables, were introduced by the respondents. We also found no significant differences in eligibility by perceived family closeness. This suggests that there was little or no bias in reports of eligibility by perceived family affect.

Overall, the results shown in Table 3.1 are heartening in terms of any potential biases in the generation of eligible three generation triads by cross-section respondents. Only three of the demographic variables revealed statistically significant differences in the proportion of the respondents reporting three generation family membership. These effects for age, marital status, and parental status were slight, however. None of the remaining demographic variables showed any significant effects. Like the findings for the demographic variables, none of the familial variables showed any effects on reported eligibility for the three generation survey. This finding is particularly noteworthy because it was possible that such familial variables as geographical proximity or family contact may have had an impact on reports of eligibility. In the next section, we turn to a closer examination of the nature of the three generation triad sampling frames.

Triad Sampling Frames

Tables 3.2, 3.3 and 3.4 describe the sampling frames from which family members of eligible cross-section members were selected for each type of triad. As shown in Table 3.2, more than two thirds of the eligible cross-section respondents who were part of a parent-child triad (G2) had only one parent, and the majority of these parents (more than three fourths) were female. These sex discrepancies are expected, given the differential in mortality rates of black men and women. There was almost no sex difference in the rate of eligibility of children. Sons and daughters appear to have been available for selection in roughly the same proportions.

TABLE 3.2
Description of Sampling Frame for Parent-Child Triads

A. Number of Eligible Parents		B. Sex of Living Parent		C. Number of Eligible Sons and Daughters		
		(For cases where only one parent is alive.)			Eligible Sons	Eligible Daughters
One	66.4%	Males	22.3%	0	24.3%	22.9%
Two	33.6	Females	77.6	1	38.3	36.9
	100%		99.9%	2	21.2	21.9
TOTAL	(423)	TOTAL	(277)	3	9.4	10.4
				4	4.8	4.3
				5	1.4	1.9
				6	0.2	1.2
				7 or more	0.2	0.5
					100%	100%
				TOTAL	(415)	(415)

TABLE 3.3
Description of Sampling Frame for Grandparent-Parent Triads

A. Number of Eligible Parents		B. Number of Eligible Grandparents	
One with living parents	66.3%	One paternal grandparent[a]	27.3%
Both with at least one living parent	33.7	Both paternal grandparents	10.9
	100%	One maternal grandparent[b]	45.0
TOTAL	(477)	Both maternal grandparents	16.8
			100%
		TOTAL	(476)

[a]For cases where one paternal grandparent is alive, 71.5% are female.
[b]For cases where one maternal grandparent is alive, 84.1% are female.

Table 3.3 shows the sampling frames for the selection of parents and grandparents for the completion of the grandparent-parent triads. Once the parent was selected, one of the selected parent's parents was selected. Selected male parents were as likely as selected female parents to have only one living parent. Maternal grandparents of the original respondents were more likely to be eligible for selection than paternal grandparents. Again, following the sex differences found among older blacks, when only one grandparent was alive, paternal or maternal, more than three fourths of them were female.

In the case of the child-grandchild triads (Table 3.4), the selected child of the original cross-section respondent generated the sampling frame for the eligible grandchildren. Here sex differences did emerge in the availability of eligible adult children of the original respondents. Eligible cross-section respondents (G1) were more likely to have daughters with eligible children than

TABLE 3.4
Description of Sampling Frame for Child-Grandchild Triads

A. Number of Eligible Sons and Daughters of Original R With Children 14 Years or Older	Eligible Sons	Eligible Daughters
0	38.5%	21.0%
1	36.6	39.7
2	17.8	19.2
3	5.7	11.7
4	0.0	3.7
5	0.9	2.3
6	0.0	0.9
7 or more	0.5	1.0
	100%	100%
TOTAL	(213)	(221)

B. Number of Eligible Children of Selected Child of Original R	Eligible Grandsons	Eligible Granddaughters
0	22.2%	27.9%
1	39.1	35.1
2	19.8	16.8
3	13.0	8.7
4	4.8	8.2
5	0.5	2.9
6	0.5	0.5
7 or more	0.0	0.0
	100%	100%
TOTAL	(207)	(208)

sons with eligible children. This disparity in availability could be a function of a combination of differential mortality rates (these children are for the most part middle aged) of men and women as well as of the possible earlier fertility of black women. Overall, the sex of available grandchildren was not too different from the availability of children by sex in the parent-child triads.

Triad Sampling Outcomes

Table 3.5 shows the triads generated and completed by triad type, gender, and region. Although the relatively low triad response rate is a cause of some concern, interviews of respondents within the three triad types were obtained in nearly the same proportions as found in the generated sample.

As shown in the last column of Table 3.5, the completion rates across the three triad types are all similar. Most importantly, however, the triads were completed in close proportions to the numbers in which they were generated.

Table 3.5 also shows a somewhat more direct test of the quality of the sampling outcomes in relation to the three generation lineage sampling frame. Although the completion rate for the all-female triads (56.0%) greatly outstripped the completion rate for the all-male triads (29.8%), the final distribution of different gender composition triads is close to the proportion of different gender composition triads generated in the cross-section survey. As in the cross-section survey response rates by gender, the all-male triads were slightly underrepresented and the all-female triads slightly overrepresented in the final distributions.

The final panel in Table 3.5 shows the generated and completed triads by region of the country. Again, the completion rates like the cross-section results, are highly skewed and indicate a higher rate of completion for all-South triads than for all non-South or mixed triads. Just as in the cross-section survey, this outcome is undoubtedly reflective of the relatively greater ease of the interviewing in the South and the greater proportion of less difficult areas (less urban) in which interviewing was conducted. Relevant to this latter point, another analysis, not presented here, indicates that approximately 60% of the three generation triads interviewed lived in the same state. Of these, 68% lived in the same city. Only 12% of those in the same city lived

TABLE 3.5
Triads Generated and Completed by Triad Type, Gender, and Region Composition

	Triads Generated	Triads Completed	Completion Rate
Triad Type			
Parent-Child	37.7%	39.4%	47.5%
Grandparent-Parent	42.6	40.4	43.1%
Child-Grandchild	19.7	20.2	46.6%
TOTAL:	100.0%	100.0%	45.4%
Triad Gender Composition			
All Males	6.1%	3.9%	29.8%
All Females	24.5	29.4	56.0%
Mixed Gender	69.4	66.7	44.7%
TOTAL:	100.0%	100.0%	
Triad Region Composition			
All South	43.5%	52.7%	62.7%
All Non-South	29.3	25.5	45.0%
Mixed Region	27.2	21.8	41.3%
TOTAL:	100.0%	100.0%	

Note. Completion rate is a simple ratio of obtained triads over generated triads. It does not include normal response rate adjustments for unavailability due to death and other non-sample situations. If this taken into consideration, the completion rate should be higher.

in the same household. These proportions, combined with the larger numbers of South triads generated and the ease of interviewing in the South, perhaps explain the observed outcomes of better completion rates in the South. As with the outcome on gender composition, the distribution of the obtained triads by region is better than the completion rate. The distribution is approximately 9% skewed in favor of the South triads and only 4% skewed less than expected in the non-South triads.

Another approach to the assessment of the overall quality of the final result sample of triads is to examine selected demographic and socio-economic characteristics of all cross-section respondents who generated triads and those for whom triads were completed. A special feature of the FNSP is that it allows eligible cross-section respondents membership in any of the three generations. This contributes some heterogeneity to the composition of the various generations. For example, because of these procedures, we have within the grandparent generation, or G1, both relatively young and very old grandparents. Differences in the characteristics of cross-section respondents for whom triads were generated and completed would thus effect the heterogeneity within generations in the result sample. Table 3.6 presents selected characteristics of these cross-section respondents by triad type for triads generated and completed.

Log-linear analysis techniques (Goodman, 1978) were used for each of the three-variable tables presented in the panels of Table 3.6 to test:

1. Whether the various types of triads were completed in different proportions than generated in the sample controlling for the selected characteristics of the cross-section respondent

2. Whether, controlling for triad type, completion of triads was related to the selected characteristic of the cross-section respondent

3. Whether there was a three-way interaction between the characteristics of the respondent, completion status and type of triad.[3]

In these analyses we were also able to test the significance of the association between selected characteristics of the cross-section respondents and the type of triad generated.

The only significant effect found for gender in Table 3.6 was the association between gender and triad type. Female cross-section respondents were

---

[3] In the three variable system, aside from marginal effects, there are three possible bivariate effects and a three-way interaction. If we use "C" as a generic notation for each characteristic of the cross-section respondent, "S" for triad completion status, and "T" for triad type, we were interested in the following effects in the assessment of impact on triad nonresponse in the final sample: ST, CS and CST. Also of interest is CT, which is the association between the characteristics of the original cross-section respondent and the type of triad generated. The analyses reported here utilized the BMDP Statistical Software Package for log-linear analysis.

more likely than male respondents to have generated parent-child triads and less likely to have generated grandparent-parent triads. The likelihood ratio chi square (LRX²) for the fit of the model with the association between gender and triad type and marginal skew of status was 3.6, with 5 degrees of freedom and a probability of .60. All three bivariate effects were included, however, in the best fitting model for age. In this analysis, structural zeros were taken into account. (See Table 3.6 for generated triads for each age group.) Respondents aged 18–25 and 26–34 did not generate any child-grandchild triads, and those respondents who were 55–64 or 65 and over did not generate grandparent-parent triads. This was expected, given known fertility and mortality or life expectancy constraints. Because of the structural zeros, measures of quasi independence were obtained for tested models for only those cells of the table which were non-zero. The all-bivariate model achieved a fit with a LRX² of 7.00, 4 degress of freedom and probability of .136. The age-triad association in this model is responsible for the structural zeros in cells for the aforementioned age groups as well as the tendency for middle-aged persons (35–54) to be more likely to have generated parent-child triads and older respondents (55 and above) to have generated child-grandchid triads. The association between age and completion status is such that triads generated by younger respondents were more likely to be completed than those by older respondents. The relationship between triad type and completion status is that parent-child and child-grandchild triads were more likely to be completed than grandparent-parent triads.

The best fitting models for region and urbanicity were those that included the effects of region or urbanicity and completion status, and region or urbanicity and triad type. These models for region and urbanicity were fit respectively with LRX² of 5.05, 8 degrees of freedom, probability of .707 and 2.71, 6 degrees of freedom and probability of .845. The association of region and urbanicity with status follows observations made earlier about the patterns of nonresponse in the cross-section study. Triads were more likely to be completed if the cross-section respondent lived in the South or in areas that were less urban and more rural. They were less likely to be completed if respondents were located in other regions or in large cities. The associations of urbanicity and region with type of triad most likely reflect migration patterns of family members and the concentration of older generations of blacks in the South and in less urban and more rural areas. Respondents in the South were more likely to have generated child-grandchild triads and less likely to have generated parent-child triads. Respondents in the North Central region were more likely than those in other regions to have generated grandparent-parent triads. Similarly, parent-child triads were more likely to have been generated by respondents in large cities and less likely by those in less urban and more rural areas. On the other hand, child-grandchild triads were less likely to be generated by respondents living in large urban areas. The similar-

TABLE 3.6
Characteristics of Cross-Section Respondents By Type of Three Generational Triad
Generated and Completed

A. Triad Type By Gender of Cross-Section Respondent

Triad Type Generated	Male	Female
Parent-Child	32.8%	40.4%
Child-Grandchild	19.3	19.9
Grandparent-Parent	48.0	39.6
	100.0%	100.0%
TOTAL	(400)	(722)
Triad Type Completed		
Parent-Child	37.7%	40.8%
Child-Grandchild	18.5	20.1
Parent-Grandparent	43.8	39.1
	100.0%	100.0%
TOTAL	(162)	(348)
Completion Rate	40.5%	48.2%

B. Triad Type by Age of Cross-Section Respondent

Triad Type Generated	18–25	26–34	35–54	55–64	65+
Parent-Child	.4%	17.0%	90.2%	39.4%	5.8%
Child-Grandchild	0.0	0.0	4.3	60.6	94.2
Grandparent-Parent	99.6	83.0	5.4	0.0	0.0
	100.0%	100.0%	100.0%	100.0%	100.0%
TOTAL	(267)	(230)	(369)	(99)	(154)
Triad Type Completed					
Parent-Child	0.8%	22.4%	93.8%	30.8%	1.5%
Child-Grandchild	0.0	0.0	1.7	69.0	98.5
Grandparent-Parent	99.2	77.6	4.5	0.0	0.0
	100.0%	100.0%	100.0%	100.0%	100.0%
TOTAL	(121)	(107)	(176)	(39)	(66)
Completion Rate	45.1%	46.5%	47.7%	39.4%	42.8%

C. Triad Type By Region of Cross-Section Respondent

Triad Type Generated	North East	North Central	South	West
Parent-Child	45.0%	36.9%	35.1%	41.5%
Child-Grandchild	15.5	11.8	25.0	16.9
Grandparent-Parent	39.6	51.3	39.9	41.5
	100.0%	100.0%	100.0%	100.0%
TOTAL	(202)	(263)	(592)	(65)
Triad Type Completed				
Parent-Child	54.5%	38.6%	35.9%	47.8%
Child-Grandchild	18.2	9.9	23.0	21.7
Grandparent-Parent	27.3	51.5	41.1	30.4
	100.0%	100.0%	100.0%	100.0%
TOTAL	(77)	(101)	(309)	(23)
Completion Rate	38.1%	38.4%	52.2%	35.4%

TABLE 3.6 (continued)

D. Triad Type by Urbanicity of Cross-Section Respondent

Triad Type Generated	Large Urban	Small Urban	Rural
Parent-Child	39.4%	37.4%	34.2%
Child-Grandchild	15.1	18.8	32.0
Grandparent-Parent	45.5	43.8	33.8
	100.0%	100.0%	100.0%
TOTAL	(523)	(377)	(222)
Triad Type Completed			
Parent-Child	42.6%	41.7%	32.5%
Child-Grandchild	15.2	18.3	28.6
Grandparent-Parent	42.2	40.0	38.9
	100.0%	100.0%	100.0%
TOTAL	(204)	(180)	(126)
Completion Rate	39.0%	47.6%	56.8%

E. Triad Type by Education of Cross-Section Respondent

Triad Type Generated	0–11	12	13–15	16 +
Parent-Child	41.4%	38.5%	28.2%	34.4%
Child-Grandchild	37.3	7.5	5.0	3.3
Grandparent-Parent	21.3	54.0	66.9	62.2
	100.0%	100.0%	100.0%	100.0%
TOTAL	(485)	(360)	(181)	(90)
Triad Type Completed				
Parent-Child	41.2%	44.2%	29.3%	36.0%
Child-Grandchild	38.4	8.5	3.7	4.0
Grandparent-Parent	20.4	47.3	67.1	60.0
	100.0%	100.0%	100.0%	100.0%
TOTAL	(211)	(165)	(82)	(50)
Completion Rate	43.7%	45.7%	45.3%	55.6%

ity of patterns in the results for region and urbanicity is no doubt due to the fact that they are highly associated. Most of the large urban areas in the cross-section study were outside of the South, and most of the rural areas were in the South.

The only significant effect in the table for education was that between education and triad type. (The LRX^2 for this model was 3.97, with 11 degrees of freedom and a probability of .971.) People with less than a high school diploma were more likely to have generated a child-grandchild triad and less likely to have generated parent-child and grandparent-parent triads. Conversely, those with at least a high school diploma were more likely to generate parent-child and grandparent-parent triads and less likely to generate child-grandchild triads. These results closely parallel those found for age and strongly suggest that they derive from the negative relationship between age and education.

All in all, these preliminary analyses suggest that where effects were found for the relationship between completion status and a demographic or socio-economic characteristic of the original respondent, they were most likely due to known patterns of nonresponse, as in the case of region and urbanicity. In the case of age, problems of completing triads with very old members may have resulted from inaccessibility due to sickness or death.[4]

Characteristics of Three Generation Family Members

Our assessment of the three generation family sample obtained using the Family Network Sampling Procedure (FNSP) began with an examination of eligibility by characteristics of cross-section respondents and then proceeded with an examination of the sampling outcomes. Our final approach to this assessment examines the characteristics of all the family members who constituted completed triads. Table 3.7 shows the distribution of age, gender, region of residence, and education within each generation of the result sample.

The majority of G1 respondents are 55 and older; the majority of G2 and G3 respondents are under 55 years of age. However, there is still some variation among age cohorts in terms of generation membership. This gives us relatively younger grandparents to be compared to older grandparents and younger parents to be compared to older parents. This also holds for G3, where the age range of the category shown in Table 3.7 is quite large. Thus, we are able to look at older and younger children in three generation families. The sex ratios within G1 and G2 tend to reflect those noted earlier for older blacks. Less difference is shown for the youngest generation. The results for region and education follow what we would expect given the known relationship between age and education, and the migration patterns of black families. G1 respondents are more likely to live in the South than either G2 or G3 respondents, for whom the proportions for South and non-South are nearly equal. The average educational level of respondents increases across generations. G1 respondents are more likely to have less than 12 years of schooling, and G3, more than 12 years of schooling. All in all, these results as expected reflect what is known about the distribution of these characteristics by age cohorts for the black population and attest to the general representativeness of our three generation sample.

Overall, these analyses of the nature of the three generation response rates and sampling outcomes suggest that our sampling procedure and field work did not yield an unduly "biased" sample of three generation family triads.

---

[4]Association between triad type and completion status was found only for the age tables and suggested that a higher order model with a three-way interaction would have fit the data better. An earlier analysis, which did not designate structural zeros, found such an effect. Further analyses of these data will hopefully clarify these relationships.

TABLE 3.7
Selected Socio-Demographic and Social Characteristics of the Three Generation
Family Members by Generation

Category	Generation		
	G1	G2	G3
AGE			
14–34	–	5.9%	95.4%
35–54	3.8%	76.8%	4.5%
55–64	24.2%	14.5%	–
65 and older	72.1%	2.8%	–
	100%	100%	100%
Total	(720)	(863)	(902)
GENDER			
Male	29.4%	31.2%	44.9%
Female	70.6%	68.7%	55.1%
	100%	100%	100%
Total	(721)	(867)	(904)
REGION			
South	68.2%	53.1%	51.5%
Non-South	31.8%	46.9%	48.5%
	100%	100%	100%
Total	(711)	(866)	(895)
EDUCATION			
1–6 years	45.5%	9.2%	1.0%
7–11 years	41.3%	43.3%	33.8%
12 years	8.8%	29.6%	34.6%
More than 12 years	4.5%	17.9%	33.6%
	100%	100%	100%
Total	(695)	(859)	(887)

From the characteristics of the sample and types of obtained interviews, it appears that interviews were obtained in about the same proportions for each type of triad and for related demographic and socio-economic characteristics of eligible respondents. Where slight deviations occurred, they were expected, based upon the demographic characteristics of the cross-section respondents, general survey nonresponse patterns, and known population differences in socio-economic status and mortality.

SUMMARY AND CONCLUSIONS

The purpose of this chapter was to highlight some of the methodological probems in current intergenerational research generally and specifically address one of them—sampling. This was accomplished through our description and evaluation of a procedure we used to generate a national sample of three generation lineage families from a national cross-section survey of the adult black population. Based on network sampling techniques (Sirkin, 1970), the Family Network Sampling Procedure provided for: the easy identification of eligible families through the original cross-section respondent; the identification of all eligible members in the appropriate adjacent generations; the use of random selection procedure for obtaining the two family members; and a set of field procedures for locating and interviewing the two selected family members and reinterviewing the original respondent to complete the three generation triad.

These procedures identified 1,122 eligible three generation triads (3,366 individuals) in which interviews were attempted. Although the predominant mode of interviewing was face to face, approximately 700 of the 2,240 completed three generation family interviews were conducted by telephone. The response rate was slightly higher in the reinterviews of the respondents. The overall response rate for the 510 completed triads was 46%. More importantly, an analysis of the completed triads by type, sex, urbanicity, education, and age indicated fairly close agreement between the obtained and generated sample, and distributions on major respondent characteristics congruent with known demographics of the black population.

Finally, the nature of the three generation respondents was examined by generation membership and basic socio-demographic characteristics. The results, as expected, reflected what is known about the distribution of these characteristics by age cohorts for the black population and suggest that structural characteristics such as gender, age, region, education, and income are sufficiently distributed across the various triads to provide adequate heterogeneity for analysis purposes.

Overall, we believe that the sampling outcomes and characteristics of the three generation triads provide strong evidence for the effectiveness of the FNSP in obtaining fairly representative national three generation family samples. Although this method was used to develop a national sample of black three generation lineage family triads, it could be used for the general population as well as for specific subpopulations in the United States. In addition to size and national character, a major advantage of this procedure is the heterogeneity of the generated sample. Although purposive samples are important and have dominated research in the three generation area, the reliance on these types of data bases could possibly result in drawing invalid conclusions (for example, overestimates of the extent of family contact and closeness) or in unknown biases, which would impair the generalizability of the findings to larger populations of interest (Bytheway, 1977). Although we did not introduce any stratification beyond the basic triad type, various sampling strata could be introduced (e.g., household composition, sex type lineages, urban/rural, etc.) depending on the study goals and design. Little difference between the telephone and face-to-face interviewing was found, suggesting even further potential reductions in costs and effort. For these reasons, we believe that the procedures and techniques described here could be easily extended to national studies of the general United States population.

ACKNOWLEDGMENT

This chapter is based upon a presentation given at the West Virginia University Conference on Life Span Developmental Psychology, Morgantown, West Virginia, May, 1984. The preparation of this chapter was supported in part by grants from the National Institute on Aging (AG 01294-04), the National Institute on Mental Health, Center for Minority Group Mental Health (MH 30706-07), and the Ford Foundation. We appreciate the assistance of Letha Chadiha, Jackie Pearlman and Cathy Jenkins in the analyses and preparation of this manuscript. We are grateful to our colleague Gerald Gurin for reading an earlier version of this chapter. His comments were particularly helpful.

REFERENCES

Aldous, J. & Hill, R. (1965). Social cohension, lineage type, and intergenerational transmission. *Social Forces, 43,* 471–482.

Allen, W. R. (1978). The search for applicable theories of Black American life. *Journal of Marriage and the Family, 40,* 117–129.

Baltes, P. & Willis, S. (1977). Toward psychological theories of aging and development. In J. E. Birren & K. W. Schaie (Eds.), *Handbook of the psychology of aging.* New York: Van Nostrand Reinhold.

Beck, P. A. & Jennings, M. K. (1975). Parents as middle persons in political socialization. *Journal of Politics, 37,* 83–107.

Bengtson, V. L. (1975). Generation and family effects in value socialization. *American Sociological Review, 40,* 358–371.

Bengtson, V. L., & Cutler, N. E. (1976). Generations and intergenerational relations: Perspectives on age groups and social change. In. R. H. Binstock & E. Shanas (Eds.), *Handbook of aging and the social sciences.* New York: Van Nostrand Reinhold.

Berk, R. A. (1983). An introduction to sample selection bias in sociological research. *American Sociological Review, 48,* 386–398.

Berk, R. A., & Ray, S. C. (1982). Selection biases in sociological data. *Social Science Research, 11,* 301–40.

Bielby, W. T., Hauser, R. M. & Featherman, D. L. (1977). Response errors of black and non-black males in models of intergenerational transmission of socioeconomic status. *American Journal of Sociology, 82,* 1242–1288.

Bytheway, B. (1977). Problems of representation in the three generation family study. *Journal of Marriage and the Family, 39,* 243–250.

Clausen, J. A. (1972). The life course of individuals. In M. W. Riley, M. Johnson & A. Foner (Eds.), *Aging and society: A sociology of age stratification, Vol. 3.* New York: Russell Sage Foundation.

Frankel, M. R., & Frankel, L. R. (1977). Some recent developments in sample survey design. *Journal of Marketing Research, 14,* 280–293.

Goodman, L. A. (1978). *Analyzing qualitative/categorical data.* Cambridge, MA: ABT Books.

Hagestad, G. O. (1981). Problems and promises in the social psychology of intergenerational relations. In R. W. Fogel, E. Hatfield, S. B. Kiesler, & S. E. Shanas (Eds.). *Aging: Stability and change in the family.* New York: Academic Press.

Heckman, J. J. (1979). Sample selection bias as a specification error. *Econometrica, 45,* 153-61.

Hill, R. (1970). *Family development in three generations.* Cambridge, MA: Schenkman.

Hill, R. (1977). Response to Bytheway. *Journal of Marriage and the Family, 39,* 251-252.

Huston, T. L., & Robins, E. (1982). Conceptual and methodological issues in studying close relationships. *Journal of Marriage and the Family, 44,* 901-925.

Jackson, J. S., Tucker, M. B. & Bowman, P. J. (1982). Conceptual and methodological problems in survey research on Black Americans. In W. Liu (Eds.), *Methodological problems in minority research.* Chicago: Pacific/Asian American Mental Health Research Center.

Jennings, M. K. (1977). Analyzing parent-child pairs in cross-national survey research. *European Journal of Political Research, 5,* 179-197.

Jennings, M. K., & Niemi, R. S. (1981). *Generations and politics: A panel study of young adults and their parents.* Princeton, NJ: Princeton University Press.

Kish, L. (1965). *Survey sampling.* New York: Wiley.

Kitson, G. C., Sussman, M. B., Williams, G. K., Zeehandelaar, R. B., Shickmanter, B. K., & Steinberger, J. L. (1982). Sampling issues in family research. *Journal of Marriage and the Family, 44,* 965-981.

Markides, K. S., Hoppe, S. K., Martin, H. W., & Timbers, D. M. (1983). Sample representativeness in a three generation study of Mexican Americans. *Journal of Marriage and the Family, 45,* 911-916.

Nathan, G., Schmelz, U. O., & Kenvin, J. (1977). *Multiplicity study of marriages and births in Israel.* (DHHS Publication Number 70, Series 2). Washington, DC: National Center for Health Statistics, Public Health Service.

Nesselroade, J. R. (1977). Toward psychological theories of aging and development. In J. E. Birren & K. W. Schaie (Ed.), *Handbook of the psychology of aging.* New York: Nostrand Reinhold.

Nesselroade, J. R. & Baltes, P. B. (Eds.) (1979). *Longitudinal research in the study of behavior and development.* New York: Academic Press.

Schaie, K. W. (1977). Quasi-experimental designs in the psychology of aging. In J. E. Birren & K. W. Schaie (Eds.), *Handbook of the psychology of aging.* New York: Van Nostrand Reinhold.

Sirkin, M. G. (1970). Household surveys with multiplicity. *Journal of American Statistical Association, 65,* 257-266.

Thompson, E., & Williams, R. (1984). A note on correlated measurement error in wife-husband data. *Journal of Marriage and the Family, 46,* 643-649.

Thompson, L., & Walker, A. J. (1982). The dyad as the unit of analysis: Conceptual and methodological issues. *Journal of Marriage and the Family, 44,* 889-900.

Troll, L., & Bengtson, V. L. (1979). Generations and the family. In W. Burr, I. Reiss, R. Hill & G. Nye (Eds.), *Contemporary theories about the family.* New York: Free Press.

II INTEGENERATIONAL RELATIONS AND CHANGE

4 Family and Community Networks in Appalachia

Dean Rodeheaver
University of Wisconsin - Green Bay

Jeanne L. Thomas
University of Wisconsin-Parkside

FAMILY AND COMMUNITY NETWORKS IN APPALACHIA

This chapter began as an exchange of the authors' experiences in conducting exploratory research in Appalachia, as well as of impressions of Appalachian culture. A common theme emerged from this exchange. In the studies described here, respondents related experiences in intergenerational networks that reflected both stability and change across generations. The same themes were apparent in considering Appalachia: although the region has changed — particularly within the last century — there are enduring cultural features. In this chapter, a survey of these regional historical changes and constant cultural themes provides a context for discussion of two studies of West Virginia elders and their family and community networks.

HISTORICAL FOUNDATIONS OF THE CULTURE

Those who write about the current ethos of Southern Appalachia suggest that we consider the character of the people who first saw the mountains as a refuge (Weller, 1965). One term useful in describing these individuals is rejection: "Instead of the hymn-singing pilgrim, we must start with the cynical, the penniless, the resentful and the angry" (Caudill, 1962, p. 6). Among the early mountaineers was a group of people who recognized no authority other than individual force and who sought a place where equal status would be ascribed to all. Rejection was their philosophy of life: organized religion, they claimed, elevated some to a status claiming to be nearer to God than others; government provided justification for the authority of one group over another; education was a means of achieving superiority. The mountains offered freedom from existing authority, sufficient opportunity for subsistence living, and isolation from all but one's kin or clan.

The isolation of the mountaineer was relatively complete, except for an excursion to fight in the Civil War, until early in the 20th century. The 20th century has brought enormous change to Appalachia; the most relevant areas of change are economic diversification and improved transportation systems.

At the turn of the century, more than half of West Virginia's population were farmers. However, just three decades later, the rural farm population was only 25.9% of the state's total (Ambler & Summers, 1965). During this period, the lumbering, railroading, and mining industries entered the region and grew in importance. Workers frequently divided their time and efforts between farming and industry or abandoned farming altogether for industry (Ambler & Summers, 1965).

However, the exposure of the mountain folk to the outside world through state industry paradoxically perpetuated isolation. The miners not only were the employees of coal companies based outside the state, but also were the wards of these companies. The company provided homes, stores, doctors, schools, funerals, and money (scrip) that was useless outside the camp. The residents of these early coal camps, consequently, found few incentives to venture elsewhere. Simultaneously, the wealth generated by mining was transported by the coal companies over the state line; neither the tax structure nor the export of coal enriched the state in any way.

It was also at this time that ventures between mountain communities and outside the mountains became easier. The 20th century also brought progress in the state's transportation network. At the turn of the century, West Virginia was arrested in the dirt road stage of its transportation history: "the state road bureau . . . said that the roads of West Virginia were the worst in the United States . . . they were then largely clouds of dust in the summer and streams of mud in the winter" (Ambler & Summers, 1965, p. 332). As the number of automobiles in the state increased, there was corresponding pressure for highway improvement. This pressure found expression in 1917 with the codification of laws and the creation of administrative bodies providing for road construction, improvement, and maintenance. The state road commission was created, and successive gasoline taxes were levied, with the eventual result that West Virginia could boast of far more adequate east-west and north-south routes, as well as interstate highways and a state turnpike, by mid-century (Ambler & Summers, 1965; Weller, 1965).

Changes in West Virginia early in the 20th century affected the social and economic context of individual life primarily in two ways. First, there was increasing diversity of lifestyle, as farming became a less predominant source of income. Second, there was the potential for decreased social isolation, as more and more individuals and communities were linked through relatively modern roadways. Although this history of the region is far from complete, it demonstrates some of the forces at work in creating the traits characteristic of the Appalachian. Considering historical change in West Virginia provides only part of the context for our discussion, however; consideration of cultural stabilities is equally important.

CULTURAL THEMES

There have been several recent portraits of Appalachia and Appalachians; this discussion is based on Henry Caudill's *Night Comes to the Cumberlands* (1962), Jack Weller's *Yesterday's People* (1965), and Kai Erikson's *Everything in its Path* (1976). All note similar outstanding themes of the Appalachian culture and regional character, and emphasize similar inherent contradictions. Erikson labels these contradictions "axes of variation". In describing the axes of variation, Erikson explains that:

> . . . the identifying motifs of a culture are not just the *core values* to which people pay homage, but also the *lines of point and counterpoint* along which they diverge. . . . the forms of contrast experienced by a particular people are one of the identifying motifs of their culture, and if one wants to understand how any given culture works, one should inquire into its characteristic counterpoints as well as its central values. . . . (pp. 82–83)

Erikson (1976) identified five axes of variation. The first is a tension between love and tradition and respect for personal liberty; in this context Erikson views the Appalachian as at once accepting restriction, as tradition is embraced, and resisting limitations as individual freedom is lauded. The second axis of variation is a contrast between self-assertion and resignation, or ambivalence between activity and submission. Third, the Appalachian is both self-centered and group centered; in other words, the mountaineer is oriented both toward individual concerns and toward a group that provides a sense of self, of security, and of belongingness. Fourth, there is a contrast between ability and disability in Appalachian culture; the people display the physical hardiness necessary for survival in the mountains, but they are also fearful of illness and physical vulnerability.

Erikson (1976) viewed the fifth axis of variation as the most important. This axis is between a sense of independence and a need for dependence. He states:

If one were to count the adjectives that appear most frequently in books and articles on the mountain character, the winner by quite a margin would be "individualistic." According to those sources, the people of the mountains are, above all else, free and independent spirits. . . . When one says that a people are independent, one is saying that they are free to do essentially as they please. This presumes, of course, that what "they please" is generated by sources from within and not molded by forces from without. Yet it is no easy matter to distinguish the inner will from the outer demand, and this particularly the case when one is discussing the people of the mountains. . . . (pp. 88–90)

Other descriptions (Caudill, 1962; Weller, 1965) of the outstanding characteristics of the Appalachian people include, essentially, the same paradoxical traits and tendencies (i.e., individualism, traditionalism, fatalism, seeking action, apprehension, and person orientation).

This was the character of the inhabitants of the southern Appalachians until the 1960s, when they were discovered by the War on Poverty. There followed a period of attempted community organization and educational reform, as well as in-migration (Caudill, 1976b). How has the regional character been altered since the "rediscovery" of the mountains? After evaluating changes in the Kentucky highlands, Caudill (1976a) suggested that changes have been few, stating that "we of the hills have in truth retreated from great possibilities and rejected great challenges" (p. 43).

We suggest that Caudill's (1976a, 1976b) observations about the lack of far-reaching change in Appalachia since the 1960s imply yet another contradiction in the Appalachian character. There is a tension between success in avoiding modernization and profound failure in realizing possibilities that might benefit offspring. Few Appalachians with exposure to the outside world can escape the feeling of having been passed by, and few Appalachians lack exposure to the world outside the mountains. Weller (1965) notes, for example, that "television brings [the Appalachian] face to face with modern American culture . . . both he and his children spend hours watching and unknowingly absorbing the ideas and values piped into his very front room" (p. 135). With the sense of missed opportunity, however, remains pride and love for cultural traditions; Weller (1965) also asserts that "in a great many ways [the Appalachian] is perfectly happy with his culture; it expresses his goals and desires quite adequately . . ." (p. 144).

In addition to describing the character of the Appalachian individual, scholars have discussed the nature of the Appalachian family (Erikson, 1976; Weller, 1965). We consider Appalachian family functioning in more detail later; however, we would like to make two general comments. First, Appalachian families are characterized by extreme closeness and belongingness, in the context of a strong sense of interdependence. Weller (1965) notes that "the mountain family is a close one, not because of shared activities, but because of emotional dependence" (p. 59). Erikson (1976) agrees, stating that the Appalachian "has invested so much in the family and is so reliant upon it for protection and support that he often does not have the personal resources to join in emotional partnerships with others" (p. 91). In addition, both Weller (1965) and Erikson (1976) stress that, together with closeness and interdependence, conflict avoidance typifies mountain families.

The remainder of this chapter describes the findings of two independent studies of the aged in West Virginia. In both studies, research participants' descriptions of their interactions with members of other generations reflected many of these cultural themes, as well as the impact of regional historical change. We do not claim that the characteristics of intergenerational relations reflecting Appalachian cultural themes and historical processes are unique to Appalachian intergenerational networks; the same or similar characteristics may well be found in a variety of cultures. Nonetheless, these respondents' awareness and expression of these features may have been fostered by congruence with Appalachian cultural themes. Two complementary Appalachian intergenerational networks are described: intergenerational relations within the context of the family, based on Thomas's research (Thomas, 1982, 1984; Thomas & Datan, 1982, 1983a, 1983b, 1985), and intergenerational networks functioning in the community, based on Rodeheaver's research (Rodeheaver, 1982, 1985).

INTERGENERATIONAL FAMILY NETWORKS

The Families

This discussion of Appalachian intergenerational family networks is based on a qualitative study of change over time in grandparenting experience (Thomas, 1982, 1985; Thomas & Datan, 1982, 1983a, 1983b, 1985) designed to identify areas of perceived change and stability in grandparents' relationships with their children. Nineteen grandparents participated in this study. All were residents of two small cities in West Virginia. Five of the six grandfathers and eight of the 13 grandmothers were long-time residents of the region and were descendants of families who had lived in Appalachia for several generations. Discussion of the intergenerational networks refers to the perceptions of these 13 grandparents. The grandparents ranged in age from 52 to 78. All had at least two grandchildren; 11 had grandchildren living in their own community, and the remaining grandparents had grandchildren living within 3 hours' automobile travel.

The grandparents' educational backgrounds ranged from completion of eighth grade through completion of graduate coursework; 11 had at least a high school education, and the grandfathers' educational levels exceeded those of the grandmothers. Three of the grandmothers were working outside the home: one was a teacher, one an office manager, and one a private household worker. The remaining grandmothers described themselves as full-time homemakers. The married grandmothers' husbands worked as physicians, business owners or managers, or manual tradesmen. All of the grandfathers were retired; one had retired during the month prior to the interview, and the rest had been retired for several years. The grandfathers' former occupations included higher education, public administration, and personnel work. Grandparents' annual family income ranged from less than $5000 to more than $26,000; income was higher for grandfathers.

The semistructured interview concerned the grandparent's perceptions of relationships with children and grandchildren, ways in which these relationships had or had not changed over time, and differences and similarities among relationships with different grandchildren. To establish a context for discussion of experiences with grandchildren, participants were asked to share memories of their own grandparents and of their parents as grandparents; these memories also served as a basis from which to consider change over time.

All of the interviews were tape recorded and transcribed verbatim. Thomas performed a content analysis and a thematic analysis of the 19 transcripts (Thomas, 1982). For the purpose of this chapter, the transcripts of the interviews with the 13 long-time residents of West Virginia were reexamined, in order to see how descriptions of grandparenting reflected regional historical processes and cultural themes.

Eleven of the 13 grandparents remembered their own grandparents. Respondents described their grandparents' life styles, the activities they remembered sharing with their grandparents, and the amount of contact they remembered having with their grandparents. With only three exceptions, respondents' grandparents had been farmers, and most of the activities that respondents remembered sharing with their grandparents were centered around farming. Six of the 11 respondents remembered having a great deal of contact with their own grandparents. These individuals explained that they had lived very close (e.g., next door, across the field) to their grandparents or that they had shared a household with a grandparent. By contrast, four of these 11 remembered having very little contact with their grandparents. Although most had lived within 100 miles of their grandparents, the poor roads and scarcity of automobiles typical of the earlier decades of the century had precluded more frequent contact.

Generational Contrasts

A comparison of respondents' characteristics and their memories of their own grandparents revealed several points of contrast. Respondents differed from their own grandparents primarily in occupation, in activities shared with grandchildren, and in constraints on frequency of contact with grandchildren. The respondents were primarily retired professionals, business or managerial workers, or service workers, and they were residents of North Central West Virginia cities of moderate size. In contrast, their grandparents had nearly all been farmers living in rural areas.

Perhaps linked to these differences in area of residence and occupation were differences in activities shared with grandchildren. All 11 of the respondents who remembered their grandparents recalled helping with farmwork, sewing, quilting, or food storage and preparation; celebrating holidays with grandparents; and reading or telling stories. All of these respondents received occasional help from their grandchildren with cooking and household chores, and all enjoyed storytelling and family celebrations with grandchildren. With those exceptions, however, there were few similarities in the activities that respondents shared with their grandchildren and the activities that they remembered sharing with their grandparents. Respondents usually entertained their grandchildren with television, board games or video games and trips to fast food restaurants, movies, swimming pools, and amusement parks. Perhaps with the state's industrialization, grandchildren became less economic assets and more exclusively sources of economic consumption and personal enjoyment.

Just as the content of interaction with grandchildren differed across generations, so also did the circumstances that permitted or inhibited frequent contact. Only one grandmother mentioned poor roads or lack of access to a car as precluding frequent contact with grandchildren, although such circumstances had limited contact with grandparents for nearly a third (four of 13) of respondents. A major generational contrast, then, was in the effort required for grandparent-grandchild contact. Nearly all of the contemporary grandparents could see grandchildren with relatively little effort, while visiting with grandchildren had been a laborious undertaking for many grandparents in the earlier generation.

Generational Similarities

Similarities as well as contrasts existed between the respondents' experiences with their own children and grandchildren and their memories of experiences with their grandparents and with their parents as grandparents. The contemporary grandparents' experiences with their children and grandchildren reflected several of the themes of Appalachian culture. Most notable are indicators of the tensions between independence and dependence, between self-centeredness and group-centeredness, and between self-assertion and resignation, as well as stress upon avoidance of family conflict. Often, the same themes were apparent in memories of relationships with grandparents and with parents as grandparents.

Grandparents described their practices in providing childbearing advice and assistance, and their perceived freedom and responsibility to discipline grandchildren. When asked whether or not they advised their children about the grandchildren's upbringing, 11 grandparents said that they did not feel free to give this sort of advice, that they advised only when their children requested information. Grandparents also said that, if they did advise, they were careful to offer their opinions about the grandchildren's upbringing in a tactful manner. Grandparents explained that they refrained from advising out of respect for their children's skill as parents and because they regarded childrearing decisions as issues that were properly the province of children's parents, not their grandparents. Grandparents also said that they attempted to avoid advising because they feared that their children would resent the advice. As one grandfather explained, "It would be worng, and it would be very easy to ruin a good relationship by grandparents [interfering] in the raising of the children . . . I wouldn't volunteer [any advice] — they have to ask me . . . I wouldn't want to do anything to wreck our relationship." Five grandparents added that they had resented childrearing advice from their own parents-in-law or that they had appreciated their own parents' reluctance to give such advice.

Two grandparents had different opinions. A grandmother said that she felt free to give advice ("Whatever I think, I spit it out"). Similarly, a grandfather said that he freely advised his children about the grandchildren's upbringing, but added, "I feel that . . . they don't have to pay any attention, but they ought to listen."

Although when asked directly grandparents generally said that they did not offer unsolicited childrearing advice, nearly all, at some point in the interview, described incidents in which they had advised. Grandparents felt free, even obligated, to advise their children when grandchildren were ill or behaving in a dangerous manner, and parents seemed unaware of possible hazards. However, grandparents said that they gave childrearing "suggestions" rather than advice or recounted their own problems in raising children and the manner in which they had dealt with these problems. One grandmother explained that "I make it look like it's [my daughter-in-law's] idea, because I don't want to be pushy, you know. And you have to do this." An even more accommodating grandfather said, "Every now and then they'll ask me what I think about something, but I usually know what they're thinking and I tell them that. I give them the answer they want to hear."

Grandparents' feelings about disciplining their grandchildren were similar to their feelings about offering childrearing advice. Respondents said that they felt free to discipline their grandchildren when they were babysitting and had assumed temporary responsibility for the children. In doing so, however, grandparents felt that it was essential to conform to their children's policies for rules the grandchildren were expected to follow and the consequences to be levied for misbehavior. As one grandmother said, "I do look after them, and . . . therefore I do make them mind when they're here, and it's approved by [my son and daughter-in-law] — it has to be!"

At other times, however, grandparents hesitated to discipline the grandchildren. When parents were present, grandparents typically refrained from disciplining. Grandparents remembered that, when their own children were young, their own parents had followed this policy. Grandparents explained that they were confident of their children's ability to deal appropriately with grandchildren's misbehavior, and that they feared that their children would resent their own efforts to discipline the grandchildren when parents were available to do so. According to one grandmother:

> I would like to have the authority to say "Now, don't do that" and "Now, don't do this" with his parents here. . . . You sort of hesitate with the parents in the room; you feel that they should. I feel like they [would] resent me ... I don't want to take a chance. . . . I don't want to do anything to hurt them. I don't want to do anything to make them think I'm critical.

Grandparents had a different attitude toward providing childrearing assistance. They gave financial help, help with grandchildren's care during family illness, and babysat. Grandparents believed that providing assistance was a crucial family function. They remembered their own grandparents and parents as important sources of support, expected to help their children and grandchildren, and found personal satisfaction in providing this assistance and in feeling that their support benefited their children and grandchildren. One grandmother, for example, said that her greatest hope for the future of their relationships with children and grandchildren was that "I just hope that for a long time I'll be able to help them any way I can. . . ." Grandparents also believed that they had grown closer to their children and grandchildren through exchanges of assistance. One grandmother said:

> [Our son] is married and has his children, and he's relying on his parents again. . . . maybe through these girls, he's seen the help that we've given him and supported him, and helped with those two when they've needed it . . . we're close now, we're all close. We depend on one another — if one need the other, we're here.

Grandparents also felt that they could count on their children and grandchildren for help. However, one grandfather worried about burdening his children, should his own needs for help become extensive as he grew older.

Several themes of Appalachian culture are reflected in these discussions of advising, disciplining, and helping. First, the tensions between independence and dependence and between self-centeredness and group-centeredness were apparent. Grandparents respected their children's autonomy, individuality, and self-determination as parents; they were reluctant to advise their children or to discipline the grandchildren in their own children's presence. At the same time, grandparents both expected and desired intergenerational assistance. In this respect, they endorsed reliance on a closely knit, interdependent family network.

The tension between self-assertion and resignation was also apparent. In their perception that they did not offer unsolicited childrearing advice and did not discipline when grandchildren's parents were present, grandparents submitted to their children's childrearing policies. However, grandparents' reported behavior reflected self-assertion. Although they denied giving unsolicited advice, the "suggestions" and descriptions of childrearing problems and solutions offered by grandparents certainly provided mechanisms through which grandparents expressed their own individuality within family networks.

Grandparents stressed the importance of avoiding family conflict. Again, grandparents hesitated to discipline grandchildren in their children's presence, abided by their children's disciplinary policies and felt cautions of offering direct childrearing advice. All of these grandparental attitudes and behaviors stemmed primarily from fear of arousing children's resentment. In his discussion of the mountaineer's orientation toward interpersonal relationships, Weller (1965) noted the importance of adult reference group life and further noted that in Appalachia there is often considerable overlap between the family and the reference group. Weller (1965) also cited conflict avoidance as a prominent feature of Appalachian reference group functioning:

> Subjects that might engender conflict are not discussed. For people so dependent on relationships, any kind of slight or hurt is devastating to both happiness and security. . . . A give and take discussion where differing opinions, honestly held, are expressed is not common to reference-group conversations. Time and again comes the statement, "I never get angry with anybody in the family," which means "We all agree to stay away from controversial subjects" or "I bottle it up inside myself." (p. 79)

In the same way that Weller (1965) portrayed the mountaineer's dependence upon the reference group and need to avoid conflict, Kai Erikson (1976) discussed the group-centeredness of the Appalachian as being partially initiated by and expressed through family dependence. According to Erikson (1976):

> Mountain people, as we have seen, are quite dependent for emotional nourishment on their families, their kin, and their immediate peers. The family in par-

ticular provides a shelter in which people almost seem to huddle for warmth and security, and this degree of attachment and closeness can be extremely impor-tant . . . to step out of that embracing surround would be like separating from one's own flesh. (p. 86)

Once more, one senses the importance of maintaining closeness through maintaining consensus within the family. One strategy of achieving harmony for the grandparents in this study was to support parental authority and thus avoid arousing their children's resentment.

It was perhaps in order to avoid family conflict — while at the same time maintaining their own individuality, self-centeredness, and tendency toward self-assertion — that grandparents adopted indirect mechanisms of social control within their families. Thus, instead of offering chidrearing advice, they "made suggestions" or recollected the time that they had faced and han-dled particular childrearing problems. Grandparents then could express both sides of these polarities of Appalachian culture. They could be at once inde-pendent and dependent, self-centered and group-centered, self-assertive and resigned.

Grandparenting in Appalachia: Concluding Thoughts

In looking back at these West Virginia grandparents' experiences in the con-text of their family histories, two conclusions emerge. First, the intergen-erational continuities are less immediately apparent than are the discon-tinuities, but these stable features of intergenerational functioning appear more fundamental than the features reflecting change. Second, the axes of variation framework implies that future generations of Appalachians will continue to express cultural themes in their intergenerational networks.

The life circumstances of these contemporary West Virginia grandparents were quite different from those shaping the experiences of their own grand-parents. Nonetheless, the unspoken norms which had guided family func-tioning (at least as West Virginia contemporaries remembered that func-tioning in 1982) in earlier generations continued to provide useful guidelines for grandparents today. It seems most useful, therefore, to describe the grandparents participating in this research as modern Appalachians, but Ap-palachians nonetheless (Thomas, 1982, 1985; Thomas & Datan, 1982, 1983a, 1983b, 1985).

Kai Erikson's (1976) axes of variation model implies that this conclusion will apply to future generations of West Virginians. Erikson (1976) noted that the continua represented by these axes are not only a framework for des-cribing culture, but also conceptual tools for understanding the impact of historical change upon culture. He suggested that historical change affects a culture through movement along these continua. Thus, even if one expects the unexpected in future regional changes, one might also expect that today's West Virginia parents and children will, in old age, find that memories of their grandparents provide useful guidelines for behavior toward their own descendents.

INTERGENERATIONAL COMMUNITY NETWORKS

Aging and Status Maintenance

Values in Appalachia, like value systems everywhere, represent a delicious paradox[1]. On one hand, these value orientations regulate social experience and contribute to the emergence of unique social problems. On the other hand, they comprise a set of possible solutions to those problems. Rodeheaver (1982, in press) considers intergenerational relations among Appalachian elders an expression of this paradox. This discussion is based on his study of status maintenance in an Appalachian community.

If, as Margaret Clark (1968) has suggested, the social experience of the aged is characterized by cultural discontinuity, Appalachian elders face that discontinuity from two directions. First, aging itself often brings a necessary shift along the axes of variation already described. For example, independence may yield to increasing dependence, or physical ability to disability. Second, Appalachian elders face discontinuity produced by social and economic changes in the region. Transportation and television, the out-migration of kin, and the in-migration of those who "aren't from around here" have created the potential for group conflicts within Appalachian communities. By virtue of aging in place, Appalachian elders come to be viewed as representatives of the tradition and history of the region, often without regard for individual values. They become the conservative element in an intergenerational conflict.

Under these conditions, the status of elders within the community is altered. This compromise in social status forms half the paradox of the social experience of Appalachian elders. Their status becomes, for them, a social problem. The paradox is completed when the discontinuity they face is accompanied by a set of culturally prescribed mechanisms by which the elders regulate their status within the intergenerational community (see also Press & McKool, 1972).

This discussion examines the paradox as it was reflected in the lives of elders in one Appalachian community (Rodeheaver, 1982). The focus of the study was not on the family but on the community as an intergenerational

---

[1]We are indebted to Richard Logan, Human Development, University of Wisconsin-Green Bay, for this phrase.

network lacking, formally at least, the obligations that often mediate family relations. If the newcomers to Eastland (the community studied) are obligated to Eastland's elders, then those obligations are not ascribed and must have been created.

The Eastland Community[2]

Eastland is a residential community of several hundred people located a few miles east of Hillton, a county seat in north central West Virginia. The first homestead in the community was settled in 1769. Early residents were farmers, but over the years small stores, repair shops, and, later, gasoline stations were established, and Eastland became a largely self-sufficient community. The centers of the community were the church, an adjacent schoolhouse, and a nearby community building.

In the late 1800s and early 1900s, Hillton and the college located there grew. Improvement of the roads between Hillton and Eastland led many of Eastland's residents to find work in the town. Those changes also led many of Hillton's residents to move to the more rural areas surrounding the town, and some of them settled in Eastland. In Eastland today, one can find residents ranging from families who trace their roots in the community to the late 1700s to families who moved to the community in the last year. The community includes a variety of occupations — homemakers, school teachers, college professors, coal miners, bankers, doctors, lawyers, and maintenance men.

Demographic changes were accompanied by changes in the social institutions in Eastland. The old school was torn down in 1940, and children now attend a larger school on the outskirts of Eastland. The residents go to Hillton for most of their entertainment; the old community building now stands unused, for sale. Thus, the concentration of church, school, and community building that was once the center of the community has dissolved; only the church is left.

Eastland United Methodist Church was created in 1843 by a group of local residents and the regional circuit preacher. It was built on land donated by one of the earliest settlers in the region and was constructed entirely through donations from church members. This kind of volunteerism has been important throughout the history of the church. A new addition was built in 1954 with the money and labor of church members. The church is currently expanding once more, again with the financial contributions and volunteer labor of church members.

Perhaps the most significant event in the formation of the Eastland community as it exists today occurred in 1974. The minister at the time deter-

---

[2]All names are pseudonyms.

mined that the church could benefit financially by withdrawing from the United Methodist Church. With the agreement of church members, he stopped sending the church's apportionment to the district bishop. The bishop responded with a threat to board up the church if the minister preached there again. The United Methodist Church owns individual churches, regardless of their origins and history, and the bishop promised to demonstrate that ownership in a lawsuit. During these difficult times, more than half of the congregation went to new churches. The group that remained, including many of the older members, had family ties to the church that made it emotionally impossible for them to leave – this group included, for example, descendants of the man on whose land the church was built. When the trouble ended without a lawsuit, they formed the core of a new church community.

Social Status Maintenance among Church Elders[3]

This research involved three groups of Eastland residents (Rodeheaver, 1982). These included members of all but three of the households of 21 church members over the age of 60, individuals in the older members' social networks (as identified by the older members), and a sample of individuals who had joined the church fewer than 5 years before the study began. A combination of face-to-face interviews, telephone interviews, questionnaires, and psychological scales was used to examine the social status of the elders in the church and the community, their relations with others in the church, and their roles in the church in general.

Social status of the elders was measured in two ways. First, each was asked to provide a list of 10 people who were important members of their social networks and to choose the three most important church members from those lists. Each of these church members, most of whom were elders themselves, was interviewed and asked to compose a social network list and to identify the three most important church members on each list. The number of times each of Eastland's elders appeared on those lists was used as a measure of individual status (position in a person's network). Second, new church members and each individual in the elders' social networks answered the following question: "Who are the people without whom there would be no Eastland church as you know it?" The number of times each elder was listed was used as a measure of community status.

The results indicated that age alone is not a determinant of status in Eastland – some of the elders were excluded from all lists; others were mentioned only infrequently. But neither did age prohibit a high status ranking;

---

[3]The term "elder" refers to the older church members, and not to a formal status in the church. The use is adapted from Erdman Palmore's *The Honorable Elders.*

the majority listed by social network members and new church members were elders. In this community, there is a group of elders consistently considered the most important people in the community.

There are four major determinants of status among the elders. First, by attending church services and club meetings, the elders maintain their visibility within the community. Second, many of the elders accorded the highest status are participants and leaders in the community. Third, the elders have a recognized historical importance to the community. Some of them are the descendants of the original founders of the church. This role is formally recognized annually on Heritage Sunday, a day set aside for learning about church history. Furthermore, although the incident in 1974 (when there was a split in the church) is not formally recognized—it is an embarrassment to church members and is often compared to the suicides in Jonestown—it is widely known and is frequently mentioned as one of the reasons the elders are important to the community. Fourth, both older and younger church members have a shared commitment to the church, the community, and their future (see also Lozier & Althouse, 1974, 1975; Ross, 1977).

Each of these four determinants of elders' status is in turn a reflection of a community whose values clash in intergenerational conflicts and are enacted by mechanisms of social influence. To understand the Eastland community, one must examine the conflicts that have emerged around differences in the meaning of the church for its members. It is their family church, either by inheritance or by adoption. Many have attended Eastland Church all their lives—some for 75 years—as did their parents and grandparents before them and as well their children and grandchildren after them. They are the middle of five generations of church members. Further, the church has a broader meaning as the remnant of the community many of the elders grew up in. As one respondent described this relationship: "People my age miss the community life we used to have. The country store and blacksmith shop were the meeting places of the community. . . . You don't meet people at the country store anymore. People go to Krogers and other shopping centers. But the church makes up for that."

These familial and historical associations with the church are widely recognized within the community. However, the church has a different meaning for some church members. It is the center of a growing community, not an historical one. Although these differences are not age based—one group of elders with strong family ties to the church considers its role one of encouraging modernization and expansion—one could suggest, nevertheless, that the differences are indeed intergenerational. These generations are not defined by years but by the values and alliances that differentiate the groups. Thus, one older member, a newcomer to Eastland, described the nature of these differences:

> When the church had problems several years ago, the older people didn't leave because it was their family church. But they don't want any change. They think that, if the church was good enough for their parents and grandparents, it's good enough for them. The church was never remodeled and many people would come in and look around and leave. The old pianist was raised here and played in the church a long time. Some of the members of the congregation moved the piano from the floor to the alter — only four feet. The pianist came in that Sunday, looked at the piano, and you could just see her reaction. She left the church and hasn't come back.

Conflicts have also arisen over carpeting the church. The idea is an abomination to people who have been associated with the church in some way or another for 132 years. Other conflicts have arisen over seating, a situation that is a literal representation of the elders' position in the conflict. The church is growing physically with additions to the sanctuary behind the place where the altar used to stand. Thus, the oldest part of the church is now farthest from the altar. Many of the older members have special seats in that old section; some have provided cushions for their pews. The church is physically moving away from them, and they do not wish to move with it. Their dilemma is illustrated in a conversation between Mr. Underwood, the oldest man in the church and one of the most prestigious elders, and the minister. Mr. Underwood commented that he would have trouble seeing and hearing when the addition was done. The minister suggested that he move forward. "I've always sat by that window," he replied. "But there's another window just like it up there." He wouldn't move; it wasn't the same to him.

The nature of these conflicts is further revealed by the history of the church. The building was also expanded in 1954. At that time, it was the elders who planned, funded, and constructed the addition. It is not change that they are resisting; it is change by outsiders.

In sum, although Eastland's elders are among the most valued members of the community, they often find themselves in conflict with other members of the church, including other elders who are encouraging change. The relationship between conflict and status in Eastland may not be a casual one: part of the elders' continued value is maintained by their use of the mechanisms of social influence available to them.

Cliques, Bake Sales, and Tradition: Mechanisms of Influence among Appalachian Elders

Social relations within the Eastland community reflect the overriding Appalachian value on group relations and person-orientation: conflict avoidance is the norm in these relations. This does not mean that negative feelings are nonexistent; it means that they will be expressed indirectly. Consequently, although there are occasional confrontations, most of the mechanisms used by older members to regulate their status in the community are mechanisms of subtle influence. These include cliques, bake sales, and tradition.

In Eastland, the elders who represent the tradition and history of the church are viewed by others as a group. The behavior and values of members of this elite group are generally interpreted as representing the behavior and values of the other older members. When the piano player left the church, for example, her action was interpreted as an expression of the feelings of all the elders. This situation suggests the importance of regulating behavior within the group—a natural expression of the group-centeredness of the region. Eastland's elders maintain themselves as a "generalized other," with common activities, common interests, and sanctions for deviance (Mead, 1934). In the words of one former church member, they are a clique. When this woman's husband died, the church members failed to ritualize the mourning of his death, as they usually do, by bringing food and socializing. She attributes this to the increasing amount of time she had spent working in the nursery her father had left her. This formerly active woman had dropped from the sight of the other church members. As she said, "If you're not a member of that clique . . . they don't know you." She was mentioned by only one other church member in any context and was not referred to by any of the new members of the church. Visibility and participation are important to the status of the elders; deviation from these norms is best not tolerated, at least from the perspective of the elders. This was particularly the case with this woman, who failed in other ways to legitimate the group's existence: "I can go out in the nursery at dusk and feel closer to God than in church," she says. "I don't need to be with other people to feel at peace with God." This statement is a contrast to the principal reason the other elders give for attending church—fellowship. Her position may also be contrasted with that of others whose participation has been restricted by physical disability but who are still considered part of the group.

The elders regulate their relations with those outside their group in other ways. Yard sales and bake sales may not appear to be mechanisms of social influence, but in a church community divided over capital improvements, control of funds places one in a stronger bargaining position. If money is to be used to carpet the church, those who have raised the money will be part of that decision. One elder, Mrs. Elliott, who considered herself an advocate of change in the church, discussed a recent bake sale. One woman had complained about the lack of help that the older women had received from younger women at this sale. Mrs. Elliott was outraged by this complaint: "They set things up so they were in charge, then complained that they didn't get any help." Perhaps such complaints call attention to the contribution of the elders to the church. Perhaps, also, permitting others to help would undermine that contribution.

History and tradition could be useful mechanisms of influence to the extent that other members of the community were familiar with the role that the elders have played in the history of the church. Their role was formally recognized through Heritage Sunday and informally recognized in other ways. For example, as part of a Women in the Community project at the college in Hillton, women in the congregation were asked to identify the women in the church who had made "both a spiritual and a personal difference" to them and to the church. The younger women left the task to the older women, claiming "they know more about it than we do." The awareness of history is also evident in the frequency with which members of the church describe the older individuals' relations with their "family church." Thus, the association of the elders with the history and tradition of the church reflects the community's consciousness. The privileged status of many of the elders is maintained by the fact that it is impossible to forget them.

This is not to suggest that these mechanisms of influence are conscious attempts by the elders to maintain their position in the community. It may be the case, though, that part of the "we feeling" in a community includes group consciousness of intergenerational relations. Perhaps the most significant single force in perpetuating the status of the older members, the trouble in 1974 that led most of the congregation to leave, illustrates this point. This event was neither intentional nor unique. It reflects personal and religious values characteristic of Appalachia. The history of many Protestant churches, particularly those that began with emotional fervor and an emphasis on individual religious experience, includes a period of expansion followed by migration to find new religious experiences (Boisen, 1940). Church members organize to express their religious needs, become dissatisfied as the church grows away from spirituality toward social organization, and express their personal dissatisfacton by leaving. Thus, the trouble in 1974 may have been an accident of culture and history, but it was integrated into the community consciousness as part of the church members' awareness of the value of the elders as those who had "held the church together."

Conflict Resolution

The first impression of the Eastland community was not the conflicts within the church, but rather the mutual respect of the generations for one another and their regard for themselves as a community. These original impressions provide a counterpoint to the examination of conflicts in the community.

The relationship between the generations in Eastland is neither exclusively conflictful nor respectful, as is illustrated in a conversation between Mrs. Ward, a member of one of the oldest families in Eastland, and the minister. "Our church has always been a community church and we want it to stay that way." The minister asked if Mrs. Ward didn't want the church to reach out to others and grow. Mrs. Ward reluctantly acknowledged that she did, revealing the ambivalence within the community. Her middle-aged son told me about his own fears for the church: "Eastland is not the same community I knew. I'm used to a small church where everybody knows each other. . . . I worry that the church will get to be a citified church." But another of the elders suggested, "You've got to get new ideas sometimes, let other people come in and examine your head." This ambivalence is shared by those elders who do seek change in the church. The same man who told me the story of the piano player claimed, "I can see their objections to modernization. It takes away from the spiritual to concentrate on the material."

This intergenerational ambivalence reflects the axis of variation we have proposed: the sense of success in avoiding the crush of modernization that is accompanied by the profound sense of failure in meeting possibilities and challenges. This is the axis along which a temporary resolution has been achieved — a mutual recognition across generations that the church would not exist were it not for the elders and that it would cease to exist without the newcomers. These contrary tendencies might be seen as the cultural equivalents of Erik Erikson's (1963) notions of generativity and ego integrity and, as such, are the essence of intergenerational relations. The lasting significance of the church as a community beyond the lives of the elders was expressed by one in the following way: "I'm just so happy to see that all these young people have come in here. They have vitality and interest where we had been struggling along."

CONCLUSIONS

The Appalachian region incorporates a set of value orientations that are resistant to change. This resistance is compellingly described by Caudill (1976a). West Virginia is often identified in travel and recreational brochures as The Switzerland of America. Caudill suggests that the comparison is not a good one:

> The Swiss mountaineers took a depressingly poor land, and by good judgement and hard work, became rich, powerful, and respected. . . . Appalachian mountaineers took a rich land and became poor. The huge achievements in the Alps flow from a popular willingness to make hard decisions and to seize and carry through burdensome responsibilities. The resounding flop in the Appalachians reflects a historic abdication of responsibility to raise up stable leaders, to fashion sound public policies, and to implement them. In both situations what might be called "cultural determinism" was hard at work and still works to impel one people toward the heights and to sink the other into dependency and degradation. (p. 47)

Generations of Appalachian families have changed. We have suggested that they have done so within the boundaries of basic value orientations — along the point and counterpoint characteristic of the region. The basic similarities between the people in Thomas' and Rodeheaver's research and their past and future generations are striking.

The values of the region also give the mountaineer a set of conflicts and strategies for dealing with them. Conflict and tension between insiders and outsiders offer perhaps the best prospects for significant change in the region. Conflict is also the tie that binds families and communities in Appalachia to families and communities elsewhere. The issues of stability and change that we have discussed suggest that conflict and ambivalence are vital signs of intergenerational relations. In Appalachia, with enormous potential for change, continuity has become so much the norm that change seems unnatural.

ACKNOWLEDGMENTS

This chapter represents a collaborative effort between the authors; names appear in alphabetical order. We are grateful to Margaret L. Rowley for clerical assistance.

REFERENCES

Ambler, C. H. & Summers, F. P. (1965). *West Virginia: The mountain state.* Englewood Cliffs, NJ: Prentice-Hall.

Boisen, A. T. (1940) Divided Protestantism in a midwest county: A study in the natural history of organized religion. *The Journal of Religion, 20,* 359–381.

Caudill, H. M. (1962). *Night comes to the Cumberlands.* Boston: Little, Brown.

Caudill, H. M. (1976a). *A darkness at dawn.* Lexington: University Press of Kentucky.

Caudill, H. M. (1976b). *The watches of the night.* Boston: Little, Brown.

Clark, M. (1968). The anthropology of aging: A new area for studies of culture and personality. In B. L. Neugarten (Ed.), *Middle age and aging.* Chicago: University of Chicago Press.

Erikson, E. H. (1963). *Childhood and society.* New York: Norton.

Erikson, K. T. (1976). *Everything in its path.* New York: Simon & Schuster.

Lozier, J. & Althouse, R. (1974). Social enforcement of behavior toward elders in an Appalachian mountain settlement. *Gerontologist, 14,* 69–80.

Lozier, J. & Althouse, R. (1975). Retirement to the porch in rural Appalachia. *International Journal of Aging and Human Development, 6,* 7–15.

Mead, G. H. (1934). *Mind, self, and society.* Chicago: University of Chicago Press.

Press, I. & McKool, M. (1972). Social structure and status of the aged. *Aging and Human Development, 3,* 297–306.

Rodeheaver, D. (1982). *Eastland's elders: Aging and status maintenance in a West Virginia church community.* Unpublished doctoral dissertation, West Virginia University, Morgantown.

Rodeheaver, D. (1985). Families as networks and communities: A developmental psychology of aging and intergenerational relations. *Contributions to Human Development, 14,* 80–85.

Ross, J. K. (Keith, Jennie) (1977). *Old people, new lives: Community creation in a retirement residence.* Chicago: University of Chicago Press.

Thomas, J. L. (1982). *The development of grandparents' relationships with their grandchildren: An exploratory study.* Unpublished doctoral dissertation, West Virginia University, Morgantown.

Thomas, J. L. (1985). Grandchildren's impact upon adult child-elderly parent relationships. *Academic Psychology Bulletin, 7,* 27–37.

Thomas, J. L. & Datan, N. (1982, November). *Stability and change in grandparent-grandchild relationships.* Paper presented at the annual meeting of the Gerontological Society of America, Boston.

Thomas, J. L. & Datan, N. (1983, August). *Change and diversity in grandparenting.* Paper presented at the annual meeting of the American Psychological Association, Anaheim, CA.

Thomas, J. L. & Datan, N. (1983b, November). *Sex roles in grandparent-grandchild relationships.* Paper presented at the annual meeting of the Gerontological Society of America, San Francisco.

Thomas, J. L. & Datan, N. (1985). Themes of stability and change in intergenerational relations. *Contributions to Human Development, 14,* 86–92.

Weller, J. E. (1965). *Yesterday's people: Life in contemporary Appalachia.* Lexington: University of Kentucky Press.

5 Asymmetrical Kin and the Problematic Son-in-Law

Corinne N. Nydegger
Medical Anthropology Program
University of California, San Francisco

At the popular level, in-law relations are a staple of comedy routines and family advice columnists. Surprisingly, students of the family have shown no interest in this topic during the past 30 years. Although network research during this period, sparked by Bott's (1957) work, expanded the narrow conjugal focus of family studies, this orientation did not encourage the examination of particular relationships among kin. Moreover, with the notable exception of Fischer's (1983) recent study of intergenerational women's relationships, in-law studies reflected the dominant perspective of the field by taking the point of view of the child-in-law rather than the parent-in-law. Thus, the studies are not readily assimilated into kinship research, which customarily takes the perspective of the mature kin group with regard to marriage of its children.

Within this child-centered point of view, theorists offered contradictory suggestions for the locus of in-law problems: Komarovsky (1950), pinpointing the wife's family; Duvall (1954), emphasizing the son's family. The conclusions from the few subsequent studies (Rogers & Leichter, 1964; Stryker, 1955) implied that in-law relations were largely a problem for women, that it was the classic wife/mother-in-law relationship that was problematic.

The data about in-law relations discussed here are derived primarily from the opposite point of view — from the traditional kinship perspective of the parental family. From this stance, the relations look different: They are at least as problematic and consequential for men as for women.

My interest in this topic arose from unexpected findings in my research on fathers. Although interpretation of these results might be limited to the context of American family structure, I could not help but be struck by certain analogues in the anthropological literature despite enormous differences in scale and social organization. I recapitulate this process here, first describing the research on fathers and then moving to a broad, cross-cultural framework to suggest a set of determinants of modal in-law problems that transcend disparate social structures, which, in turn, clarify the nature of these problems in our own society.

THE FATHERHOOD PROJECT

Let me start, then, with the Fatherhood Project. This study focused on the roles of father and the adult child.[1] The approach was explicitly *emic*: it was an attempt to achieve an "insider's" understanding. "It is *not* a method, nor is it merely the subjective perception of individuals. Rather, it is how they have given meaning to those perceptions by culturally appropriate ways of organizing, thinking, and feeling about them; literally, the phenomenology of culture" (Nydegger, 1983a, p. 452). In this case, the goal was to describe the cultural phenomenology of the reciprocal father and adult child roles.

In contrast to structural role analyses on one hand and case studies on the other, the objective was to conduct a middle-level analysis of these roles that would specify their distinctive features, their normative and experiential aspects, and their meaning to fathers and to their children. In effect, we asked: What is being a father or an adult child all about? What issues are salient for them? In what terms do they understand their experience? What principles are invoked to explain their success and failure? Methodologically, we were eclectic: We asked such "naive" questions in a variety of ways, including the use of formal measures and variables drawn from previous research. But our first concern was to be sure that we had captured the nature of informants' experience, and ways of thinking about that experience, and only then to make sense of this material in terms relevant to theory.

The Father's Perspective

Parents typically report that their relationship with each child is distinctive. Even when all relations can be characterized as good, or bad, parents maintain that they are qualitatively different. Therefore, in order to capture the full experience of fathering, we asked about all children. This means that not all parent-child relationships discussed are truly independent. However, for our purposes this is not a serious fault. First, we are not statistically correlating parent-child relationships to parental characteristics; second, we are

---

[1](MH29657) Although a primary objective of this study was to evaluate the effects of parental timing on these roles, this question is not germane to the topic here and will not be discussed.

looking for broad patterns of role experience and perception, which necessarily include experience with all children; third, dyadic father-child relationships are so varied within families that it is impossible to predict from one dyad to another except in the extreme cases. Hence, the lack of true independence is not too high a price to pay for a comprehensive view of the role.

Most of the data discussed here are drawn from lengthy, semi-structured, taped interviews. Reducing these raw materials to coded categories was a protracted, iterative process of cautious response grouping, at increasing levels of abstraction, so as not to lose those distinctions that were significant to informants. It was an arduous task, but a small, dedicated staff maintained coding reliabilities of .90 or better. Although analysts using these techniques have not developed a consistent terminology, procedures have been reported in several publications (Clark & Anderson, 1967; Nydegger, Mitteness, & O'Neil, 1983; Stolz, 1967).

The Sample.   The first phase of the project involved 267 men, aged 45 to 80 years, who had a total of 343 married children. They were initially identified via random-digit dialing within the greater San Francisco Bay area. Participants were selected according to the following stringent criteria of inclusion: All had at least one year of higher education, four years for those 45–54; by compensating for secular increases in education, the men selected represented approximately the same percentile of their respective cohorts in regard to education. The men had been functioning fathers of their first family until the children were at least in their late teens (that is, they remained married or, if divorced, had custody of their children). And all participants were native-born non-Asians.

These men were overwhelmingly middle class, and most were financially secure.[2] Occupations varied widely, from minor civil service jobs to high level professions and managerial positions; but the majority were businessmen. They had traditional marriages; few wives worked while their children were young. Thus, in terms of family, the informants represent the most stable portion of middle class fathers in this age range. They also match that urban middle class mainstream that classic American kinship studies have taken as the standard (e.g. Schneider, 1968; 1980; Wordick, 1973).

Children's Marriage as Problematic.[3]   How do these men view their children's marriages? Fathers desire marriage for all their children and worry about those who show no signs of settling down. Despite this positive view of

---

[2]All participants fall within the three highest positions on the Hollingshead (1957) scale of occupational prestige. On a 4-point scale of income adequacy developed for this study, 83% were adequate to affluent, only 17% felt "pinched"; none were objectively poor.

[3]A partial analysis of portions of these data was reported in Nydegger and Mitteness, 1982.

marriage in principle, in practice it is often problematic: It is the single most common source of tension between married children and their parents. Further, there is a persistent bias against men. Fathers are more critical of both sons and sons-in-law than they are of daughters and daughters-in-law. These conclusions are not based on a single indicator; they emerged consistently from different portions of the data.

Most relations with children are considered good, but this does not preclude dissatisfaction with one or another aspect of a child or of the child's life. About 60% of the children occasion at least moderate complaint. Fathers are more critical of sons: Given the opportunity to cite up to two specific complaints, fathers readily provide them for sons, whereas daughters elicit fewer than one and a half apiece. But of more interest than the number are the reasons for dissatisfaction. As Table 5.1 shows, the most pronounced complaint about a daughter has to do with her marriage. Even when this category is broken into its components, her parenting is responsible for few complaints; the marriage itself is the target of criticism. Although marriage also affords a good deal of dissatisfaction with sons, it is surpassed by complaints about lack of achievement. However, this distribution is only a crude kind of averaging that ignores the child's age. To take this into account, we plotted the complaints by age of child. Only one point is pertinent here: Marriage is the *only* complaint that does not decrease with age. Thus, for sons in their 30s, complaints about achievement decline, while those concerning marriage increase to the point that marriage is the primary basis of fathers' dissatisfaction. However, it never looms so large for sons as it does for daughters at all ages.

Sources of Dissatisfaction.   Why is marriage so often a subject of complaint? There are two major reasons: divorce and disapproval of a child's

TABLE 5.1
Fathers' Complaints about Married Children

	Sons (n = 123)	Daughters (n = 129)
Marriage	20% ⎫	31% ⎫
	} 24%	} 40%
Parenting	4 ⎭	9 ⎭
Lack of achievement	28	20
Goals/Lifestyle	19	19
Personal qualities	11	11
Lack of maturity	7	3
Relations with parents	6	5
Other	5	2
	100%	- 100%

TABLE 5.2
Blame for Child's Divorce

	Sons (n = 45)	Daughters (n = 44)
Child	18%	2%
Spouse	33	34
Both	4	18
Neither	27	45
No opinion	18	0
	100%	100%

spouse. At the time of these interviews, 29% of the sons and 23% of the daughters had been divorced. The pattern of assigning blame for the marital problems that led to divorce shows a clear sex bias. As Table 5.2 illustrates, in a third of the divorces, fathers refuse to blame either partner. They cite various no-fault reasons such as youth, adverse circumstances, simple incompatibility, and the like. No hostility is expressed by these fathers; the divorce is unfortunate, an occasion for dissatisfaction and regret, rather than anger.

When blame is assigned, the not-surprising tendency is to blame the child's spouse rather than the child. But sons are blamed much more often than are daughters; at most, daughters share the responsibility with their ex-husbands. Moreover, a father is twice as likely to be severely upset by a daughter's divorce than by a son's. In part, this can be explained by the greater likelihood that a daughter will return to her parents' home, often with young children, in need of financial and emotional support. But fathers also regard daughters as more vulnerable, a point to which we return later.

The second, and more frequent, source of complaint about children's marriages is disapproval of children-in-law. I should emphasize that in at least three quarters of the cases, fathers regard these in-laws fairly positively. But, as is common in the social sciences, the problematic few often tell us more than do the happy majority. In this case, as before, the reasons offered for disapproval of children-in-law are particularly revealing: Sons-in-law typically pose a different kind of problem than do daughters-in-law. This distinction is not reflected in reasons for approval, which are largely personal for both — the child-in-law is likable, has desirable characteristics, and so forth. But when the child-in-law is disapproved, sex differences appear. As shown in Table 5.3, the bases for complaint fall into three main categories. Sons-in-law are most often faulted for failure in performance of their family roles — half of all complaints.

Daughters-in-law are disliked as often for their personal qualities as for failure in family roles. Nevertheless, the latter category is the most telling one. It is a composite of three items that are distributed differentially by sex.

TABLE 5.3
Fathers' Complaints about Children-in-Law

	Son-in-law (n = 72)	Daughter-in-law (n = 45)
Personal qualities	35%	44%
Poor provider	31	0
Poor family functioning	19ᵃ	38ᵇ
Attitudes, beliefs	12	11
Other	3	7
	100%	100%

(Poor provider and Poor family functioning for Son-in-law bracketed together = 50)

ᵃMost frequently mentioned: hurtful to daughter.
ᵇMost frequently mentioned: pulls son away from parents.

For a son-in-law, the dominant item is that he is hurtful to the daughter in some way, generally in emotional terms. For the daughter-in-law, the dominant problem is that she pulls the son away from his parents, usually into closer association with her own. This complaint is accompanied by the strongest parental anger and bitterness, for it permanently disrupts family bonds and distances parents from their son. Fathers speak of having "lost" their son.

Last, because disapproval can be masked in the interests of family harmony, we probed for overt conflict or strain during visits with married children. Fathers shrugged off most of their complaints about children and children-in-law as inevitable frictions in family life. The proportion of relations they report as strained (roughly 20%) is therefore a source of serious concern. As Table 5.4 shows, children-in-law are the major locus of such strains. Here are the shiftless, alcoholic, and adulterous sons-in-law, and those daughters-in-law who have stolen sons away.

TABLE 5.4
Fathers' Reasons for Strains during Visits with Children

	Sons (n = 30)	Daughters (n = 28)
Child's spouse	37%	54%
Goals/Lifestyle	23	7
Personality conflict	17	3.5
Money	7	3.5
Conflicts due to other family members	3	21
Other	13	11
	100%	100%

Summing up these various aspects of fathers' relations with married children, we find that:

1. In almost one out of 10 cases, fathers report that a marriage has seriously strained relations with that child;
2. Fathers are consistently more critical of sons and sons-in-law;
3. Father/son-in-law relationships are most often problematic;
4. Sons-in-law pose the threat of harm to the daughter; daughters-in-law threaten the parent-child bond.

The Child's Perspective

How do children view the relations between their spouses and their parents? To answer this question, we turn now to the second phase of the Fatherhood Project, in which we obtained parallel data from children. The question also arose regarding agreement between fathers and their wives. If mothers had been interviewed, would they reverse fathers' sex bias, be more critical of women, and thus support our mother-in-law stereotypes? Although this possibility was contraindicated in the protocols, to provide some evidence on this question we expanded our focus in the second phase to include children's perceptions of mothers' relations with their spouses.

The Sample.   For the children's study, we drew a random sample from the pool of informants' children living within 60 miles of San Francisco. We interviewed one child per family, 62 sons and 62 daughters, ranging in age from the 20s to the 50s (median age 31). Because this discussion is limited to married children, the sample is reduced to 31 sons and 44 daughters. Though few in number, they are sufficient to confirm the patterns thus far described.

In-law Problems.   Children agree on pattern but paint a less rosy picture of intergenerational relations. First is the question of agreement between fathers and mothers about children-in-law. We ascertained the children's views of parental approval of spouses at the time of marriage and of subsequent changes in the relationships. Children report 77% initial agreement between their parents and even closer agreement over time. When disagreement is noted, it is the father who is generally considered more disapproving.

Children also confirm the sex bias: Fathers are considered much more likely to disapprove of sons-in-law than daughters-in-law (Table 5.5). And mothers are reported to agree with their husbands in this too: That is, although mothers are slightly more approving overall, they also are less satisfied with sons-in-law. Thus, there is no evidence of a reverse sex bias; rather, it operates in the same direction for both parents. Nor is there any evidence of a probationary period prior to approval. Over time, relations with

TABLE 5.5
Children's View of Parental Attitudes
Toward Children-in-law at Marriage

		Son-in-law (n = 44)	Daughter-in-law (n = 31)
Fathers	Approve	61%	78%
	Neutral	2	19
	Disapprove	37	3
		100%	100%
Mothers	Approve	66%	81%
	Neutral	7	13
	Disapprove	27	6
		100%	100%

children-in-law often improve, but these are almost counterbalanced by the cooling of relations with others. After some years of marriage, almost a third (30%) of the daughters report some parental dissatisfaction with their husbands; fewer than half as many sons (13%) report disapproval of their wives. Age of children is not related to parental disapproval, but, in agreement with Fischer (1983), presence of grandchildren does seem to increase complaints about daughters-in-law, though the cases are too few for confidence.

One caveat should be noted in regard to these parental agreement data. The argument can be made that being less sensitive to interpersonal relations, neither husbands nor sons are reliable informants about women and that if mothers had been interviewed, more tensions with daughters-in-law would have been reported. In other words, the conclusions here may reflect a male perspective. This interpretation cannot be ruled out, although the data (admittedly, based on small numbers) do not support it in as much as most strains reported with daughters-in-law appear to involve both parents.

TABLE 5.6
Child's Location of Strains during Visits

	(n = 75)
No strains	45%
Locus of strain	
Son-in-law	13
Father's new wife	12
Daughter-in-law	7
Father-child conflict	7
Parental marital problem	5
Mother-child conflict	3
Other	8
	100%

The second set of children's data concerns overt strains and conflict when the families get together. Here children and their fathers sharply disagree about frequency and one specific source of strain. As Table 5.6 shows, more than half the children (55%) report some strains, compared to roughly 20% of their fathers. Are fathers less aware of the tensions? Or do they want to believe that relations are smoother than they are? Or simply want us to believe this? We cannot say with certainty, but it seems to be a genuine difference in perception. As Fischer (1983) points out, children remain vulnerable to childhood points of contention, and they find it difficult to shrug off parental complaints. And they are especially sensitive to criticism of their wives or husbands. Thus, children report as strains many frictions fathers regard as minor.

The Stepmother.   Again, the qualitative data, the locus of strains or conflict, are most illuminating. In agreement with fathers' reports, relations with sons-in-law are clearly the typical problem and are much more often attributed to fathers than to mothers. But they are scarcely more problematic than one difficulty fathers had glossed over: the father's new wife. Of the 11 cases of a father's remarriage following a late life divorce or widowhood, only two did not cause major changes in relations with children. McCain (1969) showed that marriages after retirement were vulnerable to antagonism from the couple's children. This is the other side of that coin.

Informants were eloquent about the disruption of family bonds due to re marriage and drew an exact parallel to parental complaints about daughters-in-law. Children resent the new wife's pulling their father away from them to spend his time (and his money) with her and her children. Because these women are generally younger than the father, instead of playing grandfather to his own family, he is stepfathering her children or even starting a new family. His children feel they cannot compete. Again, the dominant theme is theft of love: The stepmother has stolen the father away. It is bitterly resented. Typical comments illustrate the rivalry and sense of loss: "Now that he has his new family, he's not interersted in me any more. I'm not really his daughter any more." And from another daughter: "I'm not part of his life any more. I feel like some kind of guest. It's not like I'm coming *home* to visit." From a proud young father: "He spends all his time with her kids, not mine. I still go there to see him, but I don't think he really cares. It would have been so different if Mom were still alive."

Conclusions

Summing up both fathers' and children's views, we can conclude that family members generally agree on the nature of relations with in-laws:

1. The father/son-in-law relationship is the modal source of tension; at issue is a perceived threat to the daughter's well being.

2. Although infrequent, the most serious disruptions are caused by wives alienating their husbands from their families; this threat is posed by daughters-in-law and by late-life second wives as well.

Thus the contradictory suggestions in the literature as to the locus of in-law conflict (viz., with the wife's parents or with the husband's parents) are reconciled: both are right. As Komarovsky (1950) suggested, problems with the wife's parents are typical. However, as Duvall (1954) contended, when conflicts with the son's parents do occur, they are extremely disruptive. Each problematic relationship poses its distinctive threat to the family members involved.

But these conclusions give rise to a number of questions:

1. Why is the father/son-in-law relationship typically problematic?

2. Why do sons-in-law and daughters-in-law characteristically pose *different kinds* of problems?

3. Are there patterned methods of reducing tensions between parents and children-in-law?

A partial answer to some of these questions can be found in the limited context of the father's role definition. However, to answer the questions fully, we must move to the larger context of the American kinship system. Let us deal with the father's role definition first, for it explains a major portion of the frequency and substance of father/son-in-law tension.

Paternal Responsibility

A favorable bias toward daughters runs throughout our protocols. Fathers are much less critical of daughters than of sons because they see them as vulnerable. It may be, as some have suggested (Kohn & Carroll, 1960), that men expect their wives to take the major responsibility for a daughter's development. Nevertheless, fathers regard her protection as their responsibility. As a corollary, they expect to provide for, and to retain authority over, a daughter longer than over a son.

This concern is most strikingly evidenced in men's attitudes toward a daughter's marriage. Traditionally (that is, prefeminism), a father's protective function was taken over by her husband. For many men, "giving away the bride" is still more than a mere symbolic gesture. Fathers admit, with some embarrassment, that they would prefer to screen prospective sons-in-law, although they realize that their daughters regard this as hopelessly old fashioned. Nevertheless, they watch closely for evidence of a son-in-law's ability to provide for their daughter. As we have seen, they often are unimpressed. Fathers' stronger reactions to a daughter's divorce than to a son's is another case in point. As shown earlier, a daughter is seldom held responsible for her divorce. Indeed, the father may even blame himself: "A father may feel that he failed to protect his daughter, even if his advice was not sought or was ignored" (Nydegger & Mitteness, 1982, p. 17).

It also should be remembered that the fathers in this study are typically successful, well-educated men. Even those daughters whose relations with them are not especially good generally respect their expertise. Thus, their fathers' judgments about their husbands are not easily ignored. And, despite claims of nonintrusion into children's marriages, a father's judgment of incompetence is likely to be communicated one way or another. (I suspect that the habit of offering constructive criticism to sons is readily extended to sons-in-law. Then, defensive daughters may experience strains of which their fathers are unaware — one source of the difference in reported strains.) If the daughter's husband is not merely improvident but harmful to the daughter, a father is likely to see it as his duty to intervene for her protection. Thus, fathers' definition of their role leads them to focus critical attention on sons-in-law. A son makes his own mistakes in marriage, but a daughter's marital problems raise the spectre of her father's inadequate protection — his failure in fathering.[4]

I have said that the nature of American kinship provides the fullest answers to our questions about parent/child-in-law relations. But these questions are not best resolved by remaining too close to data on American families. We can gain a clearer perspective if we step back and look at these issues in the cross-cultural context of marriage into kinship/residence systems.

MARRIAGE AND KINSHIP/RESIDENCE SYSTEMS

Kinship analysis constitutes a major bloc of the anthropological literature. No general ethnography lacks a section devoted to it. There is a well-traveled ethnologist's path through the thickets of MoFaSiSo's and the like, and many have struggled with those recondite algebraic arguments characteristic of kinship theorists, whose battles are now measured in yards of shelf space. Why all this fuss about kin?

The reason is simply that for all preindustrial populations and for a large proportion of modern societies, kinship is *the* organizing principle of social life. Its importance cannot be overestimated. In these societies, which range in scale from small, scattered bands to Dynastic China, it is kinship that determines one's social position and inheritance. And, in this context, inherit-

---

[4]In blue-collar families, mothers reputedly discharge more of these functions for daughters. Therefore, one would anticipate a higher proportion of mother/son-in-law conflict in working class samples than is reported here.

ance is not merely a matter of mother's amethyst necklace or even a handy sum of cash: it is most likely to be the very means of one's livelihood, such as land or hereditary craft. More important to the discussion here, kinship defines belonging — membership in a group — specifying to whom one owes obligations and from whom one can expect favors. Short of leaving the community altogether, the "web of kinship" (Fortes, 1949) binds its members into a lifelong support/control group.

In many parts of the world today, kinship has lost its primacy largely because of population growth, mobility, and the possibility of wage-work or its equivalent. Indeed, some have argued that in societies such as our own, kinship is of little value in explaining behavior or social organization and that, conversely, we must look to contextual factors such as friendship networks, class, and ethnicity to explain kinship behavior (Bott, 1957; Needham, 1971; Schneider & Smith, 1973). But wherever one stands on this argument, no one questions that the closest kin ties, those in what we call the nuclear family, retain their viability. They remain important in conferring social and occupational advantage, in providing emotional support, and in the caretaking of the sick and elderly. And family members continue to be involved in each other's marriages in various ways, some of which we have seen.

The second basic organizing principle of social life is residence. In anthropological parlance, this is a question about people, not geography. That is, not where, but among whom do you reside? Who shares your dwelling? Who lives nearby? When you cry out in fear or anger, who hears?

Only in the high-rise segments of modern cities are such questions irrelevant. Neighbors matter for everyone else, including many urban dwellers. Though relatively few traditional social scientists have addressed these questions in our own society (e.g., Bott, 1957; Gans, 1962), we often assume the importance of neighbors. In gerontological research especially, neighbors are central to debates about age-homogeneity (Rosow, 1967) and provision of assistance. And recently, some of the new school of ecological geographers such as Rowles (1978) have extended the meaning of location to include people as well as place.

Although we can distinguish residence from kinship theoretically, they are seldom separate in fact. Residence is rarely a free choice. Thus, for most of the world's populations, especially the rural, questions about residence continue to be answered in terms of kin. Only in the limiting case of high technology urban populations does an analytic separation reflect reality. In the context of the family, any discussion of marital units must involve both principles, for where the new unit resides is consequential for maintenance of kin ties, friendships, and for support in times of trouble (from a bad crop to invading marauders).

Both principles lend themselves to elaboration. Indeed, the ingenuity with which they have been elaborated seems remarkable to those, like us, whose cultural rules[5] about kinship and residence are minimal. The voluminous literature on kinship addresses two basic questions: how these various rules regulate social life, and how these rules have changed over time. But these are not problems that need concern us here. To focus on the narrow topic of parent/children-in-law relations, I need discuss only those aspects of marriage, kinship, and residence that are most consequential for these relationships: that is, the structural sources of in-law tension and affiliation, and the mechanisms developed to reduce tensions.

Marriage Rules

To most of us, marriage means a relationship between two people. But the notion of a universal, "natural" marital unit is as mythical as that of the "natural" nuclear family (Nydegger, 1983b). In many societies of the past and today, the marital unit has limited autonomy; control is firmly in the hands of kin group leaders. In these circumstances, marriage means a contract or alliance between kin groups and claims on children of the union. Typically, it also involves the incorporation of one spouse into the residential kin unit of the other and his or her adaptation to this group's ways.

These matters are too important to be left to youngsters. Therefore, societies have developed rules governing the selection of marriage partners. Marriage rules and their consequences for social structure have been the most hotly debated issues in kinship studies in recent years (Barnes, 1971; Levi-Strauss, 1969). These and earlier studies have emphasized the impact of various marriage rules on kin groups in terms of continuity, interrelatedness, and so forth. But there has been little interest in their meaning for parents or children-in-law. However, it is clear that these rules can facilitate or hinder incorporation into the kin/residence group.

For example, marriage rules always specify proscribed partners; lineages generally are exogamous and may extend the prohibition to other related lineages; village exogamy is not uncommon; and so on. The extension of such rules can lead to marriages wherein the partners and their in-laws are virtual strangers. Then, adaptation of a new in-law and incorporation are made more difficult.

Prescriptive rules vary considerably, but it is common to prefer marriage with lineages or villages already linked by marriage. These kinds of rules increase the likelihood of familiarity between partners and in-laws, thus facilitating incorporation of a new in-law into the group. Frequently, a cousin of one sort or another is preferred. In this case, the couple is joined by

---

[5]The term "rules" is traditional in anthropological discussions of marriage, kinship, and residence. However, the term should not be taken literally, for it includes the full range of cultural norms, from prohibitions and prescriptions to preferences.

bonds of both marriage and kinship, and the new in-law is preadapted, and the process of incorporation is eased.

Modes of Descent

Kinship can be derived from two sources: ties of blood, referred to as consanguine descent; and ties of affinity which result from one's own marriage or the marriage of one's consanguine kin. In regard to the focus of this paper, it is important to point out that the difference between consanguines and affines is not as evident as we might think. Fox (1967) makes this point forcefully: "To us, a father is genetically connected to his children in the same way as a mother: he is a consanguine. But if we took the view that the father had no part in the creation of the child, then he would not be a 'consanguine'; he would simply be the mother's husband—like a step-father in our own society—and of the same order of relationship to us as, say, a brother-in-law" (p. 35). The point is that descent "refers solely to a cultural principle whereby an individual is socially allocated to a specific group of consanguineal kinsmen" (Murdock, 1949, p. 43). It need not, and does not, always reflect genetic inheritance.

If reckoning relatives based on consanguinuity sounds simple to us, it is because our present kinship structure is one of the simplest known. From the perspective of the kinship student, we are impoverished, though our European ancestors enjoyed a more complex system. Societies have elaborated this basic notion of connection by blood in different ways to develop widely divergent systems of kin reckoning. As a first-order, gross classification, systems can be dichotomized into the lineal and bilateral types. Lineal systems are those which recognize kin along only one line of descent, either the father's or the mother's. (We will ignore the few bilineal variants.) The basic lineal forms, then, are *patrilineal* descent, which disregards the mother's kin and affiliates a child exclusively with the consanguineal kin group of the father, and *matrilineal* descent, which is the mirror opposite, affiliation being with the mother's kin group.

In sharp contrast to the unilineal is the mode of reckoning consanguine kin through both father and mother simultaneously. This is the *bilateral* mode of descent, such as we use. Bilateral descent is not a combination of two unilineal kin structures. Rather, it reflects an absence of any unilineal emphasis and produces its own distinctive kin group known as the *kindred*.

The most significant consequence of unilineal descent is the fact that the rule produces a restricted group of consanguines called a *lineage*: all are descended from a common ancestor and all are members of one kin group. This group is corporate in the sense that it has an in-perpetuity existence over and above any individual member. When it owns communal property, it is often called a clan. Because of this emphasis on the kin group in lineal descent systems, the rules are often spoken of as modes of recruitment. No member of a lineage has any doubt, or any option, about who should be considered blood kin and who are excluded — they are delineated by the lineage boundary.

Bilateral kin reckoning produces a sharply contrasting result. Traditionally called ego centered because kin are reckoned from each individual's (ego's) position, the kindred includes some and excludes some of both mother's and father's kin. Because it is ego-centered, members of a kindred group are not necessarily related to each other; their relationship is to ego. For example, my paternal uncle will include in his kindred some of his mother's relatives, to whom I am not related at all. Technically, only unmarried siblings of the same sex have identical kindreds. Thus, it is possible for one person to belong to two kindreds which are in conflict; this cannot happen in a lineage system. It is obvious that kindreds can have no corporate permanence, as do lineages, and can function as groups only in the short term.

An additional problem is the possibility of indeterminate kindred boundaries. As Murdock (1964) puts it, the boundaries "may be defined with great precision . . . or, as in American society, the boundaries may be indefinite, terminating in a sort of twilight zone" (p. 130). Schneider's (1968) study of American kinship discusses this question in detail and documents the variations that result from our flexibility of kindred inclusion. But the point here is less that bilateral systems can allow choice in definition of kin, than that these systems define kin symmetrically through the father and the mother. The importance of this point is apparent later.

Rules of Residence

Residence rules are less rigid than descent rules and are better thought of as norms or preferences. Because residence determines which, if any, kin one sees on a daily basis, unilineal societies have a stake in this question and typically have strong preferences. But residence is necessarily influenced by factors beyond kin group control, such as population pressure, shifting watercourses, depletion of game, and so forth.

Traditionally, the first-order classification of residence is patrilocal, matrilocal, and neolocal (although more accurate terms are available, these remain in common use). *Patrilocal* means that a new couple resides with or near the husband's father's kin group; *matrilocal,* that they reside in the wife's parents' location; *neolocal,* that they reside no closer to one set of parents than the other. Appropriately, the correlation between descent and residence is strong for lineage societies; bilateral systems show no marked residential preference (Murdock, 1949).

DETERMINANTS OF MODAL TENSION

Various cross-cultural studies have related kinship, residence, or marriage rules to customs such as in-law avoidance (Sweetser, 1966), outcomes such as divorce rates (Ackerman, 1963), and certain social structure variables (Farber, 1975; Murdock, 1949). These studies have utilized sophisticated indicators and drawn samples from the hundreds of societies for which categorized data are now available. My purpose here is more modest: to suggest structural determinants of modal tension among in-laws. Therefore, I will invoke only those rules of marriage, kinship, and residence that are directly and immediately consequential to the parent/child-in-law relationship. From this limited point of view, four critical questions can be posed:

1. Where, in relation to parents-in-law, will the new couple reside?
2. Is the child-in-law known (or related) to either parent prior to marriage?
3. How much autonomy do the new conjugal unit and the child-in-law enjoy?
4. What are the expectations regarding the severance of birth ties and the child-in-law's incorporation into or affiliation with the spouse's kin group (in terms of loyalty, property, authority, etc.)?

The answers to these questions largely explain the modal tension: why one kind of in-law problem is more common than another in a society. The same information suggests the choice of specific tension-reducing mechanisms. For maximum contrast, I illustrate this in brief, schematic descriptions of some basic, "ideal types" of social organization. (To simplify, I ignore polygynous marriages.) By substituting different answers to one or more of the foregoing questions, one can trace out the likely consequences for modal in-law tensions in a variety of systems.

The Patrilineal Case

The most common form of social organization is patrilineal and patrilocal (Murdock, 1949). A classic marital situation, a living "ideal case" so to speak, has been described for a Rajput village in northern India by Minturn and Hitchcock (1963). For the Rajput family, our four questions can be answered as follows:

1. The newly married couple resides in the household of the husband's father, along with other sons and their wives and children, in a village up to 100 miles from the bride's natal village. The Rajput are Moslems, and a woman maintains lifelong purdah in the village into which she marries; she need not

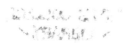

maintain purdah in her natal village, because village exogamy is the rule and all village women are classificatory sisters.

2. The bride is not personally known to her parents-in-law. In fact, she is not personally known to her husband. A moderate trend toward taking wives from the same general area means that sisters-in-law will occasionally be related or known to each other. But typically the daughter-in-law is a stranger.

3. Ideally, the new conjugal unit is totally subservient to the extended household head; the husband's primary loyalty is to his parents and lineage, not to his wife. The bride's autonomy is nil. Until she is much older, she is subservient to her mother-in-law and to those wives whose husbands outrank her own.

4. The bride is incorporated into her husband's lineage, to which she owes full loyalty and to which her chidren will belong. Although her ties to her own family and natal village are never fully severed, there is no reason for conflict: The marriage is a contract rather than a working alliance between lineages.

The modal tension is between mother and daughter-in-law. The men of the household are seldom in the living quarters except to eat or sleep and, owing to purdah restrictions, daughters-in-law have virtually no contact with their male in-laws. Household regulation is vested in the mother-in-law, who is assisted by the senior daughter-in-law. The tensions inevitably arising during the course of training a stranger to become a member of the household are exacerbated by purdah-confinement of the women in close proximity.

Tension-Reducing Mechanisms.   How is a situation with such explosive potential handled? Persistent quarrels between daughters-in-law can be settled by dividing the common courtyard and building separate hearths. But the equivalent solution for tension with the mother-in-law (i.e., a separate household) would destroy the extended family solidarity essential to the economic well being of the kin group.

Two customs have evolved in India to handle this problem. One, no longer legal, was that of the "child bride": These marriages were solemnized but were not consummated. The child grew up in her own and her marital households in a manner similar to our joint custody arrangements. By the time she was of an age to be a real wife, her mother-in-law was to some extent a mother also.

The second solution is based on the same idea of gradual incorporation. The new bride stays at her husband's village for only a month or two after the marriage and then returns to her own village for at least a year before resuming her life as a wife. Even then, her visits home are frequent and lengthy. She spends "about half of the first eight years of her married life in her mother's home" (Minturn & Hitchcock, 1963, p. 235), where she is treated as as a guest. These ties to her natal village are relinquished slowly but never altogether severed; as long as her parents are alive, she always has a bolt-hole.

The Matrilineal Case

The obverse ideal type, matrilineal and matrilocal, an uncommon form of social organization, is popular among anthropologists because it raises intriguing questions of male authority vested in mother's brother as well as conflicting claims of a man's own lineage and that of his son. The limited perspective of this discussion cannot do justice to the complex issues of authority posed by these societies. Recognizing the oversimplification resulting from a focus on in-law relations shorn of their context, we briefly sketch the outlines of a classic situation of this kind as it has been described for the Navajo of the American Southwest (Aberle, 1961; Kluckhohn & Leighton, 1962; Nydegger, 1970). For the Navajo family, the answers to the four questions are:

1. The new couple resides in their own dwelling in the camp of the wife's mother, along with other daughters and their husbands and children. The dwelling may be at any distance from the groom's mother's camp because transhumance is practiced and families have dwellings in various parts of the reservation.

2. The groom may be known to his parents-in-law. Because there is a tendency for brothers to marry into the same clan (Aberle, 1961, p. 121), brothers-in-law occasionally are related to or know one another.

3. The new conjugal unit has limited autonomy; authority is vested in the wife's mother. The groom has little autonomy inasmuch as property and control pass through the maternal line. Children are under the jural authority of the wife's brother. But the brother resides elsewhere with his wife, and the groom may, therefore, have considerable de facto authority over his own children.

4. The groom is not fully incorporated into his wife's kin group. He (and the husbands of his wife's sisters) remains peripheral, and his property (primarily sheep) often remains in the camp of his mother. On the death of his wife or divorce, his children remain with his wife's kin group, but he returns to his natal camp. His loyalties are almost permanently divided, and conflicting claims regularly occur.

The modal tension has usually been assigned to the mother/son-in-law relationship, as she is likely to be the leading clan member in her camp. However, more recent studies (Aberle, 1961; Witherspoon, 1975) suggest that the leading clan mother's husband, as second in command, shares authority and that his relationship with the son-in-law is also problematic. Thus, the major tension is not really located in the parent/child-in-law relationship as such, but between two kin groups, one headed by the mother-in-law.[6]

Tension-reducing mechanisms. How are the strains handled? The mother-in-law avoidance custom was traditionally interpreted as one method. More recent studies suggest this may be avoidance merely of eye contact and is interpreted in terms of the sexual taboo, rather than tension reduction (Witherspoon, 1975). However, polite formality in behavior and speech is strictly observed between parents and son-in-law, thus limiting overt quarrels.

The favorite method of avoiding family quarrels is by avoiding the family. Navajo men are highly mobile under the best of conditions. When tensions mount, sons-in-law simply leave camp for a while to visit their maternal families or other clansmen (Nydegger, 1970). When tensions persist, they may leave permanently. Because they are peripheral to the lineage group, it can afford to lose them. Divorce, often initiated by wives, is relatively inconsequential for all concerned and a commonplace (estimated at 75% for men [Kluckhohn & Leighton, 1962, p. 83]).

The Bilateral Case

A good contrast to these lineal systems is that of the Ilocano, agriculturalists in the northern Philippines, who have a bilateral kinship system with predominantly patrilocal residence (Nydegger & Nydegger, 1966). Again, looking at our four questions:

1. The new couple resides in their own dwelling, in the housing site of the groom's father, along with other sons and their families. This is usually no more than a day's walk from the bride's natal home.

2. The bride is personally known by, and may be related to, one of her parents-in-law (and her husband). Because community endogamy occurs, she may have known her husband and his parents all of her life. She may know one of her sisters-in-law and is probably related to other members of the community.

3. The new conjugal unit is theoretically autonomous, but cannot function well without its kindred. In matters affecting the whole family unit, the father (and/or the oldest son) is final arbiter. The mother (and/or oldest daughter-in-law) performs this function among the women. Until she has settled into the family, a new wife also is expected to defer to her older sisters-in-law.

---

[6]This is the traditional reservation pattern. Where resettlements have been established for agricultural or wage work, the conjugal family (and especially the husband) gains autonomy at the expense of the kin group (Nydegger, 1970; 1983b; Sasaki, 1960).

4. The bride is incorporated into her husband's kindred by marriage and, to a lesser extent, he into hers. Although her loyalty to her own close kinsmen is seldom affected by the marriage, should arguments arise between her consanguine and affinal kin, she is expected to support her affines — the group with whom she resides. Over time, her ties to her natal community lessen and strengthening bonds with her husband's family balance her affectional ties to her parents. If widowed, she probably remains in her husband's community unless her children are very young, in which case she may return with them to her parents' household.

In contrast to the preceding systems, tension is low and seldom persists beyond the first few years of marriage. The modal tension is between sisters-in-law (and, early in marriage, between mother and daughter-in-law). Elder sisters-in-law tend to continue to exert authority over younger women who feel they have earned their autonomy.

Tension-Reducing Mechanisms.   How are these tensions handled? An Ilocano woman is not encouraged to "go home to mother," who will send her back unless she has been mistreated. Her parents will not risk angering the in-laws, who are likely to be related by blood as well as by the daughter's marriage and also may share membership in work groups. In cases of community endogamy, her parents' home is across a few courtyards — she has no bolt-hole.

The most effective mechanism is the custom of household inviolability: "No in-law would presume to take over the management of the new bride's house unless specifically requested [to do so] during illness or childbirth. This is particularly true of the kitchen, which is a woman's private domain" (Nydegger & Nydegger, 1966, p. 49). In effect, the daughter-in-law escapes into the private recesses of her house, avoiding unpleasantness, until tempers have cooled.

But she is not without friends. In contrast to the previous examples, community members who are related to the daughter-in-law keep a friendly eye on her and her treatment. This is most noticeable during the young wife's first pregnancy, when her mother-in-law is held accountable to her parents for her health and safe delivery (Nydegger & Nydegger, 1966).

American Dispersed Kindreds

Let us now return to the American family ideal type in regard to the four questions:

1. The couple resides near neither set of parents, and their kindreds are widely dispersed.

2. Neither the bride nor the groom is likely to be known or related to the parents-in-law prior to the marriage.

3. The new conjugal unit enjoys full autonomy, although assistance is expected from one or both parents in time of need.

4. Each spouse is counted in the other's kindred as an affine. For kin outside the spouse's immediate family, this is a pro forma relationship devoid of content (e.g. my cousin's husband) — an example of the Tenuous role in Rosow's (1976) role typology. However, each spouse is expected to be incorporated into the immediate family of the other. In middle-class America today, this is defined primarily as affiliation. Prescriptively, then, the young couple should be equally involved with and affectionally tied to both sets of parents.

And there's the rub.

Asymmetry and In-Law Tension.   Each member of the new conjugal unit is a stranger to his or her in-laws, and the kin groups (in this case, the families of each generation) are dispersed. There can be little of the kind of working together that builds commonality and promotes understanding. Affiliation, especially when defined in terms of emotional involvement, is problematic and necessarily slow to develop. Under these conditions, the process takes place during visits.[7] It is the women in our society who have the responsibility for arranging them and maintaining contact, that kin-keeping function of women so often documented (Bahr, 1976; Lee, 1980).

However, given the dispersal of kin, time spent with one group of parents is usually at the expense of the other. And the mother-daughter bond appears to be stronger than that between other family members (Adams, 1968; Cohler & Grunebaum, 1981; Reiss & Oliveri, 1983). Consequently, studies of parent-child contacts show a consistent bias toward women's kin: a matrifocal asymmetry (Sweetser, 1963). This principle of American kinship, so at odds with our ideal of equal affiliation with bilateral kin, is pivotal for in-law tensions.

First, the asymmetrical involvement maximizes the likelihood of tension between father and son-in-law. A daughter's more frequent visits to her family also involve her husband. If the husband is a poor provider or otherwise unsatisfactory, his father-in-law has more opportunities to observe these faults and their impact on his daughter than he has of observing his daughter-in-law's faults. Even if contact is largely by telephone, he hears more about her life and her problems, either directly or through his wife. Thus the princi-

---

[7]This ritual of conversation and roast chicken is probably unique to modern industrialized societies such as our own and deserves intensive examination. Indeed, the entire process of evolving in-law relations is virtually unknown (Fischer, 1983; Landis, 1946) and begs for attention.

ple of asymmetry is one determinant of the location of the modal tension between father and son-in-law.

Second, if relations with a husband's family are uncomfortable, or if the daughter-in-law is unusually attached to her own family, asymmetrical involvement is likely to be marked. When the son does nothing to counteract it, we have the dominant daughter-in-law fault: She has pulled the son away from his family. Thus, the principle of asymmetry accounts for the distinctively different problems posed by sons-in-law and by daughters-in-law. (If men were the kin-keepers, would we hear similar complaints from the parents of their wives? Or would their weaker ties to their own families result in a less biased involvement?)

Third, the principle of asymmetry also produces the most dramatic in-law conflict in the context of late-life remarriage. In parallel with daughters-in-law, the matrifocal bias encourages the new wife to draw her husband into the orbit of her family. Perceiving this new interest as alienation, his own children react with great bitterness. In contrast, the few instances of mothers' remarriage were greeted by the children with relief; both sons and daughters of widows or divorced mothers were actively encouraging their remarriage.

Tension-Reducing Mechanisms.   We have only one method of reducing tensions between parents and children-in-law: avoidance. This, of course, simply aggravates the problem because it documents the very lack of affection and involvement that was the source of tension to begin with. At this point, relations are set on the downward spiral of decreasing contact, typical of tensions with daughters-in-law.

The less disruptive father/son-in-law strains seldom curtail daughters' visits: children can practice quasi-avoidance by visiting their parents without a problematic spouse. However, this technique is successfully practiced only by a daughter, who may be able to "drop by" casually during her husband's work hours, thus sidestepping the question of his feelings. Should a son too often visit his parents without his wife, it will be correctly interpreted as avoidance and exacerbate the problem.

SUMMARY

In American middle-class families, relations between parents and their children-in-law generally are good. But when tension and strain do occur, their locus typically is between father and son-in-law; at issue is perceived threat to the daughter's wellbeing. Although less common, strained relations with a daughter-in-law are more disruptive, for, in this case, the threat is to the parent-child bond itself.

Two factors account for the greater likelihood of father/son-in-law tensions and for the distinctively different kinds of problems posed by sons-in-law and daughters-in-law. The first is the way a middle class man defines his role of father to a daughter. Because he regards a daughter as more vulnerable than a son, her protection assumes paramount importance. When a daughter marries, her father anxiously focuses critical attention on the way his son-in-law performs the functions of provider and protector.

The other factor is the structure of the American kinship-residence system. Examples of in-law relations in other cultures suggest three major structural determinants of tension. First, authority over the conjugal unit leads to strains between the parent (or surrogate) charged with overseeing the child-in-law; proximity exacerbates these tensions. Second, the more familiar the in-law is to the kin group prior to marriage, the more easily is incorporation accomplished; proximity, in the absence of authority, facilitates incorporation. Unfamiliarity occasions tensions with all members of the residential group and exacerbates tensions arising for other reasons. Third, if the kin-residence system encourages divided loyalties, incorporation is most problematic and leads to strains between the in-law and the affinal kin group.

In American families, neither kin-group authority nor coresidence generally obtain; hence the first source of tension is not relevant. However, the second and third bases of tension are pertinent. Urban American families define incorporation primarily as affiliation, that is, involvement and affection. Since the child-in-law typically is a stranger, affiliation can be expected to be problematic. Although the exacerbating influence of kin-group authority is not involved, the lack of proximity to in-laws attenuates communality, retards the process of affiliation, and maintains tensions. This problem, of course, is shared equally by sons-in-law and daughters-in-law.

The pivotal factor that accounts for the distinctively different kinds of problems posed by daughters-in-law and sons-in law is the third, that of divided loyalty. Ideally, children-in-law should be equally affiliated, that is, involved and affectionally tied, to both sets of parents. But, in practice, our system has a pronounced matrifocal bias, which has two major effects. On one hand, the more frequent contact and greater involvement of a daughter with her own parents increases their knowledge of her marital problems and her husband's shortcomings, as well as occasioning more frequent contacts between father and son-in-law. Fathers' critical oversight is maximized, as is the likelihood of overt strains in their relations.

On the other hand, a daughter-in-law's strong involvement with her own family can abrogate the couple's affiliation with her husband's parents. They then perceive her as having alienated their son. In an exact parallel, a father's remarriage after his children become adults is very likely to bring the same charges of alienation by those children.

The cross-cultural examples suggest that some form of avoidance is the primary mechanism relied on to reduce strain between parents and children-in-law. In American families, tensions between fathers and sons-in-law can be reduced by scheduling, that is, by quasi-avoidance. But no mechanism has been developed to ease relations with daughters-in-law. Nevertheless, all but a handful of daughters-in-law skillfully manage these problems of kin keeping with both families. And parents of sons do their part in minimizing tension. They are well aware of the asymmetry of kin affiliation. Provided involvement is not excessively one sided, they reluctantly accept it, quoting the old (and apparently accurate) saying: "A son is a son till he takes him a wife; a daughter's a daughter for the rest of your life."

ACKNOWLEDGMENT

The author gratefully acknowledges the support of NIA grant AG00097 and NIMH grant MH29657.

REFERENCES

Aberle, D. (1961). Navaho. In D. Schneider & K. Gough (Eds.), *Matrilineal kinship* (pp. 96–201). Berkeley: University of California Press.

Ackerman, C. (1963). Affiliations: Structural determination of differential divorce rates. *American Journal of Sociology, 69,* 13–20.

Adams, B. (1968). *Kinship in an urban setting.* Chicago: Markham.

Bahr, H. M. (1976). The kinship role. In F. I. Nye (Ed.), *Role structure and analysis of the family.* Beverly Hills: Sage.

Barnes, J. A. (1971). *Three styles in the study of kinship.* Berkeley: University of California Press.

Bott, E. (1957). *Family and social network.* London: Tavistock.

Clark, M. M. & Anderson, B. (1967). *Culture and aging.* Springfield, IL: Charles C. Thomas.

Cohler, B. J. & Grunebaum, H. U. (1981). *Mothers, grandmothers, and daughters.* NY: Wiley.

Duvall, E. M. (1954). *In-laws: Pro and con.* NY: Association Press.

Farber, B. (1975). Bilateral kinship: centripetal and centrifugal types of organization. *Journal of Marriage and the Family, 37,* 871–888.

Fischer, L. R. (1983). Mothers and mothers-in-law. *Journal of Marriage and the Family, 45,* 187–192.

Fortes, M. (1949). *The web of kinship among the Tallensi.* Oxford: Oxford University Press.

Fox, R. (1967). *Kinship and marriage.* Middlesex, England: Penguin Books.

Gans, H. (1962). *The urban villagers.* NY: Free Press.

Hollingshead, A. B. (1957). *Two-factor index of social position.* Mimeo. New Haven, CT: 1965 Yale Station.

Kluckhohn, C. & Leighton, D. (1962). *The Navaho* (rev. ed.). Garden City, NY: The Natural History Library.

Kohn, M. & Carroll, E. (1960). Social class and the allocation of parental responsibilities. *Sociometry, 23,* 391–392.

Komarovsky, M. (1950). Functional analysis of sex roles. *American Sociological Review, 15,* 508–516.

Landis, J. (1946). Length of time required to achieve adjustment in marriage. *American Sociological Review, 11,* 666–677.

Lee, G. R. (1980). Kinship in the seventies: a decade review of research and theory. *Journal of Marriage and the Family, 42,* 923–934.

Levi-Strauss, C. (1969). *The elementary structures of kinship.* Boston: Beacon Press. (Original work published 1949)

McCain, W. (1969). *Retirement marriage.* Storrs, CT: Storrs Agricultural Experiment Station Monograph, University of Connecticut.

Minturn, L. & Hitchcock, J. T. (1963). The Rajputs of Khalapur, India. In B. Whiting (Ed.), *Six cultures* (pp. 203–361). NY: Wiley & Sons.

Murdock, G. P. (1949). *Social structure.* NY: Free Press.

Murdock, G. P. (1964). The kindred. *American Anthropologist, 66,* 129–132.

Needham, R. (1971). Introduction. In R. Needham (Ed.), *Rethinking kinship and marriage.* London: Tavistock.

Nydegger, C. N. (1970) *Effects of structural changes on Navajo familial roles.* Unpublished master's thesis. Cornell University, Ithaca, NY.

Nydegger, C. N. (1983a). Introduction. In C. N. Nydegger (Ed.), Anthropological approaches to aging research: applications to modern societies. *Research On Aging, 5,* 451–453.

Nydegger, C. N. (1983b). Family ties of the aged in cross-cultural perspective. *The Gerontologist, 23,* 26–32.

Nydegger, C. N. & Mitteness, L. S. (1982). Old fathers and aging children: marriage is major source of strain, *Generations, 7,* 16–18.

Nydegger, C. N., Mitteness, L. S. & O'Neil, J. (1983). Experiencing social generations: Phenomenal dimensions. *Research On Aging, 5,* 527–546.

Nydegger, W. F. & Nydegger, C. N. (1966). *Tarong: an Ilocos barrio in the Philippines.* NY: Wiley.

Reiss, D. & Oliveri, M. E. (1983). The family's construction of social reality and its ties to its kin network. *Journal of Marriage and the Family, 45,* 81–91.

Rogers, C. L. & Leichter, H. J. (1964). Laterality and conflict in kinship ties. In W. J. Goode (Ed.), *Readings on the family and society.* Englewood Cliffs, NJ: Prentice-Hall.

Rosow, I. (1967). *Social integration of the aged.* NY: Free Press.

Rosow, I. (1976). Status and role change through the life span. In R. H. Binstock & E. Shanas (Eds.), *Handbook of aging and the social sciences* (pp. 457–482). NY: Van Nostrand.

Rowles, G. D. (1978). *Prisoners of space?* Boulder, CO: Westview Press.

Sasaki, T. (1960). *Fruitland, New Mexico: a Navaho community in transition.* Ithaca, NY: Cornell University Press.

Schneider, D. M. (1968, 1980 rev. ed.) *American kinship.* Chicago: Chicago University Press.

Schneider, D. M. & Smith, R. T. (1973). *Class differences and sex roles in American kinship and family structure.* NY: Prentice-Hall.

Stolz, L. (1967). *Influences on parent behavior.* Stanford: Stanford University Press.

Stryker, S. (1955). The adjustment of married offspring to their parents. *American Sociological Review, 20,* 149–154.

Sweetser, D. A. (1963). Asymmetry in intergenerational family relationships. *Social Forces, 41,* 346–352.

Sweetser, D. A. (1966). Avoidance, social affiliation, and the incest taboo. *Ethnology, 5,* 304–316.

Witherspoon, G. (1975). *Navajo kinship and marriage.* Chicago: Chicago University Press.

Wordick, F. (1973). Another view of American kinship. *American Anthropologist, 75,* 1634–1656.

6 Daughters and Sons as Young Adults: Restructuring the Ties that Bind

A. L. Greene
West Virginia University

Andrew M. Boxer
University of Chicago and Laboratory for the Study of Adolescence
Michael Reese Hospital

Perhaps more than any other phase of the life cycle, young adulthood is considered an evanescent and easily forgotten cluster of life changes or transitions, a set of bridges extending endlessly for some and briefly for others. Indeed, few students of the life cycle, Kenniston (1970) notwithstanding, write of young adulthood without the qualifier of "transition to" or "transition from." In the United States there is no one event that formally marks the transition to adulthood (Featherman, Hogan & Sorenson, 1984; Marini, 1978). Beginning in late adolescence a number of role entries, punctuate this rather unroyal road to adulthood: The end of mandatory schooling, entry into higher education, exit from the parental home, the establishment of an independent household, entry into full-time labor, marriage, and parenthood.

Several historians of the family have noted that at one time transitions were more a family matter (Hareven, 1982; Modell, Furstenberg & Herschberg, 1976). The critical aspect of such transitions was not the age at which they occurred, but how such transitions related to those of other family members. Across adjacent and nonadjacent generational positions, family members share expectational sets about the advent and timing of individual and shared life events (Hagestad, 1981; Neugarten, Moore & Lowe, 1965; Pruchno, Blow & Smyer, 1984; Riley & Waring, 1976). One example of this shared expectancy is the advent and timing of leaving home. Parents and children share mutual expectations of when and how children leave home.

The congruence between such expectations and actual behavior contributes to the psychological well being of all family members (Cohler & Boxer, 1984). Within a web of family consociates (Plath, 1982), the transition to adulthood may be viewed as a set of counterpoint transitions (Riley & Waring, 1976), which although initiated by young adults, affect parents and other family members as well.

Examined in this manner, a critical dimension of young adulthood is the alteration in family relationships produced by the transition. However, as Hagestad (1981) has noted, "After the voluminous research on early childhood and adolescence, we seem to drop the relationship and not pick it up again until the parents are old and the children are middle-aged" (p. 33). This lacuna may stem, in part, from the hypostatized view of adolescents as needing to make enduring psychological and physical separations from parents, a critical developmental task necessitated by the demands of a successful adult life. The impact of a young adult's leaving the parental home has been closely examined from the perspective of the mother, but seldom from that of the father or child. We turn our attention to dimensions of the parent-child relationship in the context of changing life course configurations.

SOCIAL AND HISTORICAL CONTEXTS OF YOUNG ADULTHOOD

Many historians of the family have a special interest in transitions. Thus, more than many other phases of the life course, adolescence and youth have been the subject of numerous studies examining the ways in which sociocultural changes have altered, reordered, and shaped these periods of life (e.g., Boxer, Gershenson & Offer, 1984; Elder, 1980). It seems clear today that the current age grading that occurs, for example, in school and in the ascription of social maturity related to such behaviors as drinking, driving, and voting, has increased the significance and use of chronological age as a demarcation of social status, accentuating the distinctiveness of subgroups of adolescents. It is no surprise that we now find developmentalists further differentiating the stage into early, middle, and late adolescence (e.g., Hamburg, 1974; Kagan, 1971; Thornburg, 1983).

Twentieth century contemporary social myths would lead us to believe that adolescence and youth have become more extended phases of life. Protracted schooling, economic dependency on the family, and the complex nature of career decisions are often taken to indicate that the timing of the adulthood transition has become more prolonged and the sequence of changes less clearly prescribed. This enduring myth has been addressed, perhaps most compelingly, by Modell and his colleagues (Modell, Furstenberg & Hershberg, 1976). Drawing on contemporary census data and data from an

1880 Philadelphia Federal Population Manuscript schedule restricted to white populations, Modell and his associates found that growing up in contemporary America has become less prolonged, and that the sequence of transitions, including departure from the family of origin, marriage, and the establishment of an independent household has become more concentrated. It seems that the protracted transition into adulthood was more a phenomenon of centuries past (Katz, 1975; Kett, 1977).

Leaving the parental household itself has only recently become a subject of historical investigation. Richard Wall (1978) has suggested that a century or more ago movement from home was a gradual and "revolving door" process. It was the gradual nature of this process, rather than the proportion of children of particular ages at home, that distinguished these communities from those of today. There was, however, a much greater probability of finding fewer young children at home than is now the case. In preindustrial Europe, many children left the parental household for domestic and apprentice service. Yet, as Kertzer and Schiaffino (1984) point out, we know little about the consequences of these arrangements on the interweaving of family lives or about their impact on the relations between parents and children (see also Mogey, 1976).

Katz and Davey (1978) have argued that the impact of industrialization was to lengthen the portion of the life course during which children lived with their parents. Currently, children may reside in the parental household longer, but their departure appears now to be a more abrupt one. Young (1974, 1975), examining contemporary survey data from Australia, suggests that it is the suddenness of physical departure that differentiates leaving home today from that of past centuries. In the 1970s (Young, 1974), the average age of leaving home for males was about 23 years, and for females, 21 years. A greater proportion of daughters left home for marriage than for other reasons.

Young adults today must negotiate a complex set of decisions about the sequencing of events in the transition to adulthood. Such decision making and the consequent transition may be significant sources of psychological distress (Hauser, 1980; Pearlin, 1980). Young men or women in Modell's 1880 Philadelphia would enter the work force and contribute to the income of their families of origin for about 7 years. Currently, the family economy is more dependent on husband and wife (Modell, et al., 1976; Oppenheimer, 1981). Children today typically do not contribute economically to their families of origin, but rather, are more likely to spend their money on consumer goods or create savings for investments in their education (Modell, et al., 1976; Oppenheimer, 1974, 1981).

There are many nonfamilial institutions today that are part of the transition to adulthood (Demos, 1979; Featherman, Hogan & Sorenson, 1984; Skolnick, 1979). Rising levels of education and declining age at marriage are associated with the "latent function" (Marini, 1978) of a marriage market which educational institutions serve in bringing together large numbers of students, self-selected for social homogeneity. Growing up into an adult has become briefer, not longer, and, as Modell et al. (1976) state, "more normful and bounded" (p. 31).

While the constraints of age appear to be taking on less significance generally (Neugarten, 1979), it has been argued that the early part of adulthood is more clearly age graded now than it was in the nineteenth century (Hagestad & Neugarten, 1984; Hogan, 1982; Neugarten & Hagestad, 1976). Hogan (1982) found that high school-aged adolescents normatively prefer to traverse the life course in terms of school, work, and marriage. There are, however, decreasing numbers who follow this clear cut order; a large number of diverse sequencing patterns are found among today's youth (Abeles, Steel, & Wise, 1980). School, career, and family-related transitions appear to be interwoven. Thus, young adulthood is a time in which there often occurs a pileup of role changes (Neugarten & Hagestad, 1976).

Changing demographic realities indicate that an increasing proportion of the population lives out the course of life within a family context (Uhlenberg, 1978). Changing mortality and fertility rates mean that family members can expect more long-lasting and enduring relationships. Consequently, the family has become a smaller unit with less disruption by the death of a sibling or parent. It has been suggested that intergenerational relations not only have come to be more extensive, but more intensive as well (Hagestad, 1981; Skolnick, 1978).

Young Adults and Their Parents

The parent-child relationship undergoes many transformations across the life course of its members. If relationships can be thought to have critical periods, adolescence can be seen as a time in which maturational changes may exert influences on the adolescent in relation to all family members. (Hill, 1980; Steinberg, 1981; Steinberg & Hill, 1978). Changes in the parent-child relationship also may be initiated by parents' reactions to their adolescents and to their own (parents') developmental concerns and preoccupations (Boxer, Solomon, Offer, Petersen, & Halprin, 1984). As Rossi (1980) and others (e.g., Johnson & Irvin, 1982) have commented, parents of adolescents may be "winding down" while young adolescents are "winding up." Findings from several normative studies of adolescents and parents have shown that most report fairly stable and smooth relationships with one another and that conflicts are negotiated without major disruptions in the parent-child bond (Douvan & Adelson, 1966; Kandel & Lesser, 1969; Offer & Offer, 1975).

Changes in the parent-child relationship during adolescence are thought to be important precursors to interactions in adulthood. Moving into young adulthood, adolescents seem to develp a more extensive network of consociates (Plath, 1980; Pruchno, Blow, & Smyer, 1984). The parent-child relationship can be examined, from the perspectives of both parent and child, in terms of the intermeshing of lives. The task, as Plath (1982) suggests, is one "of reconciling at least two types of contradictions; that one's partners are in different seasons of life and that one is moving simultaneously on several career pathways with each of these partners" (p. 298).

FAMILY ATTACHMENTS, BONDS AND BINDS IN YOUNG ADULTHOOD

Writers have frequently conceptualized the task of young adulthood as that of separation from the family (that is, the parents) and the successful assumption of new, autonomous social roles (e.g., Bettelheim, 1965; Blos, 1962; Freud, 1914/1957; Mead, 1970). Erikson (1956), for example, describes this process as "the selective repudiation and mutual assimilation of childhood identifications, and their absorption in a new configuration . . . " (p. 65). Following the tradition of Mahler (1972a, 1972b; Mahler, Pine, & Bergman, 1975), Blos (1962, 1967) characterizes young adulthood as part of a second individuation process, recapitulating many of the conflicts of earlier parental ties and attachments. As he states, it is "the shedding of family dependencies, the loosening of infantile object ties in order to become a member of society, or, simply, of the adult world" (Blos, 1967, p. 163). As attachments to parental figures (or to mental representations thereof) decrease during this transition, attachments first to self and subsequently to others increase (Freud, 1914/1957).

At the sociological level, this perspective is complemented by the use of extrafamilial markers (e.g., marriage, the establishment of a separate household, or parenthood) to index both the degree and timeliness with which the young adult has effected this transition (e.g., Hill, Foote, Aldous, Carlson, & MacDonald, 1970; Neugarten & Moore, 1968; Wall, 1978). Correspondingly, there is a presumption of loss to the family, most particularly to the mother, as the child's departure is thought to have substantive effects on the mother's role and responsibilities (Bart, 1970; Blau, 1973; Lidz, 1968; Spence & Conner, 1971; Rose, 1962). Indeed, several authors describe this as a "mourning period" for both mother and child, in recognition of their mutual loss consequent to the separation (Laing & Esterson, 1964; Stierlin, Levi & Savard, 1971). Repeated findings, (e.g., Neugarten & Datan, 1974), suggest, however, that mothers anticipate and experience the transition with satisfaction, relief, and a notable lack of depressive episodes (Campbell, Converse, & Rodgers, 1976; Glenn, 1975; Hagestad, 1978).

At both psychological and sociological levels of analysis, then, the developmental expectancy of this period remains that of the child's distantiation from the family—a shift in primary attachment from the family of origin to peers, and, finally, to the family of procreation. Indeed, the metaphors invoked to describe this transition capture not only *researchers'* perceptions of its impact, but certain of their misperceptions, as well. Consider the use of such phrases as "the family as a launching pad," or "the empty nest." Both metaphors evoke an image of objects hurled into space, struggling valiantly against the gravitational pull of early attachments. Both metaphors describe a transition that is seemingly abrupt and characterized by physical distance.

The use of such metaphors to describe this transition reflects a rather odd assumption about the nature of intergenerational attachments, that is, attachments between parents and their young adult children are assumed to have an implicitly dichotomized quality. Successful transition to adulthood and separation from the parents is presumed to entail disruption of, if not an end to, attachments between generations (Bettelheim, 1965; Mead, 1970). Conversely, the maintenance of strong or cohesive parental attachments is thought to be suggestive of an inadequate or unsuccessful transition to adult status (Levinson, Darrow, Klein, Levinson, & McKee, 1978; Panel, 1973a, 1973b).

Seemingly in consequence, two decades of intergenerational research has focused on relations between parents and their adult children (e.g., Adams, 1968; Aldous, 1967; Hagestad & Snow, 1977; Harris & Associates, 1975; Kalish & Knudtsen, 1976; Litwak, 1965; Shanas, 1979; Sussman & Burchinal, 1962; Troll, 1971; Troll, Miller & Atchley, 1979; Troll & Smith, 1976), presumably to determine how "empty nests" get refilled through filial obligations.

Maintaining Parent-Child Bonds in Adulthood

Troll and Bengtson (1982) point to an increasing corpus of research that suggests the maintenance of parent-child bonds over the life course. "Despite differences in maturational levels, geographic propinquity, gender, and socioeconomic mobility, as well as possibly confounding effects of cultural change and peer interaction, parent-child solidarity appears to represent consistently an important interpersonal bond in contemporary American Culture" (p. 907).

Paradoxically, several investigators have observed increased levels of affection and attachment between parents and their children following separation from the family (Levi, Stierlin & Savard, 1973; Murphey, Silber, Coelho, Hamburg, & Greenberg, 1963; Stierlin, 1974; Stierlin, Levi & Savard, 1971). Sullivan and Sullivan (1980), for example, report that boys who go away to college (boarders) report significantly increased affection for and from their parents as compared to their preseparation report and as compared to boys who stay at home to attend college. Moreover, mothers of boarders perceived their sons as more affectionate after the separation than before it. Curiously, fathers whose sons moved more than 200 miles away perceived their sons as significantly more dependent than fathers whose sons lived at home and commuted to college.[1] Distance does seem to make the heart grow fonder.

Where researchers have examined the maintenance of family attachments during young adulthood, the focus has been primarily on the parents' role and activities. Thus, we find that while there is a good deal of interaction across the life course, parents are typically described as the primary givers to younger generations (Adams, 1968; Litwak, 1965; Rosow, 1965; Sussman & Burchinal, 1962). We suspect that this finding and the resultant picture of intergenerational relations have obtained for several reasons. First, much of this research has been conducted by investigators whose "cohort affinities," if they may be so termed, are closer to those of adult parents than to those of young adult children. The typical orientation is that of the parents and not that of the young adult children, or, preferably, that of both parents and children. The assumptive emphasis of verticality in this regard is noteworthy. That is, the transition to adulthood is examined only with respect to its intergenerational impact, and there only with regard to parents. We may safely assume that the transition of one child also has implication for other siblings within the family—or what may be termed intragenerational impacts—which, as yet, remain largely unaddressed in the literature.

Second, as several authors have noted (Hagestad, 1981; Kalish & Knudtsen, 1976; Knudtsen, 1976; Troll & Bengtson, 1982; Troll & Smith, 1976), we lack both theoretical and empirical understanding of dyadic attachments in adulthood. In consequence, the predominant tendency has been to apply child-based models of attachment processes to adult family functioning (Cohler & Geyer, 1982; Hagestad, 1981; Knudtsen, 1976).

Finally, those studies that have examined intergenerational bonds, have focused primarily on the occurrence of intergenerational exchange. Such exchanges are typically defined in terms of their more concrete aspects, that is, the provision of material goods and services (e.g., child care, monetary sup-

---

[1]Although this research is one of very few to focus on the young adult's separation from the family, the authors overlook the influence of economic factors upon perceived dependency/autonomy. Families who send their children away to college (i.e., boarders) are more likely to incur greater educational expenses than are families whose children remain at home. Perhaps, therefore, it is not too surprising that parents of boarders also might perceive their children as more emotionally dependent.

port). In this light, parents are seen as the major providers to and maintainers of the relationship, as compared with their young adult children (Bengtson & Kypers, 1971).[2]

Differentiating the Generational Stake

The dual tendency to focus on the parents' perspective in the child's transition to adulthood and upon the more material aspects of subsequent exchanges has resulted in a thematic assumption that pervades much of this literature. Family attachments are thought to be maintained after the child's transition to adulthood largely, if not exclusively, through the differentially greater affective, psychological, and economic investment of parents (Bengtson & Kypers, 1971; Bengtson, Olander & Haddad, 1976; Troll & Bengtson, 1982; Troll & Smith, 1976).

An example of this formulation can be seen in the generational stake hypothesis forwarded by Bengtson and Kypers (1971). These authors suggest that parents and their young adult children remain attached, but that their respective levels of investment in that attachment are considerably different. Parents, whose concerns focus primarily on self-extension and generational continuity, minimize essential differences between generations. "In the face of behavior which, in reality, reflects both difference *and* continuity, the middle generation [parents] is constrained to believe and perhaps to fabricate the continuity" (Bengtson & Kypers, 1971, p. 257). In contrast, adult children, whose concerns center on the establishment of individual life styles and attitudes, maximize essential intergenerational differences. Parents, Bengtson and Kypers (1971) argue, have a differentially greater investment in attachment qua similarity/continuity than do their young adult children.

There are, however, several social and familial factors that modify or obviate the investment of parents described by these authors. The asymmetry of family relationships, for example, is an important consideration. Although the child may have only one set of parents from whom to separate, the parents may have several children (Hagestad & Dixon, 1980; Sweetser, 1963). Even in the instance of only children, the asymmetry persists. (It is, however, intriguing to speculate what the circumstance might be in single-parent one-child families).

We may speculate that the more asymmetrical the relationship becomes, the greater the likelihood that the parents' generational stake will lessen for

---

[2]We must, however, consider the economic realities that may underlie intergenerational exchanges. Middle-aged parents are more likely to occupy higher levels of income and financial security than either their older adult parents or their young adult children. It is not surprising therefore that the middle generation would and frequently does serve as a material resource to both the eldest (e.g., by way of filial obligation) and youngest generations (e.g. by way of exchanges).

each child — as the number of children increases, so too increases the assurance of generational continuity for the parents. Cook (1982), for example, observed that parents' adjustment to the death of a child was positively correlated to the number of children in the family. The greater number of surviving children, the better was the parents' adjustment.

We may further speculate that the generational stake in a given child will vary considerably both with the child's sex (Hagestad & Speicher, 1981; Hill et al., 1970; Komarovsky, 1964; Sweetser, 1964), and with the child's intragenerational position (Lowenthal, Thurnher, & Chiriboga, 1975). Cook (1982) also notes that the death of either the eldest or the youngest child significantly attenuated the level of adjustment parents were able to achieve one year later. In both instances, parents, particularly mothers, felt that loss of the child (whether first or last born) had disarranged a primary social role. Similarly, Lowenthal et al.'s (1975) oldest male respondents reported greatest affectional preference for their eldest sons.

The point of consideration here is the assumption that the child's transition to adulthood in some way differentially affects, for parents and their young adult children, both the perception and quality of intergenerational attachments. In this manner, the assumption of disrupted parental bonds persists, and the child's contributions to the maintenance of that bond are largely ignored.

Filial Contributions to the Parent-Child Bond

Where researchers (and they are few) have examined the more subtle lineaments of adulthood attachment, the child's participation as a comparable "giver" becomes more apparent (Hagestad, 1978, 1979; Hagestad & Snow, 1977; Hill et al., 1970; Troll, 1971; Troll, Miller, & Atchley, 1979; Troll & Smith, 1976). Hagestad (1978), for example, found that young adult children contributed a good deal to maintaining the bond between themselves and their mothers. The majority of mothers who could identify the child's impact described their children as "interpersonal resources." "Most commonly, the child was seen as a source of personal change in the mother, such as increased knowledge or changed attitudes. On this, daughters were slightly higher than sons" (Hagestad, 1978, pp. 19–20). Curiously, whereas daughters were reported to have influenced personal changes in the mother, sons were seen as a greater source of emotional support and sense of self-competence. Researchers (e.g., Hagestad, 1981) also have described the role of young adult children within the family as that of a "cohort bridge", a link to a changing social context, with its accompanying changes in norms, attitudes, and lifestyles. Hill et al. (1970) report similar patterns of affective contribution to the parent-child bond. Indeed, in their analysis, the youngest generation (i.e., children) occupies a uniquely healthy reciprocal status, high in receiving (child care, economic assistance) *and* high in giving (emotional support, companion-ship).

Nor are the child's contributions to the maintenance of parental bonds lim-ited to the vagaries of affect. Many young adult children prefer to live in pro-pinquity to their parents (Fischer & Fischer, 1963; Leichter & Mitchell, 1967; Smith, Britton & Britton, 1958; Sweetser, 1966)—a phenomenon we term *child preference for propinquity* (CPP)—frequently relocating at considera-ble expense, to serve as proximal interpersonal resources (Troll, Miller & Atchley, 1979). Taken together, these findings suggest not a disruption of pa-rental bonds following the child's transition to adulthood, but rather an alter-ation in its more subtle features (Cohler & Geyer, 1982).

Each family has a shared history that both bonds and binds them (Bengtson & Black, 1973; Hess & Handel, 1959; Troll, 1971; Troll & Smith, 1976; Turner, 1970). Parents and their young adult children contribute equally to its maintenance, although in very different ways. As Boszarmenyi-Nagy and Spark (1973) suggest,

> Loyalty commitments are like invisible but strong fibers which hold together complex pieces of relationship "behavior" in families as well as in larger socie-ties. To understand the functions of a group of people, nothing is more crucial than to know who are bound together in loyalty and what loyalty means to them. Each person maintains a bookkeeping of his perception of the balances of past present and future give-and-take. What has been "invested" into the sys-tem through availability and what has been withdrawn in terms of support re-ceived as one's exploitative use of others, remains written into the invisible ac-counts of obligations. (pp. 39–40)

Perhaps, then, the task of young adulthood is not the achievement of familial autonomy, but rather familial interdependence (Cohler & Geyer, 1982)—a state of differentiation rather than separation, in which the maintenance of parental bonds and independent functioning are dual achievements. The question thus is not one of separation, or its timeliness, but the processes by which the *family's* interdependence is renegotiated over successive *mutual* transitions (Lerner & Ryff, 1978).

In the remaining section of this paper, we examine some of the processes and strategies by which this familial interdependence is renegotiated during the child's transition to adulthood. For illustrative purposes, we make use of two data sets. The first is drawn from a preliminary analysis of intergen-erational family conflict (Boxer, 1982), which is part of a larger investigation of 148 three generation urban American families conducted by Hagestad, Cohler and Neugarten (1983). In this study a grandparent, a middle-aged fa-ther and mother, and one young adult child from each family were individu-ally interviewed to examine patterns of influence and communication across generations. We refer to these data as the Chicago three generation study.

The second data set comes from individual pilot interviews conducted by the authors in Morgantown, West Virginia and Chicago, Illinois, with a non-random sample of young adults and their parents.

THE SAMPLE CASE OF LEAVING HOME

Although leaving home appears to be a rather straightforward transition, little is known about its psychology. For many, this move occurs in the context of going to college, getting married, or entering the military. For most, this event is probably anticipated and rehearsed, and the transition is made with relative ease. It is in the context of leaving home that the process of bilateral negotiation (Bengtson & Black, 1973; Bengtson & Treas, 1980) between parent and young adult in transition takes place. One middle-aged mother succinctly described this process in discussing her 24-year-old daughter:

> Her going to school for 4 years gave us more of a perspective on each other. She has always been a very good girl, and since she's the youngest and my only daughter, she has always been very special to me. Because of her experience at school and her learning to become more *independent* there, she appreciates her *home life more now*. I also think that I changed my reaction to her and to her reactions. I've toned things down and relax more with her now.

It is interesting to note that this mother discusses increasing independence while adding that her daughter has an increased appreciation of "home" life. It is unfortunate that we did not ask the daughter where she actually considered her home to be.

The ideal of autonomy in young adulthood is often equated with physical separation. "Separation is usually encouraged from the culturally supported point of view that if the offspring and parent can sustain physical separation, they will develop coping mechanisms which eventually will make them emotionally less mutually interdependent" (Boszormenyi-Nagy and Spark, 1973, p. 32). This idea seems to have originated in child-based observations of mothers and infants. Beginning in the earliest strange situation, infants seek proximity to a primary caregiver (Ainsworth, Blehar, Waters, & Wall, 1978). Gradual accruals in the ability to tolerate physical separations from mother and father are noted as milestones in the child's development. In our clinical experience, however, first separations of a prolonged nature may be more traumatic to the parents than to the infant. Whether in the form of home care or day care or in the later entry into kindergarten and primary grades, the developing autonomy of a young child is usually a prized and cherished aspect of psychological differentiation (Mahler, Pine, & Bergman, 1975). Sleepovers, overnight camps, visits to relatives, and, for the wealthy perhaps, boarding school are only some of the punctuation marks in the child's progress toward leaving home.

Leaving home means more than simply leaving one's parents. It may mean leaving significant others, such as siblings or grandparents. Separation has horizontal as well as vertical generational dimensions. It also may mean leaving comforts or important material or symbolic object attachments (Csikszentmihalyi & Rochberg-Halton, 1981; Furby, 1978). Pets, one's bed, or one's own room are all objects that provide a sense of continuity or comfort and, in times of distress, also may serve soothing and caregiving functions.

The periodic psychological refuelings discussed by Mahler (Mahler, Pine, Bergman, 1975) and Ainsworth et al., (1978) have been compared to the young adult's periodic return to family or household of origin. To parents, the child's departure from home appears to signify an increased freedom (Lowenthal & Chiriboga, 1972), as well as a benchmark of their own success as parents. Wilen (1979) has noted that it was when the child did not leave home on time, or in the expected manner, that parents experienced strain and a sense of personal failure.

Due to economic conditions, many young adults may return home for a period of time between college and the establishment of an independent household. In our exploratory pilot interviews, we spoke with several parents whose children had returned to the parental household after an extended absence. One mother described this, in joyful terms, as a time when she could get to re-know her child. She added, "I could become a mother once again. . . . I could even become a cook." Another mother found it quite annoying and felt disappointed in the unanticipated return. Thus, it appears that the conditions under which the child returns, rather than the fact of the return itself, form the critical features of this process. As parents have a stake (Bengtson & Kypers, 1971) in their child's future, a return home may signify defeat to them, as well as to the young adult.

Parents and young adults seem to actively anticipate departure from the parental home. One young man interviewed in the Chicago three generation study discussed his relationship with his mother, saying:

> My mother and I talk about the future and what she thinks I should do. I want to take things as they come. She doesn't say that is wrong . . . but doesn't think it's good or what I really want to do. She might live through me what she wants to see me do well at. Talk doesn't get things resolved, but we do discuss things. I think I might be happy just doing something not that prestigious — maybe living in the country, farming.

While this young man is preoccupied with many issues, the prospects of downward mobility, of something "not that prestigious" is of concern to both the parent and child. This is an issue of concern to most parents: What is the child leaving home for? For some young adults it may be college, for others marriage, for others the establishment of an independent household, or entry into the labor force. The psychological terminus at which one's parental home becomes one's former home, and at which young adults begin to consider having their own home is little understood. It seems clear, however, that this psychological reality is not necessarily restricted to, or associated with, marriage. Many married young adults still refer to visits to the family of origin as "going home."

The prospects and expectancies of leaving home and beginning an independent household are viewed differently by parent and child. Another young man in the Chicago three generation study described a disagreement he had had with his father about leaving home: "I'll be going to college next year, and a few weeks ago he told me he wanted me to plan to live in the dorms instead of an apartment, because so much will be going on in the dorms. Also, he doesn't want me to take my car to school, because he thinks I'll drive down too much to see my girlfriend. I got really angry but I held it back."

This father may have been concerned not so much about what was going on in the dorm, but rather about what might go on in his son's apartment. His concern, like most parents', was that his son enjoy a smooth transition and successful entry into adult roles. For many young adults, leaving home seems to highlight a kind of enforced dependency that is as much psychological as it is material. The physically abrupt nature of leaving home itself presages a rather gradual transformation of relationships between young adults and their parents.

Multiple Pathways from the Parental Home

There are many variations in patterns of leavetaking, each of which may be mediated by social class as well as ethnicity. Hagestad, Smyer and Stierman (1984) found that when parents divorced during the young adulthood of their children, mothers often turned to the children for a kind of accelerated filial maturity. The premature need to depend on one's child for economic or psychological support seemed to produce a strong sense of guilt in the mothers studied. Even in Levinson et al.'s (1978) sample of 40 men, there were many variations in the relationships between young adult men and their parents. Only seven men stayed close to their parents, personally and geographically. Eight men reported major conflicts with their parents (especially with the father) that had continued for many years. Between these extremes, 25 men had moved a considerable distance, geographically or socially, from their parents' world. "For most of them, however, the ties to parents steadily eroded during their twenties" (Levinson et al., 1978, p. 74). Nonetheless, many young men maintain primary residence in the homes of their parents or close relatives for a considerable part of the transition to young adulthood. Working class men, for example, enter the labor force sooner than those who are more affluent (Neugarten & Moore, 1968), and this early entry may have implications for the maintenance of family ties in later life.

Based on observed sex differences in parent-child relationships during adulthood, (Troll & Bengtson, 1982), daughters may experience their leaving home in quite different ways than sons. Daughters seem to maintain more involved relationships, particularly with their mothers, after departure from the parental household. In the Chicago three generation study (Wilen, 1979), the mother-daughter bond was not unique in terms of the frequency of relationships, which family members reported as nonconflictual. However, when the relationship was perceived as nonconflictual, it was much more strongly bonded than was a nonconflictual relationship between father and son, and was more intense than cross-sex parent-child relationships.

A critical issue, then, for parents and young adult children seems to be whether the child is able to meet the parents' expectations in assuming adult roles and whether parents and children are able to develop a new mutually supportive relationship. The processes by which this relationship is transformed or altered are little understood. It is to those processes that we now turn our attention.

RESTRUCTURING THE TIES

We have seen in previous sections of this paper that the task of young adulthood is reciprocally defined for parents and children as involving a renegotiation of the interdependencies that bond and bind them. And, in the sample case of leaving home, we saw that although physical departures are likely to be abrupt, these renegotiations occur gradually and within a context of strong attachment, whether positive or negative (Bengtson et al., 1976; Lowenthal et al., 1975).

Hill al. (1970) suggests that at each stage of family life cycle there exists a complex of roles within which family members participate. Individual life cycle transitions, therefore, produce reverberations throughout the complex, affecting the role definitions and responsibilities of other participating members (Hagestad, 1978; Hill et. al, 1970). Rosow's (1976) discussion of the changes within a given role nicely illustrates this point. As he states,

> . . . being a son or daughter involves progressive role changes as people traverse the life cycle . . . different normative standards govern the expectations *and* reciprocities of a daughter and her parents when she is a child, an adolescent, a young woman, a wife, a mother, a matron and a grandmother. She remains a daughter during all those periods, but her role and its content are steadily modified. (Rosow, 1976, p. 472)

We may add that as the daughter's role is steadily modified, so too are the roles and role contents of her parents modified.

Within this framework, the family's renegotiation of roles and role definitions would most favorably result in the child's assumption of a collegial role (Hagestad, 1978) or a companion status (Nydegger & Mitteness, 1979). It also would, of necessity, involve the parents' acceptance of the child's new role (Murphey et al., 1963). In such instances children, and implicitly their parents, appear to be "high in autonomy and high in relatedness; able to function independently of their parents yet aware of a growing sense of equality between them" (Murphey et al., 1963, p. 646). Complementarily, the parents of these youths appear to establish clear boundaries and to encourage the growth of personal responsibility.

The foci of concern in this discussion are the strategies by which children and their parents achieve this and similar role changes. Unfortunately, the literature most pertinent to this framework generally stresses the assumption of role obligations, rather than role transitions, in young adulthood (Hagestad, 1978). The exception is those studies that have focused on the psychological enmeshment of parents and children (e.g., Anthony, 1971; Cohler & Grunebaum, 1981; Stierlin et al., 1971). Little attention has been paid to the strategies underlying the intergenerational role relationships of the kind described by Murphey (1963) or implied by Rosow (1976).

In the following section, we present for consideration several strategies by which this transition, or role renegotiation, may be affected. This discussion centers on the means by which the child achieves adult status within the context of parental attachment. Those instances in which the child achieves that status through a literal repudiation of the parents are not included here, as they have been extensively discussed in the clinical literature concerning pathogenic families (e.g., Johnson & Irvin, 1982; McGoldrick & Carter, 1982; Stierlin, 1974).

Role Renegotiation Strategies in the Transition to Adulthood

Two broad venues suggest themselves as the means by which the child's transition to adulthood may be affected within the context of family attachment. Each appears to contain a subset of strategies which may be used, or responded to, in that process. The first we term the *intrafamilial venue,* in which renegotiation appears centered primarily within the family's interaction. In contrast, the *extrafamilial venue* is based on changes in the social roles which the child occupies *outside* the family. It is, we suggest, within the framework of these extrafamilial role changes that transitions within the family's role complex occur. Two caveats must be noted in our discussion of these venues and strategies. First, these are working hypotheses in our exploration of intergenerational attachments. Although we make conservative use of pilot interviews, these data are limited at best. Second, the strategies discussed are not considered to be mutually exclusive; their meaning and use differs within and between families, as does the timing and duration of the process itself.

The Intrafamilial Venue

Two strategies appear to fall within this venue of role renegotiations: (a) what Hagestad (1979) refers to as *demilitarized zones* or DMZs, and (b) a less implicitly conflictual strategy we refer to as *boundary recognition*. Both strategies are notable in that the impetus for each appears to be derived from an ongoing process of family interaction and a mutual desire to maintain that interaction.

Hagestad (1979) describes DMZs as "silent mutually understood pacts regarding what not to talk about" (p. 30). Through the use of DMZs, parent and child avoid disruptive conflicts over differences of opinion, lifestyles, etc.

In contrast, the *boundary recognition* strategy appears to enjoy use in families where there is tolerance for disagreement and individual differentiation. The child's lifestyle, opinion or behavior may be disagreeable to the parents (assuming it is not criminal), but those opinions and that lifestyle are accepted as his or her own. Parents may discuss, even argue, their differences, but there appears to be a kind of marker beyond which they do not proceed and beyond which they are not invited to do so. The following quotation from the mother of a then college dropout illustrates this point:

> The period when he was in between schools and not doing anything was a problem. He would sleep until noon. I told him to get off his rear end and get a job. He got some insight into his own feelings. I [would] say "what are you going to take in school, what are you planning?" But I can only go so far. He won't allow me to go any further — that's when it's better not to press.

The apparent distinction between *boundary recognition* and DMZs is twofold. First, boundary markers appear to be more flexible. Renegotiation around issues of the child's employment and social life, for example, can resume and continue past previous boundaries, without reversions to dependency on the child's part. As the strategy is anchored within the interaction, so it appears mutable by subsequent interactions. Second, as young adults and their parents proceed through the transition, increasing aspects of the young adults' lives fall under this rubric — and increasing aspects of their lives are recognized as such by the parents.

The Extrafamilial Venue

Two types of role renegotiation strategies appear to fall within this venue. In contrast to intrafamilial strategies, these mechanisms appear to be impelled by the role or status (Rosow, 1976) the young adult occupies outside of the family context. In this manner, extrafamilial strategies act as reverberative reflections of external changes, which facilitate or exacerbate internal processes.

The first of these strategies, *boundary facilitators,* is reflective of what Rosow (1976) describes as the child's status or role ascension. Markers of this change in social role include full-time employment, marriage, or childbirth. External markers though they may be, they also differentiate the perceived quality of parent-child interactions following their occurrence. In the following quotation, Molly, a 24 year old newlywed, reflects on what she perceives to be the impact of her recent marriage. "My mother really treats me differently now . . . before she would want to know what I was doing, who I was with . . . you know . . . personal stuff. Now she starts to do it and she stops and says, "oh . . . you're a married woman, I can't say that anymore. You have your own life now." Wasn't it my life before?"

Notice how the mother's recognition of her daughter's new status differentially influences her response to various aspects of her daughter's life, aspects previously open to question. In turn, the daughter must signal to her mother that advice, as distinct from influence, is both appropriate and desired. She continues: "Sometimes, you know, I just want to talk about things . . . not everything, but some things . . . so when she stops like that . . . like I told you, I say "It's ok mom . . . what do you think about it?" Then she tells me, only sometimes she doesn't . . . I never thought I'd ask for her advice . . . what a change!" As this exerpt suggests, both parent and child are renegotiating the features of their interaction consequent to the daughter's new social status. Molly's extrafamilial role ascension elicits different, less directive, behaviors in the parents and facilitates more independent behaviors in Molly. Her new marital status can be seen as an instance in which the extrafamilial venue facilitates the development of boundaries between parent and child. Molly's closing comment eloquently captures this point, "If I'd known getting married would give me this much weight [in the family], I'd've done it when I was 12."

The child's upward social mobility vis á vis the parents also may influence role renegotiation during this transition. Sennett and Cobb (1972) describe the more negative impacts on the family's role complex following the child's entry into a higher socio-economic status. As they state, " . . . if a father's sacrifices do succeed in transforming his children's lives, he then becomes a burden to them, an embarrassment" (p. 133). We may speculate that the estrangement between parent and child in such circumstances is reflective not of the child's transition to role colleague status (Hagestad, 1978), but rather his or her assumption of an apparently higher role within the family complex than the parents occupy.

The second role renegotiation strategy apparent within this venue is *boundary disruptors*. In this strategy, changes in the family's role complex are reflective of the child's loss of some externally defined status, what Rosow (1976) refers to as role attrition. Examples of role attrition include such events as dropping out of school, divorce, separation, or loss of full-time employment. We suggest that the advent of role attrition external to the family offsets the transition process for both parent and child, with subsequent reverberations throughout their interactions. Susan, a 31-year old-woman, discusses the continuing impact of her divorce: "They see me as . . . I don't know . . . more helpless? than I was before [when I was married] . . . especially my father. They call a lot more than they used to . . . It's like I'm going to have troubles if they don't watch out for me . . . ."

Although Susan's divorce occurred several years before this interview, its impact upon interactions with her parents continues: "I thought after a while it would stop . . . you know, they'd see I was okay . . . I have my own car and a different job . . . but I think they'll just keep on going until . . . someone . . . takes care of me [I get married] I feel like I let them down . . . like . . . so I don't always stop it." Note that Susan's status attrition, if it may be so termed, facilitates both her parents' assumption of a quasi-caretaker role and her, albeit ambivalent, acceptance of less autonomous functioning.

Both strategies within the extrafamilial venue have several interesting aspects. They reflect a concrete referent of the child's new adult status (positively or negatively), on the basis of which role renegotiation within the family context can occur. The advents of such markers provides both parents and children adaptive leverage in the differentiation process.

In certain instances this may be the only means through which the child is able to affect role renegotiation within the famiy. Early or impulsive marriages, adolescent pregnancy and parenthood, and certain mentoring relationships are some examples of this process (see Levinson, et al., 1978, for an interesting discussion of this point). We colloquially refer to such instances as "familial end-runs", where the child must venture beyond the family role complex to achieve differentiation, and, it is hoped, recognition of adult status. We would note, however, familial end-runs most probably have the opposite effect — for both parents and children — as a critical aspect of this transition is its recognition and acceptance within the family complex. Familial end-runs thus can be seen as a special instance in which extrafamilial role ascensions may have the paradoxical effect of decreasing the child's standing within the family.

SUMMARY

In the preceding sections of this paper, we have examined changes in the parent-child relationship in the child's transition to young adulthood. Although writers (e.g., Bettelheim, 1965; Erikson, 1956; Freud, 1914) often have characterized the task of young adulthood as that of separation from the family, our analysis suggests that the task is reciprocally defined for parents and children and involves a renegotiation of the interdependencies that bond *and* bind them. In the sample case of leaving home, we saw that although physical departures may be abrupt, they also are often rehearsed and occur over a span of years. Familial renegotiations thus are seen to occur only very gradually and within a context of strong and continuing attachment (Bengtson et al., 1976).

In the final sections of this paper, several strategies of familial role renegotiation were discussed. In particular, two venues and their composite strategies were described as examples of the means by which familial role negotiations may take place during the transition process. A primary assumption in our conceptualization of these strategies is that changes in the adult child's social roles outside of the family context (e.g., labor market entry, marriage, parenthood) differentially effect patterns of interaction and influence between parents and their young adult children. We presume that the employment of and response to these strategies within the family and between family members will, of course, vary in consequence of the child's sex, intergenerational position and prior relationship with the parents, as well as with the age, sex and life cycle position of the parents themselves. It is, however, this range of familial variation that offers new areas of exploration in our continuing efforts to understand the lineaments of adulthood attachment.

We suggest these venues and their corresponding strategies as new perspectives from which to view the child's transition to adulthood. They offer new areas of research and provide an interesting way to conceptualize the transition process and its ripple effects across a web of family consociates.

ACKNOWLEDGMENTS

We gratefully acknowledge the contributions of the following people: Charles Jaffe, M.D., for his insights in the conceptualization of this paper; Bertram Cohler, Ph.D., Judith Cook, Ph.D., Mark Freeman, M.A. and Doris Gruenewold, Ph.D., for their comments on previous drafts of this paper; and Michelle Nichols for her tireless reproduction of multiple revisions.

The first author wishes to emphasize that this paper represents a collaborative effort and not a senior-junior relation between authors.

Portions of this research were supported by a grant awarded to Bernice L. Neugarten, Gunhild O. Hagestad and Bertram J. Cohler by the National Institute of Aging (POL-A6-123).

REFERENCES

Abeles, R. P., Steel, L. & Wise, L. (1980). Patterns and implications of life-course organization: Studies from Project Talent. In P. B. Baltes & O. G. Brim (Eds.), *Life-span development and behavior, Volume 3*. New York: Academic Press.

Adams, B. N. (1968). *Kinship in an urban setting*. Chicago: Markham.

Ainsworth, M. P. S., Blehar, M. C., Waters, E., & Wall, S. (1978). *Patterns of attachment: A psychological study of the strange situation*. Hillsdale, NJ: Lawrence Erlbaum Associates.

Aldous, J. (1967). Intergenerational visiting patterns: Variation in boundary maintenance as an explanation. *Family Process, 6,* 235–251.

Anthony, E. J. (1971). Folie a deux: A developmental failure in the process of separation-individuation. In J. McDevitt & C. Settlage (Eds.), *Separation-individuation: Essays in honor of Margaret Mahler*. New York: International Universities Press.

Bart, P. (1970). Mother Portnoy's complaints. *Transaction, 8,* 69.

Bengtson, V. L. & Black, O. (1973). Intergenerational relations: Continuities in socialization. In P. B. Baltes & K. W. Schaie (Eds.), *Life-span developmental psychology: Personality and socialization*. New York: Academic Press.

Bengtson, V. L. & Kypers, J. A. (1971). Generational difference and the developmental stake. *Aging and Human Development, 2,* 249–260.

Bengtson, V. L., Olander, E., & Haddad, E. (1976). The generation gap and aging family members: Toward a conceptual model. In J. F. Gubruim (Ed.), *Time, roles and self in old age*. New York: Human Sciences Press.

Bengtson, V. L. & Treas, L. L. (1980). The changing family context of mental health and aging. In J. Birren & R. B. Sloan (Eds.) *Handbook of mental health and aging*. Englewood Cliffs, NJ: Prentice-Hall.

Bettelheim, B. (1965). The problem of generations. In E. Erikson (Ed.), *The challenge of youth*. New York: Anchor Press.

Blau, Z. S. (1973). *Old age in a changing society*. New York: New Viewpoints, Franklin Watts.

Blos, P. (1962). *On adolescence: A psychoanalytic interpretation*. New York: Free Press.

Blos, P. (1967). The second individuation process of adolescence. *The psychoanalytic study of the child, 22,* 162–186. New York: International Universities Press.

Boszarmenyi-Nagy, I. & Spark, G. (1973). *Invisible loyalties: Reciprocity in intergenerational family therapy*. New York: Harper & Row.

Boxer, A. M. (1982). *Intergenerational conflicts in three generation families*. Unpublished Master of Arts Thesis, University of Chicago, Chicago.

Boxer, A. M., Gershenson, H. P., & Offer, D. (1984). Historical time and social change in adolescent experience. In D. Offer, E. Ostrov & K. I. Howard (Eds.), *New directions for mental health services: Patterns of adolescent self-image*. San Francisco: Jossey Bass.

Boxer, A. M., Solomon, B. C., Offer, D., Petersen, A. C., & Halprin, F. (1984). Parent's perceptions of young adolescents. In R. Cohen, B. J. Cohler, & S. Weissman (Eds.), *Parenthood: A psychodynamic perspective*. New York: Guilford Press.

Campbell, A., Converse, P. E., & Rodgers, W. L. (1976). *The quality of American life*. New York: Russell Sage Foundation.

Cohler, B. J. & Boxer, A. M. (1984). Middle adulthood: Settling into the world—person, time and context. In D. Offer & M. Sabshin (Eds.), *Normality and the Life Cycle*. New York: Basic Books.

Cohler, B. J. & Geyer, S. (1982). Psychological autonomy and interdependence within the family. In F. Walsh (Ed.), *Normal Family Process.* New York: Guilford Press.

Cohler, B. J. & Grunebaum, H. (1981). *Mother, grandmothers and daughters: Personality and child care in three generation families.* New York: Wiley.

Cook, J. A. (1982). *The long term adjustment of parents following the death of a child from cancer.* Paper presented at the annual meetings of the National Council on Family Relations, Washington, DC.

Csikszentmihalyi, M. & Rochberg-Halton, E. (1981). *The meaning of things: Domestic symbols and the self.* New York: Cambridge University Press.

Demos, E. (1979). Images of the American family, then and now. In V. Tufte, & B. Myerhoff (Eds.), *Changing images of the family.* New Haven, CT: Yale University Press.

Douvan, E. & Adelson, J. (1966). *The adolescent experience.* New York: Wiley.

Elder, G. H., Jr. (1980). Adolescence in historical perspective. In J. Adelson (Ed.), *Handbook of adolescent psychology.* New York: Wiley.

Erikson, E. (1956). The concept of ego identity. *Journal of the American Psychoanalytic Association, 4,* 56–121.

Featherman, D. L., Hogan, D. P., & Sorenson, A. B. (1984). Entry into adulthood: Profiles of young men in the 1950's. In P. B. Baltes & O. G. Brim, Jr. (Eds.), *Life-span development and behavior,* (pp. 159–200). New York: Academic Press.

Fischer, J. & Fischer, A. (1963). The New Englanders of orchard town. In B. Whiting (Ed.), *Six cultures: Studies of childrearing.* New York: Wiley.

Freud, S. (1957). *On narcissism: An introduction.* Standard Edition, Vol 14. (pp. 69–102). London: Hogarth. (Original work published 1914).

Furby, L. (1978). Possessions: Toward a theory of their meaning and function throughout the life cycle. In P. B. Baltes (Ed.), *Life-span development and behavior, Vol. 1,* New York: Academic Press.

Glenn, N. D. (1975). Psychological well-being in the postparental stage: Some evidence from national surveys. *Journal of Marriage and the Family, 37,* 105–111.

Hagestad, G. O. (1978). *Role change and socialization in adulthood: The transition to the empty nest.* Unpublished manuscript, Committee on Human Development, University of Chicago.

Hagestad, G. O. (1979). Patterns of communication and influence between grandparents and grandchildren in a changing society. Paper presented at the World Congress of Sociology, Uppsala, Sweden.

Hagestad, G. O. (1981). Problems and promises in the social psychology of intergenerational relations. In R. W. Fogel, E. Hatfield, S. B. Kiesler & E. Shanas (Eds.), *Aging: Stability and change in the family.* New York: Academic Press.

Hagestad, G. O., Cohler, B. J. & Neugarten, B. L. (1983). [The Chicago three generation family study]. Unpublished raw data.

Hagestad, G. O. & Dixon, R. A. (1980). *Lineages as units of analysis: New avenues for the study of individual and family careers.* Paper presented at the NCRF Theory Construction and Research Methodology Workshop, Portland, OR.

Hagestad, G. O. & Neugarten, B. C. (1984). Age and the life course. In E. Shanas & R. Binstock (Eds.), *Handbook of aging and the social sciences,* Second Edition. New York: Van Nostrand, Reinhold.

Hagestad, G. O., Smyer, M. A., & Stierman, K. L. (1984). Parent-child relations in adulthood. The impact of divorce in middle age. In B. Cohen, B. J. Cohler, & S. Weissman (Eds.), *Parenthood: A psychodynamic perspective.* New York: Guilford Press.

Hagestad, G. O. & Snow, R. (1977). Young adult offspring as interpersonal resources. Paper presented at the Gerontological Society Meetings, San Francisco.

Hagestad, G. O. & Speicher, J. L. (1981). *Grandparents and family influence: Views of three generations.* Paper presented at the bienniel meeting of the Society for Research on Child Development, Boston, MA.

Hamburg, B. A. (1974). Early adolescence: A specific and stressful stage of the life cycle. In G. Coehlo, D. A. Hamburg, & J. E. Adams (Eds.), *Coping and adaptation*. New York: Basic Books.

Hareven, T. (1982). The life course and aging in historical perspective. In T. Hareven & K. J. Adams (Eds.), *Aging and life course transitions: An interdisciplinary perspective*. New York: Guilford Press.

Harris, L. & Associates (1975). *The myth and reality of aging in America*. Washington: National Council on Aging.

Hauser, P. M. (1980). Our anguished youth: Baby boom under stress. In S. C. Feinstein, P. L. Giovacchini, J. G. Looney, A. Z. Schwartzburg, & A. D. Sorosky (Eds.), *Adolescent psychiatry: Developmental and clinical studies, Volume III*. Chicago: University of Chicago Press.

Hess, R. & Handel, G. (1959). *Family worlds*. Chicago: University of Chicago Press.

Hill, J. P. (1980). The family. In M. Johnson (Ed.), *Towards adolescence: The middle school years*. The Seventy-ninth Yearbook of the National Society for Study of Education. Chicago: University of Chicago Press.

Hill, R. N., Foote, J., Aldous, R., Carlson, R., & MacDonald, R. (1970). *Family development in three generations*. Cambridge, MA: Schenkman.

Hogan, D. P. (1982). Subgroup variations in early life transitions. In M. W. Riley, R. P. Abeles & M. s. Teitelbaum (Eds.), *Aging from birth to death, Volume II: Sociotemporal Perspectives*. Boulder, CO: Westview Press.

Johnson, C. & Irvin, F. S. (1982). The interface between adolescence and midlife transition. In H. Morrison (Ed.), *Parents of depressed children*. New York: Grune & Stratton.

Kagan, J. Z. (1971). A conception of early adolescence. *Daedalus, 100,* 997–1012.

Kalish, R. & Knudtsen, F. W. (1976). Attachment vs. disengagement: A lifespan conceptualization. *Human Development, 19,* 171–181.

Kandel, D. B. & Lesser, G. S. (1969). *Youth in two worlds: United States and Denmark*. San Francisco: Jossey-Bass.

Katz, M. B. (1975). *The people of Hamilton, Canada West: Family and class in a mid-nineteenth century city*. Cambridge, MA: Harvard University Press.

Katz, M. B. & Davey, Q. E. (1978). Youth and early industrialization in a Candian city. *American Journal of Sociology, 84,* 581–591.

Kenniston, K. (1970). Youth: A "new" stage of life. *The American Scholar, 39,,* 631–654.

Kertzer, D. I. & Schiaffino, A. (1984). Industrialization and coresidence: A life-course approach. In P. B. Baltes & O. G. Brim, Jr. (Eds.), *Life-span development and behavior, Vol. 5,* New York: Academic Press.

Kett, J. F. (1977). *Rites of passage*. New York: Basic Books.

Komarovsky, M. (1964). *Blue-collar marriage*. New York: Random House.

Knudtsen, F. W. (1976). Life-span attachment: Complexities, questions, consideration. *Human Development, 19,* 135–142.

Laing, R. D. & Esterson, A. (1964). *Sanity, madness and the family*. London: Tavistock.

Leichter, H. & Mitchell, W. (1967). *Kinship and casework*. New York: Russell Sage Foundation.

Lerner, R. M. & Ryff, C. D. (1978). Implementation of the life-span view of human development: The sample case of attachment. In P. B. Baltes (Ed.), *Life-span development and behavior, Vol. 1*. New York: Academic Press.

Levi, L. D., Stierlin, H., & Savard, R. J. (1973). Fathers and sons: The interlocking crisis of integrity and identity. *Psychiatry, 35,* 48–56.

Levinson, D., Darrow, C., Klein, E., Levinson, M., & McKee, G. (1978). *Seasons of a man's life*. New York: Knopf.

Lidz, T. (1968). *The person*. New York: Basic Books.

Litwak, E. (1965). Extended kin relations in an industrial democratic society. In E. Shanas & G. F. Streib (Eds.), *Social structure and the family: Generational relations*. Englewood Cliffs, NJ: Prentice-Hall.

Lowenthal, M. R. & Chiriboga, D. (1972). Transition to the empty nest: Crisis, challenge or relief? *Archives of General Psychiatry, 26,* 8–14.

Lowenthal, M. R., Thurnher, M., & Chiriboga, D. (1975). *Four stages of life.* San Francisco: Jossey-Bass.

Mahler, M. (1972a). On the first three phases of the separation-individuation process. *International Journal of Psychoanalysis, 53,* 333–338 (a).

Mahler, M. (1972b). Rapproachement subphase of the separation-individuation process. *Psychoanalytic Quarterly, 41,* 487–506 (b).

Mahler, M., Pine, F., & Bergman, A. (1975). *Psychological birth of the human infant.* New York: Basic Books.

Marini, M. M. (1978). The order of events in the transition to adulthood. *Sociology of Education, 57,*

McGoldrick, M. & Carter, E. A. (1982). The family life cycle. In F. Walsh (Ed.), *Normal Family Processes.* New York: Guilford Press.

Mead, M. (1970). *Culture and commitment: A study of the generation gap.* New York: Doubleday.

Modell, J., Furstenberg, J. & Hershberg, T. (1976). Social change and transitions to adulthood in historical perspective. *Journal of Family History, 1,* 7–32.

Mogey, J. (1976). Residence and family kinship: Some recent research. *Journal of Family History, 1,* 95–202.

Murphey, E. B., Silber, E., Coelho, G. V., Hamburg, D. A., & Greenberg, I. (1963). Development of autonomy and parent-child interaction in late adolescence. *American Journal of Orthopsychiatry, 33,* 643–652.

Neugarten, B. L. (1979). The middle generation. In P. K. Ragan (Ed.), *Aging parents.* Los Angeles: University of Southern California Press.

Neugarten, B. L. & Datan, N. (1974). The middle years. In S. Arieti (Ed.), *American handbook of psychiatry, Vol. 1.* New York: Basic Books.

Neugarten, B. L. & Hagestad, G. O. (1976). Age and the life course. In R. H. Binstock & E. Shanas (Eds.), *Handbook of aging and the social sciences.* New York: Van Nostrand Reinhold.

Neugarten, B. L. & Moore, J. W. (1968). The changing age status systems. In B. L. Neugarten (Ed.), *Middle age and aging.* Chicago: University of Chicago Press.

Neugarten, B. L., Moore, J., & Lowe, J. (1965). Age norms, age constraints and adult socialization. *American Journal of Sociology, 20,* 710–717.

Nydegger, C. N. & Mitteness, L. (1979). Transitions in Fatherhood. *Generations, 4,* 14–15.

Offer, D. & Offer, J. B. (1975). *From teenage to young manhood: A psychological study.* New York: Basic Books.

Oppenheimer, V. K. (1974). The life-cycle squeeze: The interaction of men's occupational and family life cycles. *Demography, 11,* 227–245.

Oppenheimer, V. K. (1981). The changing nature of life-cycle squeezes: Implications for the socioeconomic position of the elderly. In R. W. Fogel, E. Hatfield, S. B. Kiesler, & E. Shanas (Eds.), *Aging: Stability and change in the family.* New York: Academic Press.

Panel, (1973a). The experience of separation-individual in infancy and its reverberations through the course of life. II: Adolescence and maturity. *Journal of the American Psychoanalytic Association, 24,* 155–167.

Panel, (1973b). The experience of separation-individuation in infancy and its reverberations through the course of life. III: Maturity, senescence and sociological implications. *Journal of the American Psychoanalytic Association, 21,* 633–645.

Pearlin, L. I. (1980). Life strains and psychological distress among adults. In N. J. Smelser & E. H. Erikson (Eds.), *Themes of work and love in adulthood.* Cambridge, MA: Harvard University Press.

Plath, D. V. (1980). Contours of consociation: Lessons from a Japanese narrative. In P. B.

Baltes & O. G. Brim, Jr. (Eds.), *Life-span development and behavior, Vol. 3*. New York: Academic Press.

Pruchno, R. A., Blow, F. C., & Smyer, M. A. (1984). Life events and interdependent lives. *Human Development, 27*, 31–41.

Riley, M. W. & Waring, J. (1976). Age and aging. In R. K. Merton & R. Nisbet (Eds.), *Contemporary social problems* (4th ed.). New York: Harcourt, Brace & Jovanovich.

Rose, A. M. (1962). A social-psychological theory of neurosis. In A. Rose (Ed.). *Human behavior and Social Processes*. Boston: Houghton-Mifflin.

Rosow, I. (1965). Intergenerational relationships: Problems and proposals. In E. Shanas & G. F. Streib (Eds.), *Social structure and the family*. Englewood Cliffs, NJ: Prentice-Hall.

Rosow, I. (1976). Status and role change through the life span. In R. H. Binstock & E. Shanas (Eds.), *Handbook of Aging and the Social Sciences*. New York: Van Nostrand Reinhold.

Rossi, A. (1980). Aging and parenthood in the middle years. In P. B. Baltes & O. G. Brim, Jr. (Eds.), *Life-span development and behavior, Vol 3*. New York: Academic Press.

Sennett, R. & Cobb, J. (1972). *Hidden injuries of class*. New York: Vintage Press.

Shanas, E. (1979). Social myth as hypothesis: The case of the family relations of old people. *The Gerontologist, 19*, 3–9.

Skolnick, A. (1979). Public images and private realities: The American family in popular culture and social science. In V. Tufte & B. Myerhoff (Eds.), *Changing images of the family*. New Haven: Yale University Press.

Smith, W., Britton, J., & Britton, J. (1958). *Relationships within three-generation families*. University Park: Pennsylvania State University College of Home Economics.

Spence, D. & Conner, T. (1971). The "empty nest": A transition within motherhood. *The Family Coordinator*, 369–375.

Steinberg, L. D. (1981). Transformations in family relations at puberty. *Developmental Psychology, 17*, 833–840.

Steinberg, L. D., & Hill, J. (1978). Patterns of family interaction as a function of age, the onset of puberty, and formal thinking. *Developmental Psychology, 14*, 683–684.

Stierlin, H. (1974). *Separating parents and adolescents*. New York: New York Times Book Co.

Stierlin, H., Levi, L. D., & Savard, R. J. (1971). Parental perceptions of separating children. *Family Process, 10*, 411–427.

Stierlin, H., Levi, L. D., & Savard, R. J. (1973). Centrifugal versus centripetal separation in adolescence: Two patterns and some of their implications. In S. Feinstein & P. Giovacchini (Eds.), *Adolescent psychiatry, Vol. 2: Developmental and Clinical Studies*. New York: Basic Books.

Sullivan, K. & Sullivan, A. (1980). Adolescent-parent separation. *Developmental Psychology, 16*, 93–99.

Sussman, M. & Burchinal, L. (1962). Parental aid to married children: Implications for family functioning. *Marriage and Family Living, 24*, 320–332.

Sweetser, D. (1963). Asymmetry in intergenerational family relationships. *Social Forces, 41*, 346–352.

Sweetser, D. (1964). Mother-daughter ties between generations in industrial societies. *Family Process, 3*, 332–343.

Sweetser, D. (1966). The effect of industrialization on intergenerational solidarity. *Rural Sociology, 31*, 156–170.

Thornburg, H. D. (1983). Is early adolescence really a stage of development? *Theory into Practice, 22*, 79–84.

Troll, L. E. (1971). The family of later life: a decade review. In C. Broderick (Ed.), *A Decade of Family Research and Action*. Minneapolis, MN: National Council on Family Relations.

Troll, L. E. & Bengtson, V. L. (1982). Intergenerational relations throughout the life span. In B. Wolman (Ed.), *Handbook of developmental psychology*. Englewood Cliffs, NJ: Prentice-Hall.

Troll, L. E., Miller, S., & Atchley, R. (1979). *Families of later life.* Belmont, CA: Wadsworth.

Troll, L. E. & Smith, J. (1976). Attachment through the life span: Some questions about dyadic bonds among adults. *Human Development, 19,* 156–170.

Turner, R. H. (1970). *Family interaction.* New York: Wiley.

Uhlenberg, P. (1978). Changing configurations of the life course. In T. Hareven (Ed.), *Transitions: The family and the life course in historical perspective.* New York: Academic Press.

Wall, R. (1978). The age at leaving home. *Journal of Family History, 3,* 181–202.

Wilen, J. (1979). *Changing relationships among grandparents, parents and their young adult children.* Paper presented at the annual meetings of the Gerontological Society, Washington, DC.

Young, C. M. (1974). Ages, reasons and sex differences for children leaving home: Observations from survey data for Australia. *Journal of Marriage and the Family,* 769.

Young, C. M. (1975). Factors associated with the timing and duration of the leaving home stage of the life cycle. *Population Studies, 29,* 61–73.

7 Family Ties and Life Chances: Hard Times and Hard Choices in Women's Lives Since the 1930s

Glen H. Elder, Jr.
Department of Sociology
University of North Carolina at Chapel Hill

Geraldine Downey
Department of Human Development and Family Studies
Cornell University

Catherine E. Cross
Carolina Population Center
University of North Carolina at Chapel Hill

INTRODUCTION

Problems of interdependence between family ties and individual achievement are common in the life course. Family relations both enhance and curtail the life chances of individuals by influencing their opportunities for achievement through education, occupation, and marriage. Individual achievement, in turn, can strengthen or weaken family bonds. This social dynamic has appeared in women's scheduling of family events and individual achievement since at least the 1940s. In this paper, we view women's lives across three generations from the vantage point of family ties and life chances.

Times of adversity, such as the Great Depression, accentuate the fateful interdependence of family and individual concerns. Depression mothers became central figures in their households following the income loss of husbands, and older children frequently assumed adult-like responsibilities, filling a role once occupied by parents (Elder, 1974). Changes in family roles also had implications for the presence or absence of opportunity for personal achievement — mothers went out to work, and older daughters gave up their education for an earner's role in the household.

The problems of balancing work and family demands created by the Great Depression have much in common with those facing women today. In the 1930s, however, paid work for wives was portrayed as merely an extension of the household. Few Depression mothers of young children worked, even when times were desperate. For women of that era, family demands took precedence over individual achievement. Since the 1930s, women's opportunities for educational and occupational achievement have expanded dramatically. Over the past 2 decades graduation from college has become commonplace, and career lines once restricted to men have become more open. In addition, high divorce rates have made combining work and family careers an economic necessity for many.

The daughters of Depression mothers entered the middle years during this period of rapidly expanding opportunity. For them, problems of interdependence include the scheduling of work and childbearing, the choice between part- and full-time jobs, and, in some cases, the continuous management of work and family careers. The postwar daughters of Depression offspring are more apt to take college for granted and to consider a career that excludes children and even marriage itself. These exclusions provide one solution to the continuing challenge of managing individual pursuits and family obligations.

In this study, we explore the problem of interdependent family and individual needs by focusing on women who were children during the Great Depression in the city of Berkeley, California. These women started their own families in the baby boom era of postwar America, a time of renewed domesticity and prosperity. Using the Guidance archive (Eichorn, Clausen, Haan, Honzik, & Mussen, 1981) at the Berkeley Institute of Human Development, we follow 95 women from their Depression childhoods to middle age and relations with adolescent daughters. For comparative purposes, we include the Berkeley males in much of the analysis. Three propositions guide the analysis.

Family Relations and Life Chances

The first proposition addresses the interrelations of family ties and life chances. Depression hardship strengthened the affectional ties between mother and daughter while weakening the ties between mother and son and especially between father and son (cf. Elder, 1979). We suggest that combined with limited resources for higher education, these conditions oriented the Berkeley girls toward achievement through marriage, rather than through individual attainments, (e.g., education, worklife).

Family Continuity and Women as Kin-Keepers

Consistent with the mother-daughter bond in the 1930s, we expect the Berkeley women to show greater continuity than men in affective ties with parents from their Depression childhood to midlife. This outcome reflects the centrality and continuity of family roles in women's lives, in contrast to the primary role work plays in men's lives. This differential continuity should extend to the women's relations with mother in old age and with their own daughters in the postwar generation.

Mother-Daughter Ties and Youthful Aspirations

Some Berkeley women from the Depression generation broke with the conventional life style during the baby boom era through late childbearing, higher education, and work experience after marriage. We hypothesize that these women were likely to transmit this pioneering orientation to daughters in the form of aspirations for a career, even one without marriage and children. But career-centered aspirations may also increase tension between mother and daughter.

Across these problem foci, our objective is to investigate whether and how economic hardship influences the family ties and life chances of Depression-reared women and their postwar daughters. Building on studies that have used the Berkeley archives over the past decade, we first examine conceptual issues and examples of this interdependence and then take up some measurement issues.

FAMILY RELATIONS AND INDIVIDUAL ACHIEVEMENT

We highlight the interplay of individual and family functioning by attending to individual lives and their mutual interdependence through evolving family relationships. An appreciation of this interdependence is central to an understanding of family experience in the Great Depression, and in the subsequent life course of Depression children. One account of such interdependence appears in the experience of Oakland families reported in *Children of the Great Depression* (Elder, 1974). The drastic income loss experienced by men in the 1930s led to three modes of adaptation among the nearly 170 Oakland families and their children (born in the early 1920s).

First, household operations shifted toward a more labor intensive economy, which enlarged the roles of mother and of older children. Adolescent daughters in hard-pressed families assumed more responsibility in the home; some held jobs in the community. Household involvement increased girls' exposure to domestic influences and to family strife. From this experience grew a sense of industry and responsibility, sensitivity to others, and a desire to grow up quickly. Hardship increased the paid employment of boys as well as their independence from the family. Employment offered boys a way to achieve some control over their life situation.

The second mode of change occurred in power and in affectional relations. Mothers gained centrality as authority and affectional figures in the lives of children, as fathers lost earning power and effectiveness within the family. Family income loss sharply diminished the perceived status of fathers, especially among sons. In deprived households, girls were strongly influenced by mothers and by changing social roles, while boys gained more freedom from family regulation and supervision.

The third change involved an increase in social and emotional strains, conflicts, and social ambiguities within the family. Consciousness of self increased among boys and girls in response to these changes. These modes of adaptation to family hardship had implications for female solidarity and for the manner in which children played out their life chances, the concerns of our first proposition.

Female Solidarity in Hard Times

Under economic pressure girls in the Oakland sample, formed closer ties to mothers, while boys developed weaker ties to both parents (Elder, 1974). One explanation for the heightened affiliation between mothers and daughters is that hard times increased rather than diminished the importance of women. From the unemployed mill village of Marienthal, Austria (Jahoda, Lazarsfeld & Zeisel, 1971) to the Great Depression in the United States (Bakke, 1940), family survival hinged largely on the activities of women. Repeatedly in studies of hard times, wives and mothers emerged as the central figures, the copers and managers (Jahoda et al., 1971; Stack, 1974). The role of women in maintaining family relationships is consistent with a central developmental theme in their lives, the idea that "women's sense of self becomes very much organized around being able to make and then maintain relationships" (Miller, 1976, p. 83). By contrast, job and income loss undermined a core dimension of men's sense of self. Men in the Berkeley cohort responded to such loss with irritable, explosive, tense, and unstable behavior (Liker & Elder, 1983).

In addition to affecting family relationships, adaptations to hard times influenced the way in which the Oakland girls worked out their life chances. Specifically, the experience oriented them *toward achievement through people and marriage* (Elder, 1974, especially chap. 8). In the middle class, these girls were more apt to marry early and to embrace family activity as a favored role. Were the life chances of Berkeley daughters influenced in the same manner by Depression hardship?

Family Continuity and Women as Kin Keepers

The second proposition regarding family continuity is linked to the kin-keeper function attributed to women. The evidence at hand suggests that the primary kin carriers and integrators are women (Bott 1971; Hill, Foote, Aldous, Carlson, & MacDonald, 1970; Young & Willmott, 1964). Women are more active than men in maintaining communicative ties through letters, phone calls, and visits. They invest more in keeping track of the family history, dates, people, and events. Noting that women play a more dominant role in the kin system than men, Adams (1968) asserts that "young wives tend to express a closer affectional relation to all degrees of kin, and are more likely to feel that kin are an important part of their lives" (p. 169–170).

Affectional orientation toward kin represents an important component of the family continuity issue, but it does not directly address the question of continuity across an individual's life span. Do women show greater continuity in family ties with parents from their Depression childhood to the middle years than do men? Two factors favor such continuity in women's lives, especially when compared with the work-centered trajectories of men. First, a woman's central and enduring involvement in family roles represents an orientation strongly encouraged from early childhood (Komarovsky, 1950, 1956). Second, relationships are more central to women's self-concept, in contrast to the importance of occupation in men's self-definitions. At present, however, the life-span stability of affectional ties between parent and child is largely a matter of speculation, as are correlates of affection for parents (Troll & Smith, 1976). The transmission of affectional relations across the generations is also a matter of conjecture. Thus, we do not know whether women who have positive feelings toward parents are more likely than other women to hold positive feelings toward their own children.

Youthful Aspirations and Family Ties

With our last proposition we move to the family relations and aspirations of postwar women whose mothers grew up in the Depression era. Do such relationships vary by the girls' own aspirations for a career? In an age of domesticity, some Berkeley women managed to break with family tradition by extending their formal education, delaying marriage and childbearing, and combining work and family. This life course can be regarded as a distinctive socialization environment for daughters — an environment that favored self-enhancement and occupational achievement. From prior research (Bennett & Elder, 1979), we know that mothers who supported the idea of a dual career for their daughters were likely to be college educated. If formal education delayed family events, and if work experience in a mother's life raised the career aspirations of her daughter, are such aspirations compatible with mutual support and understanding between mother and daughter?

SAMPLE AND MEASUREMENT ISSUES

The Berkeley Guidance Study is known for its longitudinal assessment of a cohort of children born in 1928–29. The archive also contains detailed information on three additional generations: the grandparents (G1), parents (G2), and children (G4) of the Berkeley subjects (G3). A summary of key information on these four generations is contained in Table 7.1.

The Guidance Study was launched in 1928 by selection of every third birth in the city of Berkeley over a period of 18 months. It represents one of the oldest panel studies in operation. The original sample includes an intensively studied group ($N = 111$) that provided detailed information on family patterns in the 1930s, and a less intensively studied group ($N = 103$). The two groups were matched on social and economic characteristics in 1929. Most members of the sample had white, Protestant, native-born parents. Slightly more than three fifths of the families were positioned in the middle class in 1929. Although Berkeley is dominated by a large state university, the Berkeley fathers typically commuted to work settings in other Bay Area communities.

When the study was initiated in 1929, family income for households in the sample averaged $2,300; all but a few fathers were employed full time. Three years later, in the trough of the Great Depression, family income had declined by approximately 30%, a figure comparable to that of California families in general. Available evidence on the Berkeley sample indicates that deprived (loss greater than 34% of 1929 income) and nondeprived families did not differ before the Great Depression on such factors as personality, marital quality, and family size. Hence, we view the Depression as a natural field experiment which created an exogenous change in the social and economic well-being of families.

Berkeley parents (G2) and their children (G3) were studied annually from 1929 to 1945. This archive includes annual information on income, worklife of father and mother, annual teacher ratings regarding academic and social behavior, annual interviews with mother and child within the intensive sample, and staff assessments based on observations and interviews. Most of the children participated in two adult follow-ups (1959–60 and 1969–70), which included lengthy interviews and a battery of psychological, medical, and mental tests. Educational, occupational, and family histories were constructed from the interview materials. Of the 214 original subjects, 95 females and 87 males provided information at age 40. A comparison of the child and adult samples produced no significant differences in distributions of IQ, social class, and ethnicity.

By the 1969–70 follow-up, a large number of the Berkeley subjects (G3) had become parents of the G4 generation. The Institute staff at Berkeley at-

TABLE 7.1
Four Berkeley Generations

	Grandparents (G1)	Parents (G2)	Children (Ss) (G3)	Grandchildren (G4)
Birth year	Before 1890	1890–1910	1928–29	post–1946
No. of cases	844	422 (211 couples, 1928)	182 (1928–1970)	122 (age 14–18, 1969–1970)
Main Source of Data	Reports by parents, 1930 interview	Annual and periodic measurements 1928–1946; 1969–70	Annual and periodic measurements 1928–1946, Adult contacts in 1960, 1969–70	Contacted 1969–70: interviews, question- naires

tempted to interview all of the subjects' children (G4) between the ages of 14 and 18. Using the criterion of one son and one daughter from a family, we selected for this study 60 boys and an equal number of girls who had completed interviews. These boys and girls came from 87 different families. Data on the fourth generation also include questionnaires and a California Q-sort.

The analysis involves three components that correspond to the propositions previously outlined (see Fig. 7.1). The first part examines the impact of Depression hardship on family relations in the 1930s, specifically, parents' significance for girls and for boys. We next examine the interrelation of a Depression childhood and individual events and accomplishments along the life course, such as education, marital timing, occupational status, and, for women, work after marriage. These events and achievements are analyzed in terms of childhood ties with each parent and in terms of family misfortune during the 1930s.

The second part of the analysis focuses on the intergenerational ties of the Berkeley subjects at midlife. Here we consider the issue of life-span continuity: Do childhood orientations toward parents endure into the middle years of adulthood? We begin with an empirical test of this question among members of the G3 generation (born in 1928–29). Then we examine respondents' views of intergenerational ties in 1970, first with elderly mothers and then, in the postwar years, with adolescent children. These extensions enable us to determine whether family ties are based on a shared reality; that is, the extent to which both parties in a relationship hold similar views of its strength or weakness. The guiding question is whether the preceding ties are more likely to be true for middle-aged women, from the G3 generation, than for men of similar life stage.

The third and last part returns to the theme of life chances and examines the implications of mothers' (G3) unconventional life course for the aspirations of their daughters (G4). We also consider the link between family ties and individual achievement in the lives of mothers and daughters, completing our analysis of the Great Depression's influence across 40 years and three generations.

FAMILY HARDSHIP AND PARENTAL SIGNIFICANCE: PART I-A

Two issues warrant consideration in our examination of the ties between parents and children in the wake of the Great Depression. First, men frequently respond to income loss with erratic and explosive behavior, straining wives' coping skills (Liker & Elder, 1983). Did these women seek comfort in strengthened affectional bonds with their daughters? Second, the role de-

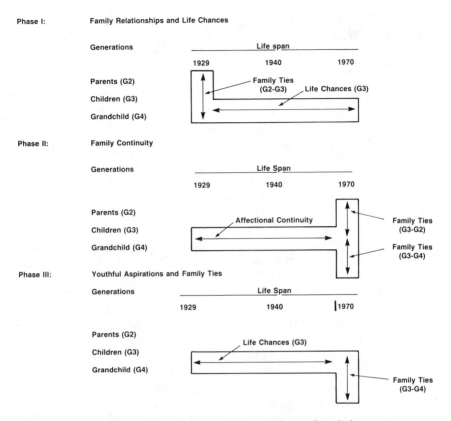

FIG. 7.1 Orienting Propositions and Phases of Analysis.

mands of women increase considerably when they assume responsibility for the family economy, while those of men diminish under income and job loss. Did a corresponding change occur in the status of mother as a role model for children?

To address these questions, we assess the effects of income loss during the Depression on two dimensions of parental significance. The first dimension concerns the child's perception of the affectional tone of parent-child relations. The second dimension is parental efficacy as a role model. These two dimensions bear on the core themes of the chapter: family relations and individual achievement.

The association between economic deprivation (loss greater than 34% of 1929 income) and parental significance may occur directly (without family mediation) and indirectly by intensifying problems of family relationships (Elder, Caspi & Downey, 1984). To specify these problems, we include in the analyses a measure of family instability.[1] The measure taps three types of parental behavior occurring from 1932 to 1935 that were strongly influenced by heavy income loss: the role of father in the explosiveness of the home, the inconsistency and extreme variability of parental discipline, and the irritability of father. Since all three measures are highly intercorrelated, the scores were averaged to produce a single index.

Family Hardship and Family Affection

The affectional tone of relations with mother and with father is assessed using two 5-point scales: warmth expressed toward mother and toward father, respectively. These ratings are based on interviews with the Berkeley children over the period 1936–38, when they were 8–10 years old. A low score denotes a relationship characterized by hostility on the part of the child, whereas a high score denotes a relationship perceived as warm. An additional measure included in the analyses is the child's perception of security in the home. A high score on this 5-point scale indicates perceived security, a fitting in with the family. This perception hinges on parental acceptance of the child.

Table 7.2 presents the effects of income loss and family instability on three family outcomes: warmth toward mother, warmth toward father, and security in the home. Separate statistical models were computed for sons and daughters. Income loss appears to draw mother and daughter closer together, leaving affection toward father unaffected among children of either sex. While hard times in boys' lives did not directly affect warmth toward either parent, the father-son relationship was vulnerable to unstable family circumstances. Boys in such homes were hostile toward their fathers and felt insecure. Girls' perceptions of parents and home were not, on the other hand, weakened by family explosiveness.

An explanation for the enhanced mother-daughter relationship may come from sex differences in response to stress between mothers and fathers, and between daughters and sons. With instrumental achievement an organizing principle of men's self-concept (e.g., Maccoby & Jacklin, 1974), fathers lost a core dimension of their social significance when they lost their jobs. Deprived

---

[1]Prior research has demonstrated the negative consequences of economic hardship for family relations operated primarily through the fathers (Elder, Caspi, & Downey, 1985). The explosive home index represents an average of three indicators; frequency and intensity of physical and verbal domestic violence in 1929–32 (scores range from 0 to 6), financial conflict in 1932–34 (scores range from 1 to 5), and marital tension in 1933–35 (scores range from 1 to 5). The two 5-point ratings of father's arbitrariness or inconsistency in 1933–35 were averaged (father arbitrary and extreme). Scores on father irritable in 1933–35 range from 1 to 5. All three scores were averaged to produce a single measure of an unstable home.

TABLE 7.2

Girls' and Boys' Perception of Parents' Affectional Significance by Economic Deprivation and Family Instability: Regression Coefficients in Standard Form (G3)[a]

1936–1938	Girls (n = 49)				Boys (min. n = 40)			
	Economic Deprivation		Family Instability		Economic Deprivation		Family Instability	
	Beta	r[b]	Beta	r	Beta	r	Beta	r
Warmth to father	−.10	−.11	−.03	−.06	−.26	−.18	−.39**	−.43
Warmth to mother	.42**	.43	.02	.18	.05	.18	−.14	−.06
Secure in home	.23	.24	.14	.21	−.16	−.03	−.32*	−.30

[a]Social class is a covariate in all regression analyses.
[b]Zero-order correlations are in parentheses.
*p<.05
**p<.01

fathers became worrisome, explosive, and irritable, whereas little change of this sort was observed in women (Liker & Elder, 1983). Unlike men, women could fall back on an activity of central concern in their lives: forming and maintaining relationships (Gilligan, 1982).

In the case of children, sex differences in response to family stress have been demonstrated repeatedly (Porter & O'Leary, 1979; Rutter, 1979). These findings suggest that in stressful times, parents have much greater difficulty in maintaining an affectional relationship with sons than with daughters. Consider the case of divorce. Boys react to disruption in family problem solving by becoming increasingly oppositional and aggressive; girls, on the other hand, become more compliant and complaining (Hetherington, Cox, & Cox, 1981). These differences in response to family changes are compatible with Martin's (1974) conclusions: coercive parental responses are more likely to socialize inhibition in girls and aggression in boys. The internalizing response style of girls appears easier for parents to manage than the external response style of boys.

Considered together, sex differences both in parents' and in children's response style produce a scenario where mothers' and daughters' reactions to financial stress and to its consequences facilitate an affectionate relationship that may protect daughters from the harshness of their fathers. In contrast, the disruptive response style of both fathers and sons are conducive to hostile family relations. The data indicate that such negative relations occur in unstable families. Mothers appear less capable of handling sons' aggressive responses to family stress than they are of handling daughters' responses. Hence, mothers are less apt to strengthen their affectional bond with sons. Overall, the findings confirm the gender differences of previous research which show an increased vulnerability of males to family conflict and an enhanced female solidarity in hard times.

Family Hardship and Parent as Role Model

The second aspect of parental significance is parental efficacy as a role model. Two relevant measures were obtained during the junior high school years. *Attractiveness* refers to the child's overall perception of the parent as an attractive person. *Prestige* measures the child's evaluation of the extent to which a parent is an esteemed figure in the community. Evaluations of attractiveness and prestige were obtained for each parent. Each score is based on a 9-point Q-sort rating (Block, 1971). The measures are intended to index children's evaluation of parents at a time when they (children) are becoming more concerned with issues of personal identity (Erikson, 1963).

Table 7.3 shows the effect of income loss and family instability on parental prestige and attractiveness. As before, separate analyses were carried out for

TABLE 7.3

Girls' and Boys' Perception of Parental Efficacy as a Role Model by Economic Deprivation and Family Instability: Regression Coefficients in Standard Form (G3)[a]

Junior High	Girls (min. n = 35)				Boys (min. n = 27)			
	Economic Deprivation		Family Instability		Economic Deprivation		Family Instability	
	Beta	r[b]	Beta	r	Beta	r	Beta	r
Attractiveness of father	.05	-.14	-.54**	-.59	.02	-.16	-.40*	-.40
Prestige of father	-.08	-.25	-.31*	-.50	.08	-.28	-.38**	-.38
Attractiveness of mother	.12	.11	-.19	-.05	.33	.30	.02	.10
Prestige of mother	.26	.24	-.10	-.02	.10	-.11	-.48*	-.47

[a]Social class is a covariate in all regression analyses.

[b]Zero-order correlations are in parentheses.

*p<.05

**p<.01

boys and for girls. The results again reveal differences in outcome by sex of parent and sex of child. Income loss in the early 1930s has no significant effect on perceived paternal attractiveness or prestige 10 years later for either sons or daughters. This is contrary to what one might expect: that fathers who lost their positions during the Depression would also lose status in the eyes of their children. However, paternal status is diminished for both boys and girls in unstable homes. As we have indicated previously, family instability in the early 1930s was accentuated when fathers lost income. Thus, the effect of a troubled home on parental status appears to represent an indirect consequence of financial hardship.

Despite the enlarged role mothers played in Depression families, daughters' evaluation of them is unaffected by income loss during the 1930s. For boys, however, economic hardship increased the perceived attractiveness of mothers (beta = .66, $p < .01$), whereas an unstable home diminished their social prestige (beta = $-.52$, $p < .01$). The effect of mothers' augmented family role on daughters appears to operate through relationships rather than through a process of role modeling.

Summary

The Depression experience had direct consequences only for the significance of mother. Income loss drew mother and daughter closer together and enhanced mother's attractiveness for sons. Paternal significance was more responsive to family disruption when compared to the significance of mother. An unstable atmosphere, fueled by economic hardship, diminished sons' affection for fathers and lessened their status in the eyes of both boys and girls. In what ways did these relational patterns emerging from the Great Depression influence the individual achievement of daughters and sons? Before addressing this question, we must first consider the consequences of Depression hardship for career beginnings and midlife status.

SOCIAL ORIGINS, LIFE CHANCES AND FAMILY TIES:
PART I-B

The Berkeley children reached adulthood during the postwar era, a time of renewed domesticity and prosperity in America. Many had experienced the childhood constraints of economic pressure and diminished opportunities, the precariousness of male earnings and the competence of a mother who took the family helm during hard times. Did the Depression experience continue as an influence in adulthood, delaying or accelerating early life transitions and diminishing opportunities for social attainment? Did limited resources in deprived families orient girls toward social mobility through marriage, as asserted in the first proposition?

To examine these questions, we focus on the timing of four key transitions among the Berkeley daughters and sons: completion of education, first full-time employment, marriage, and parenthood. In addition, two indicators of status attainment are included in the analysis: educational and occupational status[2] by midlife. Since few women were employed in positions carrying status equal to that of husbands by midlife, the husband's occupation is taken as an indicator of their social status. Because life patterns vary by class origins, we define social class in 1929 as a family context in the analyses (Bennett & Elder, 1979; Elder, 1974). The average timing of early life transitions and mean levels of status attainment for deprived and nondeprived sons and daughters within each social class are presented in Table 7.4. Hard times left their marks on the early life transitions, education, midlife status, and employment history of Berkeley women who grew up during the 1930s. However, the effect typically varied by class origins. Consider the transition to adulthood. Economic hardship accelerated entry into family roles among women from the middle class, as indexed by early marriage and parenthood. In the working class, the pattern is reversed: hardship postponed these family events, and the same type of delay appears among the Berkeley males from working class homes. In the middle class, the results are consistent with the hypothesis that girls from hard-pressed families sought adult status through marriage. In the working class, the pattern of family delay corresponds with a traditional practice in which older daughters postponed marriage in order to help support parents (Hareven, 1981). The corresponding delay among sons from the deprived working class may be rooted in the same pressures; the need to help parents and to become economically self-sufficient before marriage.

Despite the contrasting marriage timetable of women from deprived families in the middle and working classes, they share a common path to adulthood, a pathway through marriage and husband's status. In the middle class, mate selection was more likely to occur on the college campus. Over four fifths of the women entered college, compared to only a third of the women from working-class homes. The latter were more likely to meet husbands through work settings. Though little is known about this mating process, it is clear that Depression hardship did not entail a status disadvantage through marriage among working-class offspring. The only social disadvantage appears in the life course of women from the middle class. Likewise, we find no ill effects of Depression hardship in the midlife status of Berkeley men, even

---

[2]Social class is indexed using the Hollingshead measure: middle class includes strata I-III; working class includes strata IV and V.

TABLE 7.4

Early Life Transitions and Status Attainment of Berkeley Women and Men: Means, Standard Deviations, and Percentages (G3)

| | Berkeley Women by Class Origin and Economic Deprivation | | | | Berkeley Men by Class Origin and Economic Deprivation | | | |
| | Middle Class | | Working Class | | Middle Class | | Working Class | |
	Nondeprived $\overline{X}$	Deprived $\overline{X}$	Nondeprived $\overline{X}$	Deprived $\overline{X}$	Nondeprived $\overline{X}$	Deprived $\overline{X}$	Nondeprived $\overline{X}$	Deprived $\overline{X}$
	(Min n = 34)	(Min n = 26)	(Min n = 12)	(Min n = 10)	(Min n = 27)	(Min n = 15)	(Min n = 14)	(Min n = 19)
Early Life Transition								
Age at completion of education	21.5	22.9	18.2	20.5	25.3	24.7	22.9	22.4
	(3.6)[b]	(7.0)	(1.5)	(6.4)	(5.9)	(5.9)	(6.4)	(5.8)
Age beginning full-time employment	21.3	21.1	18.8	19.1	22.8	21.7	20.0	19.2
	(3.8)	(5.1)	(3.3)	(2.1)	(3.3)	(3.3)	(3.2)	(2.9)
Age at first marriage	22.9	21.2	19.8	20.9	23.4	23.5	21.8	24.7
	(3.7)	(2.7)	(2.6)	(1.9)	(3.5)	(2.7)	(2.7)	(4.6)
Age at parenthood	25.3	23.4	22.5	23.9	25.0	25.3	22.5	26.9
	(4.0)	(3.0)	(3.8)	(3.7)	(3.7)	(2.9)	(2.4)	(6.2)
Educational Attainment								
Entering college, %	79%	87%	36%	29%	86%	83%	37%	44%
Graduating from college, %	a	a	a	a	71%	56%	37%	12%
Status Attainment								
Status attainment by midlife	6.0	5.4	4.2	5.0	5.6	5.6	4.8	4.4
	(1.3)	(0.3)	(1.7)	(1.6)	(1.3)	(1.0)	(1.3)	(1.5)

[a]Subgroup size is too small for calculation
[b]Standard deviations in parentheses

though men from deprived homes failed to go as far in higher education as the nondeprived.

Parents' Aspirations for Their Children

The low level of college completion among daughters reflects the prevailing belief that formal education was more critical for sons than for daughters. It was a prerequisite to a son's "making something of himself," as a Berkeley mother put it. For daughters in the postwar decade, the primary avenue of social mobility was marriage, with a wife's social status being determined by her husband's occupation. These differential expectations for sons and daughters often emerged in interviews with the Berkeley parents during the early 1940s.

Though many expressed the wish that their children would receive training beyond high school (and indeed succeeded in providing them with higher education), the purpose and type of educational aspirations expressed for boys and for girls differed considerably. Aspirations for sons centered on training for established male-dominated occupations, (e.g., medicine, science, engineering, farming, and the trades). In contrast, parents expressed the hope that daughters would receive training appropriate to the traditional female occupations: teaching, secretarial work, dress designing, and the arts. Support for a daughter's nontraditional aspirations was qualified, as the following quote from an upper-middle class father illustrates: "I think it would be fine for her to go into lab work or become a physician but I really don't expect her to do much of anything . . . I expect she will be married."

Marriage and family were central themes in paternal aspirations for daughters, in sharp contrast to sons, for whom there was not a single reference to family ties. The life trajectory commonly desired for girls is expressed in the following quote from an upper middle-class Berkeley mother: "[I want her to] get a good education, choose a good occupation, and finally have a home and family of her own." This Berkeley daughter fulfilled her mother's ambitions by attending college, marrying a professional man, and holding a sales job until the birth of her first child.

One function of education for daughters was to enable them to work until parenthood — in order, as one mother put it, "to learn the value of money." A second purpose of "training" was expressed by a lower middle-class mother who wanted her daughter "to prepare in some line of work so if anything goes wrong in her life she would be able to be self-supporting." A third function of higher education for daughters (i.e., a means of forming suitable social contacts) is implied in the aspirations of an upper middle-class mother for her daughter: "College, social popularity, and an early marriage." This daughter met her professional spouse at college and left school to marry. These views of education and training for daughters share the assumption that occupation was not to play a central role in their lives. Judging from the scarcity of women in full-time occupations at midlife in the Berkeley sample (25%), this was, in fact, the case.

Despite the centrality of marriage and family in parents' aspirations for daughters, nearly three out of five women had some experience with gainful employment by midlife. Only one fifth of the wives, however, maintained a stable work pattern uninterrupted by motherhood. Two socioeconomic factors influenced employment after the first child: (1) husband's occupational status and (2) a childhood background of Depression hardship (Bennett & Elder, 1979). The first condition is reflected in the familiar association between women's involvement in the labor force and in the economic pressures accompanying marriage to low status men (e.g., Mason, Vinovskis & Hareven, 1978). Whether from a deprived background or not, the wives of lower status men were more likely to be employed than women in the upper-middle class (61% vs. 42%, respectively) at midlife.

Depression hardship increased the likelihood of maternal employment among women who were "least apt" to be faced with strong economic pressures to work—those in the upper middle class. Here, two thirds of the women from deprived homes were in the labor force at midlife, as compared to one fourth of the women from nondeprived homes. The effect of Depression hardship on women's employment in the upper middle class is generally consistent with the proposition that hard times foster an orientation toward work outside the home, an orientation that incorporates an ability for economic self reliance.

Linking Family Ties and Life Chances

Up to this point we have examined the Depression's effects on the two themes of this study, life chances and family ties. We turn now to relations between them. Are affectional ties to parents and to parental efficacy important factors in the life accomplishments of Depression-reared women and men? Three aspects of the life course were used to measure achievement along social and instrumental dimensions: age at first child, educational level, and occupational status (husband's status, if respondent was female). We calculated correlations between these indices of attainment and four measures of orientation toward parents in the preadult years of the Berkeley children: (a) warmth toward father and mother; (b) security in the home, for 1936–38; (c) attractiveness of father/mother and (d) social prestige of father and mother for the junior high years. In each case, we partialed out the effect of class origin in 1929.

TABLE 7.5

Linking Family Ties and Aspects of Life Course Among Berkeley Females and Males: Zero-order and Partial Correlations Controlling for Social Class, 1929 (G3)

| | Aspects of Life Course | | | | | |
| | Education | | Age at First Birth | | Occupation[a], 1968 | |
Family Ties	Female partial r	Male partial r	Female partial r	Male partial r	Female partial r	Male partial r
	min. $n = 49$	min. $n = 45$	min. $n = 42$	min. $n = 39$	min. $n = 38$	min. $n = 42$
Affectional Ties, 1936–1938						
Warmth to Father	−.51***	−.12	.10	−.16	.12	−.06
Warmth to Mother	−.11	.02	.03	−.04	−.11	−.11
Secure in Home	.22+	.00	.32*	−.18	.34*	−.19
Efficacy of Parents, Junior High School	min. $n = 38$	min. $n = 34$	min. $n = 35$	min. $n = 31$	min. $n = 33$	min. $n = 33$
Father Attractive	.27*	−.29*	.39***	.08	.28+	−.06
Father has Prestige	.17	−.07	.23+	.28+	.28+	−.03
Mother Attractive	.09	−.01	.34*	.11	.23	.06
Mother has Prestige	.15	−.01	.08	.21	.09	−.08

[a]For females, occupation refers to that of husband in 1968.

+ $p < .10$
* $p < .05$
** $p < .01$
*** $p < .001$

169

Affectional ties with parents during the Depression decade (Table 7.5) were of little direct consequence for the timing of parenthood and status attainment, as well as education and occupational status, among women and men in the Berkeley cohort of 1928–29. Literally, the only exception involves the reported warmth of girls toward father and girls' subsequent educational achievement. The correlation is strongly negative and remains so with class origin statistically controlled (partial $r = -.51$, $p < .001$). How did emotional distance from father and even hostility play a role in women's educational attainment? One answer may involve the pervasive tendency for fathers to devalue their daughters' aspirations for a higher education that leads to work. The young women who were emotionally distant from their fathers could, if necessary, break free to choose a different future, one with higher education and even a career. On the other hand, the girls who felt secure in their homes and attracted to their fathers were likely to delay family events, acquire a higher education, and marry well in terms of husbands' eventual status at midlife. This orientation toward father is clearly an important element in a life course of achievement among women, both through marriage and independently. Adolescent girls who perceived mother as an attractive person were also likely to follow a course of achievement, one involving late family events and mobility through marriage. But unlike such perceptions of father, an attractive mother was not a factor in the educational achievement of women.

Summary

Three conclusions emerge from the analysis and relate to the first proposition. First, hard times in the 1930s strengthened affectional ties between mother and daughter. However, mother's status as a role model for her daughter was not directly affected by economic deprivation, despite the central role many women adopted in hard-pressed homes. Second, the Depression experience oriented daughters toward achievement through marriage. However, Berkeley women from hard-pressed families were also directed toward instrumental achievement; a finding most pronounced among some upper middle-class women who worked, despite economic sufficiency. Third, the significance of mothers as objects of affection and respect for daughters during the 1930s and early 1940s had few consequences for the daughters' accomplishments (G3 generation). This implies that mother-daughter relational patterns (at least in the domains we have examined) established as an adaptation to financial crisis do not represent mechanisms through which the Depression influenced life chances. The question remains, however, whether or not the long-term effects of mother-daughter relational patterns emerge more strongly in the arena of family ties?

FAMILY CONTINUITY AND WOMEN AS KIN-KEEPERS: PART II

This part of the analysis begins with continuity of the Berkeley women's perceptions of relations with parents from childhood to midlife. The focus is on continuity in affectional bonds, since data are available on this dimension of parental significance in the middle years (1969–70 interview). Using interviews with the aged mothers (1969–70) and with adolescent children of the middle-aged Berkeley women, we address the following questions: Do mothers (G2) and daughters (G3) show greater agreement in the assessment of their joint relationship than mothers and sons? Do Berkeley women demonstrate a stronger degree of continuity in affectional relations across three generations than Berkeley men?

Family Continuity Across the Life Course

In 1969–70, the men and women of the Berkeley cohort (G3) were asked two general questions regarding their parents. First, they were to define the importance of mother and father as reflected in the degree of parent-child involvement, regardless of emotional tone. A high score on this 5-point scale indicated that parents were extremely involved in their children's lives. Second, the perceived quality of relations with mother and with father was also assessed using a 5-point scale. A score of 5 indicated a relationship of "exceptional friendliness, closeness and agreement." Stress and conflicts were located at the other end of the continuum. Table 7.6 presents the zero-order correlations obtained between warmth toward mother and father at ages 8–10, Depression hardship, and the midlife measures.

The principal continuities in attitudes toward parents across the life course occur in two areas: the importance of parents for the Berkeley males, and relations with both parents among the Berkeley females. The relative unimportance of parents is a noteworthy legacy of Depression hardship among men. Those who grew up in hard-pressed families were least likely to report meaningful involvement with parents at midlife. Men who claimed involvement with parents generally had felt some affection for mother and especially for father in their Depression childhood.

By comparison, midlife involvement with parents shows little relation to the Depression experience of women, whether in terms of economic hardship or warmth toward parents. For them, continuity appears in the quality of relations with parents. Women with affectionate feelings toward father in the 1930s were likely to report similar attitudes at midlife. This contrasts sharply with the total lack of continuity of men's attitudes toward their fathers. Likewise, emotional ties with mother show little stability for men between child-

TABLE 7.6

Midlife Orientations toward Parents by Childhood Attitudes toward Parents and Family Hardship: Zero-order Correlations (G3)

Childhood Factors	Attitudes toward Parent at Midlife by Sex					
	Importance of Parents		Relations with Father		Relations with Mother	
	Female r	Male r	Female r	Male r	Female r	Male r
	$n = 64$	$n = 48$	$n = 55$	$n = 42$	$n = 66$	$n = 50$
Economic Depreviation	.03	− .41**	− .08	− .23	.16	.12
	$n = 27$	$n = 29$	$n = 25$	$n = 25$	$n = 29$	$n = 30$
Warmth to father	.11	.49**	.44**	.05	.25	.20
Warmth to mother	.09	.26	.16	.31	.43**	.21

*$p < .05$
**$p < .01$

hood and midlife, whereas much greater stability appears in the sentiments of women toward mothers.

Continuity in the quality of daughters' relations with parents across the life course is consistent with an argument for the salience of family ties in daughters' lives. However, the following point should be borne in mind when considering this finding: The power of parent-daughter relations to predict relational quality at midlife does not necessarily imply anything about the quality of the relationship in the intervening years. Similarity in parent-daughter relations during these life stages may mask a turbulent transitional stage, as daughters seek to establish their independence from family (e.g., Fischer, 1981). By 1970, most of the Berkeley subjects were parents of school-age children. According to Freud (1933), motherhood may revive a daughter's identification with mother, something she has striven against until marriage. This reorientation may put the mother-daughter relationship back on the course established in childhood.

Do we find greater family continuity between the midlife reports of women and the reports of their aged mothers about the mother-daughter relationship? Do these family members share the same view of their relationship? In the 1970 follow-up, the Berkeley mothers who were born around 1900 were asked to describe the quality of their relationship with offspring (i.e., 1 = "below average" to 5 = "above average"). Mothers' perceptions correlate strongly with daughters' reports of relations with their mothers ($r = .49$, $p < .01$). By comparison, there is no correspondence between mothers' and sons' evaluations of their relationship ($r = -.05$). The same gender contrast is evident when the "importance of parents" in middle age is correlated with mothers' reports of the relationship ($r = .56$, $p < .001$, $r = -.16$, $p > .05$, for daughters and sons, respectively). This disparity may reflect a difference in expectations, with mothers expecting more from relations with sons than their sons expect. Only 7% of mothers disenchanted with their daughters had a daughter who did not share their view of the poor or average quality of social relations. When daughters reported an above average relationship, nine tenths of the mothers agreed. Among the sons who reported such a relationship, the percentage of mothers who agreed is little more than one third.

The picture emerging from our analysis of family ties at midlife is one of greater continuity over the life course for daughters. Given the family themes evident in mothers' aspirations for their daughters in the 1940s, it is not surprising that mothers evaluate daughters in terms of family ties. Do mothers evaluate sons, on the other hand, in terms of their individual achievements? A significant correlation between occupational status at midlife and mother's perception of relationship quality suggests this may be the case ($r = .33$, $p < .01$). No relationship was found between daughters' status attainment and mothers' perception of their relationship.

Berkley Daughters (G3) and Their Children (G4) in Postwar America

The affectional bonds that daughters form with parents in childhood are evident in their adult lives. Is the affectional tone of this relationship re-created in the mother-child relations of postwar families, where the role of Berkeley children is reversed (i.e., they are parents)? Do the data support an argument that women act as kin keepers, as agents of intergenerational continuity in family themes? The 1970 interview with the Berkeley men and women includes information on perceived affection toward spouse and children. Affection is measured on a 5-point scale, with a high score denoting affectionate relations and a low score denoting an undemonstrative orientation to family members. Perceived quality of relations with mother and with father at midlife predicts daughter's affection toward her spouse (mean $r = 32$, $p < .05$) and toward her children (mean $r = .42$, $p < .01$). Sons' evaluations of relations with parents do not generalize to affection toward wife and children. These findings are consistent with the proposition of greater family continuity among daughters.

Do the postwar Berkeley children (G4) share their parents' perception of the parent-child relationship? Two measures from the interviews with G4 respondents (1969–70) are relevant to this point: affectional and value orientation[3] toward mother and toward father. Mothers' affection toward their children significantly predicts their children's maternal affectional orientation ($r = .39, p < .01$). Fathers' affection predicts their children's affectional and value orientation toward fathers ($r = .43, p < .01; r = .39, p < .05$, respectively). These findings strengthen our argument that women play a kinkeeper role in families by maintaining family relational themes across generations. They also indicate that the father's failure to accurately perceive his relationship with the mother does not generalize to other relationships.

Summary: Female Continuity and Male Discontinuity

The picture that emerges when we piece together available data on family ties highlights the central role women play in preserving family relational ties across time and in the face of family hardship. In the 1930s, the Depression experience drew mother and daughter closer together. The affectional tone characterizing mother-daughter relations in childhood was carried across 30 years to 1970, when the Berkeley daughters were themselves middle-aged parents and their mothers had reached old age. We also see intergenerational continuity along the female lineage, with affection toward mother predicting affection toward children. In contrast, the family ties of Berkeley sons are characterized by discontinuity. Quality of relations with parents in childhood does not predict quality of relations at midlife. Sons' and mothers' perceptions of their joint relationship in 1970 show marked discrepancies. Son's perceptions of this relationship do not reflect relations with their children. This summary brings us to the third part of the analysis: examination of the tensions between achievement and family ties in the third and fourth generations of the Berkeley study.

YOUTHFUL ASPIRATIONS AND FAMILY TIES: PART III

In this third and final part of the analysis we return to the theme of individual achievement, and examine continuity in this domain across the generations. We conclude by delineating the interconnections between family ties and individual pursuits, as they emerge in the lives of middle-aged Berkeley

---

[3]a. *Affectional orientation* toward mother is obtained by averaging the following interview scales (scores range from 1 to 5): positive evaluation of mother, personal satisfaction with mother, mother has disappointed child, and wishes to change mother. A high score on the index indicates low affectional orientation toward mother. b. *Value orientation* is obtained by averaging the following ratings of mother (scores range from 1 to 5): views mother as a role model, mother has influenced child as a person, spends time talking with mother, shares ideas with mother. A high score indicates low valuation of mother's influence.

women and their adolescent offspring. Two questions structure the analysis:[4] First, are nontraditional women (G3) likely to raise daughters (G4) with nontraditional career aspirations? Second, are career orientations that emphasize individual concerns likely to introduce tension into the mother-daughter relationship?

Pioneering Mothers and Their Postwar Daughters

To investigate the first question, we identified three indicators of a nontraditional life pattern among the Berkeley women (G3): late childbearing, higher education, and employment after the birth of the first child. In the immediate postwar era, well-educated mothers who delayed childbearing and who were employed after the birth of their children were clearly breaking from the customary life course of women during the baby boom era. As we have seen, those who married late for educational reasons were likely to come from nondeprived middle-class homes, whereas postponement of marriage and motherhood among lower-class daughters tended to occur in response to Depression hardship. The lives of mothers who worked were also likely to have been touched by financial hardship. Such women were the wives of men in low status jobs or upper middle class wives from deprived backgrounds (Bennett & Elder, 1979). The third indicator of a nontraditional life pattern, educational attainment, appears to be most affected by the Depression experience of deprived middle-class girls, restricting their achievement in this domain.

The adolescent daughters of Berkeley women were asked, in 1970, whether they had plans for combining work and marriage. Two fifths expressed an interest in a career as well as the expectation of marriage. Only two girls had career plans without plans for marriage. Slightly more than a quarter of the girls claimed that marriage and family would come before any interest in a career activity. A surprisingly large number of girls had plans for marriage, but not for careers (30%). Were these traditional girls most likely to have traditional mothers? In order to estimate the influence of maternal orientation on the goals of daughters, we used mother's education, age at first birth, and work after marriage, to obtain an "induced single factor measure" (Heise, 1972) of a nontraditional life course trajectory.

As can be seen in Figure 7.2, mothers who broke with custom or tradition tended to have daughters whose aspirations emphasized individual achievement in the work domain, rather than simply a family-centered life course

---

[4]In order to increase the sample size, female (G3) subjects and spouses of male subjects (i.e., *all* mothers of postwar daughters) were included in this part of the analysis. Corresponding analyses were performed using female subjects only, with comparable results.

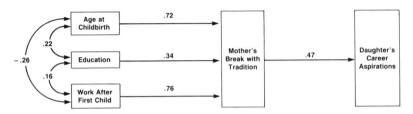

FIG. 7.2 Effect of Mother's Break with Tradition on Daughter's Career Aspirations; Heise's Induced Variable Approach.

(Sheaf coefficient = .47).[5] Closer examination of the relative contribution of the three indicators of nontraditional mothers to the career plans of daughters shows that late childbearing and work are the principal factors. Note that both of these variables are more closely associated with Depression hardship than with level of education. As such, they may represent one process by which family hardship in the 30s influenced family ties and individual achievement in the next generation.

Personality Correlates of a Career Orientation

Do the career-oriented aspirations of daughters with pioneering mothers reflect a general orientation toward individuality rather than toward social relationships? To address this question, we examined the relationship between career aspirations, educational plans, and a number of personality attributes. Educational plans were measured on a 6-point scale with the highest score indicating plans for graduate school. All personality measures are based on 9-point Q-sort ratings by clinicians (Block, 1971). Ratings in the analysis were intended to tap four domains commonly associated with instrumental and agentic behavior (e.g., Spence & Helmreich, 1978): Independence, Breadth of Perspective, Assertiveness and Identity. The correlations presented in Table 7.7 show moderate to strong associations between career aspirations and instrumental qualities.

The emerging profile of a daughter who places career before marriage can be summarized as follows: She is likely to value independence, to have wide interests and value intellectual matters, to be assertive and view the self as

---

[5]The "sheaf coefficient" was developed as part of the "induced variable" approach (Heise, 1972) for use in problems where indicator variables are clearly *determinants of* an abstract construct (e.g., socioeconomic status or ethnicity), instead of being *determined by* the underlying construct (e.g., intelligence). The indicator variables are assumed to define perfectly the latent construct (induced variable), and the total effect of the induced variable on the dependent variable is represented by the sheaf coefficient. Sheaf coefficients are interpreted as standardized regression coefficients and therefore may be compared with the betas of other independent variables in the model.

causative, and to feel ambitious. She is not inclined to be other-directed, dependent, or highly feminine. A similar profile appears among daughters who plan to pursue advanced education. However, the association between educational plans and the attributes of an instrumental personality is less marked, particularly in the domain of dependence. A possible explanation for this finding is that college completion and postgraduate education were less an issue for women in general in the 1970s than were career aspirations, which may or may not have included marriage.

Family Ties and Individual Achievement

Women with postwar children were faced with the question of whether a mother should work. A primary dilemma of the 1970s was whether a career woman could also cope with maternal obligations. We have seen that daughters with nontraditional aspirations in the 1970s had mothers who broke with

TABLE 7.7
Vocational Orientation by Personality of Daughters: Zero-order
Correlations (G4)

	Girls' plans in 1970 (n = 47)	
Girls' Q-Sort Ratings, 1970	Educational Plans r	Career Plans r
Independence		
Values independence	.11	.31**
Thinks unconventionally	.18	.23*
Other-directed	− .12	− .43**
Aloof	− .03	.23*
Breadth of Perspective		
Wide interests	.36**	.43**
Values intellectual matters	.32**	.48**
Uncomfortable with uncertainty	− .33**	− .23*
Assertive		
Assertive	.15	.35**
Views the self as causative	.23*	.44**
Withdraws from frustration	− .24*	− .40**
Dependent	− .16	− .43**
Power oriented	.33**	.50**
Identity		
Satisfied with self	.20	.22*
Feels ambitious	.43**	.62**
Feminine	− .38**	− .38**

*p < .05
**p < .01

tradition in the postwar years, especially by working. Such daughters were also likely to approach the world in a traditionally masculine instrumental manner. Does a pioneering orientation, as reflected in the behavior of mothers and in the aspirations of daughters, weaken the mother-daughter relationship?

Consider, first, the consequences of mother's nontraditional behavior for family ties. A pioneering orientation, indicated by higher education, late parenthood, and maternal employment, is not associated with diminished affection for either spouse (mean $r = -.07$) or child (mean $r = -.04$). In fact, late parenthood significantly accentuated mother's affection toward her children ($r = .27$, $p < .01$). What were the consequences of mother's nontraditional behavior for daughter's perception of her relationship with mother? Mothers who worked were less likely to be viewed affectionately by their adolescent daughters ($r = -.29$, $p = < .05$). By contrast, daughters were no less affectionate toward well-educated mothers who became parents relatively late. A possible explanation for the apparently contradictory consequences of nontraditional behavior among mothers may lie in the different meaning of the three indicators of altering the tradition of family involvement. Although college completion and late parenthood were not commonplace in the baby boom era, many well-educated women who postponed parenthood did not attempt to combine career and motherhood. In fact, there is some evidence that these women were most strongly influenced by the family-centered *zietgeist* of the 1940s and 1950s (Campbell, 1984). Working mothers, in contrast, were expending energy on individual pursuits away from the family, which may have undermined their relationship with adolescent daughters. The reasons that such mothers went against the spirit of their times have not been fully explored.

What were the consequences of daughter's career-oriented aspirations for family ties? Mother's affection for daughter was unlikely to be affected by her daughter's career aspirations ($r = .08$). To examine whether pioneering daughters were likely to perceive weakened relations with mothers, we focused on three measures of family ties: perception of mother as a source of affection, of values and of support.[6] Our analysis was limited to those girls for whom a career (as opposed to work) was likely to be a viable prospect: those in the upper two thirds of the sample distribution of intellectual ability. For comparative purposes we included fathers in the analysis. The data provide moderate but consistent support for the proposition that career-centered aspirations among intellectually capable girls are associated with a weak-

---

[6] *Supportiveness* indexes the degree to which parent is perceived as supportive. Values were obtained by averaging the following scale scores (range from 1 to 5): child's perception of mother's evaluation of him or her, understanding and support provided by mother, extent of confidence in child. A high score indicates mother is perceived to be unsupportive.

ening of the mother-daughter bond (mean $r = -.31$, $p < .05$). A positive evaluation of paternal significance is not, however, incompatible with aspirations centering on an individual agenda (mean $r = .05$).

Summary

Two conclusions emerge from this part of the analysis. First, mothers and daughters showed moderate continuity in orientation towards individual achievement: Mothers who broke with tradition in the 1940s and 1950s were likely to have pioneering daughters in the 1970s. Second, breaking with tradition did not affect mothers' perceptions of relations with family members. However, adolescent daughters were likely to view the situation differently, perceiving themselves as less affectionate toward mothers who worked. Daughter's career plans were also likely to generate tension in the mother-daughter relationship, as perceived by the daughter; mother's view of the relationship was unaltered. It is possible that this tension is transient, arising from the pressures of adolescence and young adulthood.

OVERVIEW

A central theme in human society involves the competing claims of group membership and individual desires. These conflicting pressures are most vividly expressed in the lives of women, especially since the 1930s with the large-scale entry of mothers into the work force. Using archival data from three generations of the Berkeley Guidance Study, this research examined the interplay of family ties, on the one hand, and individual achievement, on the other, as played out in the lives of women. The first proposition viewed hard times as an influence on family relations and on life prospects. We hypothesized that family adaptation to father's role loss strengthened the mother-daughter bond, and oriented daughters toward people and relationships as the preferred avenue of achievement. The second proposition centered on the continuity of relationships in women's lives, relative to men. Our final proposition depicted individual aspirations as a factor in undermining the strength of mother-daughter ties.

The first part of the analysis showed that female solidarity and a family-centered life course represent independent modes of adaptation to a Depression childhood among females. Across the life course, from childhood to the middle years, and across the generations, the Berkeley women demonstrated continuity in affectional ties from the 1930s. This stands in contrast to the lack of continuity in men's affectional ties. Men's poor relations with parents in childhood did not anticipate poor relations with spouse and children. Overall, these findings support the kin-keeper role attributed to women.

Continuity in women's lives also appears in the domain of individual achievement. Women (G3) whose life course departed from the family-centered ideal of the postwar era (i.e., started their family late, were highly educated, and worked after children were born) conveyed this orientation toward individual achievement to their adolescent daughters (G4). This achievement did not diminish Berkeley women's (G3) identification with family. However, conflicts between the pull of family obligations and a desire for individual achievement do have consequences for mothers' relations with teenage daughters. The daughters are less likely to perceive working mothers in an affectionate light, and their own career aspirations are negatively correlated with a view of mother as a source of affection, values, and support.

Although the propositions orienting our analyses are generally supported by the data, the moderate cross-time and intergenerational relationships leave much of the variance unexplained. Not all daughters were drawn closer to mothers by the Depression experience. The nature of the mother-daughter relationship established in childhood did not always set the tone of affectional ties to significant others at midlife. Not all postwar daughters of pioneering mothers adopted nontraditional aspirations relative to their cohort.

What are the family and contextual factors that affect continuity in relationships? What factors moderate the transmission of values relevant to the dilemma of balancing family and work demands among women? These questions have significant implications for understanding the changes observed in women's lives over the past forty years and as such represent an important agenda for subsequent investigation.

Our analysis has been restricted by the givens of archival data. Data on the affectional dimension of parent-child relations were available only during childhood and again at midlife. Thus, the nature of the relationship in the intervening years could not be established. Research based on retrospective data (e.g., Fischer, 1981) indicates that the mother-daughter relationship may be quite turbulent in the adolescent years. Parent-child relations over the life course are not well documented, although the importance of such research is recognized (e.g., Hagestad, 1982; Caspi, 1983). Hagestad (1982) has drawn attention to the data gaps between research on young children and their parents and between older people and their middle-aged children. These empirical strands must be bridged if we are to understand the transformation of parent-child relations through individual development and generational change.

Another restriction of the data concerns the limited number of dimensions along which family ties can be explored. We focused primarily on affectional bonds as an indicator of attachment. Yet other important indicators of relationships have been identified; for example, residential propinquity, degree of interaction and assistance, and respect (Troll & Bengtson, 1979). Our failure to treat social ties as a multidimensional construct may account partly for the strength of sex differences in family continuity. Affection may be a highly salient parameter along which to assess women's attachment to family, but not men's.

Interview material was not available on how Depression-reared women (G3) perceived and balanced the claims of individual aspirations and family obligations. Thus, our analyses of hard choices in these women's lives were restricted to their behavior vis à vis education, age at marriage, parenthood, and maternal employment. In contrast, data were available on how their daughters (G4) intended to resolve this dilemma, but we were unable to determine the extent to which their subsequent behavior reflected aspirations in adolescence. The question of how the fulfillment of individual aspirations is modified by the constraints of family obligation and by social options cannot be fully addressed by the data collected to date.

Beyond these limitations, the study provides an overdue temporal perspective with which to view the interrelation of family ties and life chances in women's lives. Instead of viewing this interplay at a single point in time, we have moved as far as possible toward a perspective that views family ties, life chances, and their relationship across the life span and across generations. Among women who were born shortly before the Great Depression (1928–29), we see their affective ties to parents in childhood and again during the middle years. Depression hardship had much to tell us about women's life chances, but limitations of background were soon challenged by their achievements through education and marriage mobility. From an intergenerational standpoint, hardship in this G2 generation shaped both family ties and life chances in the daughter generation (G3); these influences made a difference in the family ties and life opportunities of daughters from the G4 generation. Women who surmounted the barriers of a Depression childhood, through higher education, late marriage, and work experience after the birth of children, were likely to have daughters with ambition; but this transfer was not without cost to mother-daughter ties.

ACKNOWLEDGMENTS

This study is based on a program of research on social change in the family and life course.

Support from the National Institute of Mental Health (Grant MH-34172, Glen H. Elder, Jr., principal investigator) is gratefully acknowledged. The manuscript was prepared during the senior author's Guggenheim Fellowhsip.

We are indebted to the Institute of Human Development (University of California, Berkeley) for permission to use archival data from the Berkeley Guidance Study.

REFERENCES

Adams, B. N. (1968). *Kinship in an urban setting.* Chicago: Markham Press.

Bakke, E. W. (1940). *Citizens without work.* New Haven: Yale University Press.

Bennett, S. K. & Elder, G. H., Jr. (1979). Women's work in the family economy: A study of Depression hardship in women's lives. *Journal of Family History,* 153–176.

Block, J. (1971). *Lives through time.* Berkeley, CA: Bancroft.

Bott, E. (1971). *Family and social network: Roles, norms, and external relationships in ordinary urban families* (2nd ed.), New York: Free Press.

Campbell, D. (1984). *Women at war with America: Private lives in a patriotic era.* Cambridge, MA: Harvard University Press.

Caspi, A. (1983). Parent-child resemblance over the life course: Some comments and data on the study of intergenerational relations. Paper presented at the annual meeting of the American Sociological Association, Detroit.

Eichorn, D. H., Clausen, J., Haan, N., Honzik, M., & Mussen, P. (Eds.) (1981). *Present and past in middle life.* New York: Academic Press.

Elder, G. H., Jr. (1974). *Children of the great depression.* Chicago: University of Chicago Press.

Elder, G. H., Jr. (1979). Historical change in life patterns and personality. In P. Baltes & O. Brim (Eds.), *Life-span development and behavior* (Vol. 2, pp. 117–159). New York: Academic Press.

Elder, G. H., Jr., Caspi, A., & Downey, G. (1985). Problem behavior and family relationships: A multi-generational analysis. In A. Sorensen, F. Weinert, & L. Sherrod (Eds.), *Human development: Interdisciplinary perspectives.* Hillsdale, NJ: Lawrence Erlbaum Associates.

Erikson, E. (1963). *Childhood and society* (2nd ed.). New York: Norton.

Fischer, L. (1981). Transitions in the mother-daughter relationship. *Journal of Marriage and the Family, 43,* 613–622.

Freud, S. (1933). *New introductory lectures.* New York: Norton.

Gilligan, C. (1982). Adult development and women's development: Arrangements for a marriage. In J. Giele (Ed.), *Women in the middle years: Current knowledge and directions for research and policy.* New York: Wiley.

Hagestad, G. O. (1982). The continuous bond: A dynamic, multi-generational perspective on parent-child relations between adults. Presented at the Minnesota Symposium on Child Development, October.

Hareven, T. (1981). *Family time and industrial time.* New York: Cambridge University Press.

Heise, D. (1972). Employing nominal variables, induced variables, and block variables in path analyses. *Sociological Methods and Research, 1,* 147–173.

Hetherington, E. M., Cox, M., & Cox, R. (1981). The aftermath of divorce. In E. M. Hetherginton & R. Parke (Eds.), *Contemporary readings in child psychology* (2nd ed.). New York: McGraw-Hill.

Hill, R., Foote, N., Aldous, J., Carlson, R., & MacDonald, R. (1970). *Family development in three generations.* Cambridge, MA: Schenkman.

Jahoda, M., Lazarsfeld, P. F., & Zeisel, H. (1981). *Marienthal: The sociography of an unemployed community.* New York: Aldine.

Komarovsky, M. (1950). Functional analysis of sex roles. *American Sociological Review, 15,* 508–516.

Komarovsky, M. (1956). Continuities in family research: A case study. *American Journal of Sociology, 62,* 466–469.

Liker, J. K. & Elder, G. H., Jr. (1983). Economic hardship and marital relations in the 1930s. *American Sociological Review, 48,* 343–359.

Maccoby, E. E. & Jacklin, C. (1974). *The psychology of sex differences.* Stanford, CA: Stanford University Press.

Martin, B. (1974). Parent-child relations. In F. D. Horowitz and E. M. Hetherington (Eds.), *Review of child development research*. (Vol. 4). Chicago: The University of Chicago Press.

Mason, K. O., Vinovskis, M. A., & Hareven, T. (1978). Women's work and the life course in Essex County, Massachusetts, 1880. In T. Hareven (Ed.), *Transitions* (pp. 187–216). New York: Academic Press.

Miller, J. B. (1976). *Toward a new psychology of women*. Boston: Beacon Press.

Porter, G. & O'Leary, D. K. (1979). Marital discord and child behavior problems. *Journal of Abnormal Child Psychology, 8,* 287–295.

Rutter, M. (1979). Maternal deprivation, 1972–1978: New findings, new concepts, new approaches. *Child Development, 50,* 283–305.

Spence, J. & Helmreich, R. (1978). *Masculinity and femininity*. Austin: University of Texas Press.

Stack, C. (1974). *All our kin*. New York: Harper & Row.

Troll, L. E. & Bengtson, V. (1979). Generations in the family. In W. Burr, R. Hill, F. I. Nye & I. Reiss (Eds.), *Contemporary theories about the family* (Vol. 1). New York: Free Press.

Troll, L. E. & Smith, J. (1976). Attachment through the life span: Some questions about dyadic bonds among adults. *Human Development, 19,* 156–170.

Young, M. & Willmott, P. (1964). *Family and kinship in East London*. Baltimore: Penguin.

8 The Role of the Family in the Development of Mental Abilities: A 50-year Study[1]

Marjorie P. Honzik
Institute of Human Development
University of California, Berkeley

For over half a century I have been interested in the mental development of infants, children and, in more recent years, adults. My research has been largely analyzing the mental test records of individuals who were tested repeatedly over long periods of time. This chapter presents an overview of what we now know about individual differences in mental growth, based on longitudinal research at the Institute of Human Development at the University of California at Berkeley; at other centers in the United States, such as Fels; and at five research centers in Europe coordinated by the International Children's Center in Paris (Falkner, 1955). The five European longitudinal studies are situated in London, Stockholm, Brussels, Paris and Zurich. These investigations all began in 1955, when the children to be followed were born. The children's physical, mental, and behavioral development was assessed until age 17.

Fifty years ago, when the Berkeley and Fels studies were initiated, we thought we knew a great deal about the development of intelligence. Terman (1919) and others had provided excellent tests that were reliable, and he reported that the test scores were highly predictive over the age periods studied (the average correlation was .93). In other words, he stated that on the basis of the evidence, the IQ is constant. However, an early finding in the field of mental testing was that although the trend is for individuals to maintain their relative positions in the group over time, there are always instances of changes, even marked changes, in scores. These changes do not appear to be

---

[1] An earlier version of this chapter was presented as the Tryon Memorial Lecture at the University of California, Berkeley, November 9, 1983.

random, inasmuch as the gains or losses tended to be maintained for fairly long periods of time.

Before discussing the determinants of individual patterns of mental growth, I would like to report briefly on the group findings for individuals in the several longitudinal studies. My research has been based largely on the Guidance Study. This is one of three longitudinal investigations sponsored by the University of California's Institute of Human Development during the past 50 years. The random sample of 248 children in this long-time study included every third child born in Berkeley in 1928 and in the first six months of 1929. These children were given their first mental test at the Institute at the age of 21 months and were retested at specified ages to age 18 years. They have been tested in recent years at ages 40 and 50 years on versions of the Wechsler Adult Intelligence Scale.

PREDICTION OF 40-YEAR IQS

The first question in a longitudinal study of mental growth is: How well do IQs or mental test scores at an early age predict scores at later ages, for example – at 40 or 50 years? Figure 8.1 provides the answer for the Guidance Study sample. Tests given at 1 3/4 years, or 21 months, do not predict IQs at age 40 years. This is true for both boys and girls. However, prediction increases markedly during the preschool years and, by age six, the correlations are relatively high (approximately .60 for both boys and girls). Results shown in this figure suggest that the girls' IQs are more predictive of their 40-year IQs than are the boys' during the early preschool years (2–4), and then the boys catch up. This finding is discussed in more detail later in this chapter.

We have not yet drawn a figure showing the prediction of the 50-year IQs, but we can report that the correlations between the 40- and 50-year IQs are very high: .88 for the women and .89 for the men.

Cross-validation

Figure 8.2 provides cross validation of the results reported in the first figure. Results in three different studies are compared. Prediction of IQs at 8 years from IQs obtained at earlier ages is shown for the Guidance Study, the Stockholm study mentioned earlier (Klackenberg-Larsson & Stensson, 1968), and the Berkeley Growth Study directed by Nancy Bayley (1949) at the Institute until she retired. The results are very similar in all investigations, despite the fact that the children in the Stockholm study not only were born in a different country, but were born more than 25 years later than the children in the two Berkeley samples.

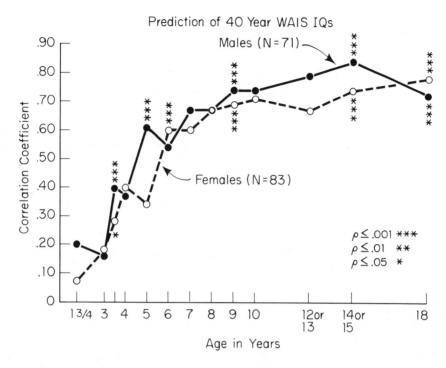

FIG. 8.1   Correlations showing prediction of 40-year IQs from IQs obtained at earlier ages.

INFANT TESTS

Long-term prediction from tests given in infancy is negligible. Nancy Bayley pioneered her intensive study of mental growth during the first few years of life. There were approximately 70 children in the Berkeley Growth Study sample. These children were given their first test at 1 month and were retested every month of the 1st year and then at increasingly longer intervals until age 40 years, when they received the same Wechsler test as the Guidance Group. The fact that infant test scores are not related to test scores of older children and adults suggests that they are unreliable and lack validity. However, the more likely explanation is that prediction is limited during periods of very rapid growth. Actually, there has been remarkable cross validation of Bayley's findings in other longitudinal studies, which attests to both the reliability and the validity of her findings. For example, Bayley reported a correlation of .57 between test scores on her test (Bayley Scale of Infant Development) at 3 and 6 months. In the Stockholm Study, the correlation for the same age period (using the Brunet-Lezine infant test) was .51 (Klackenberg-

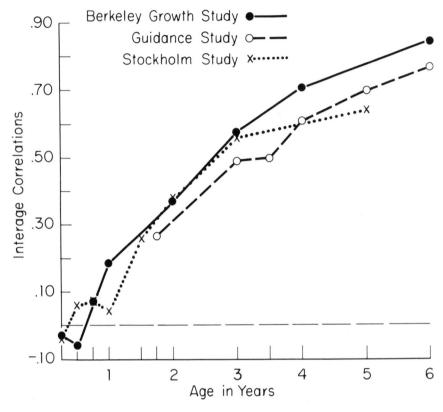

FIG. 8.2   Prediction of 8-year mental test scores from test scores given at earlier ages in the Berkeley Growth Study, Guidance Study, and Stockholm Study.

Larsson & Stensson, 1968). Hindley (1965) in London, using the Griffiths Scale, reports a correlation of .53 for this same 3- to 6-month period. In other words, testers using three different tests in different parts of the world at different time periods all find that the correlation between tests given at 3 and 6 months range from .51 to .57 (Honzik, 1983).

FACTORS RELATED TO IQ CHANGES BETWEEN 2 AND 40 YEARS

The next question concerns the factors related to changes in mental test scores. These factors may suggest a genetic basis or the effects of experience. Table 8.1 shows the age changes in the correlations between the years of schooling of the parents and the children's mental test scores at successive ages. This table notes an increase with age in the correlations of the children's test scores and parental education. Further, the correlations become statistically significant for the girls at age 3, but not until age 5 for the boys.

Parental education appears to be an environmental variable, but Fig. 8.3 suggests a somewhat different interpretation. Figure 8.3 compares the increasing relationship of the mother's education and the child's mental test performance in the Guidance Group with that obtained in the Skodak-Skeels Study of Adopted Children (Honzik, 1957). In both studies, the education of the biological mother is increasingly related with age to the test scores of her child. Note that the children in the Guidance Study were living with their biological parents whereas the children in the Skodak-Skeels Study had been adopted in the first year of life (Skodak & Skeels, 1949). The adopted children's IQs do not show a significant relationship to the adoptive parents' education. This finding suggests that the basis for the correlation between the education of the mother and the children's test scores is biological rather than environmental. Education, occupational status, all measures of socioeconomic status, and the intelligence of the parents are intercorrelated at statistically highly significant levels (Eichorn, Hunt, & Honzik, 1981). Thus the increasing correlation between the education of the parents and the children's IQs is most probably a function of the relationship of the intelligence of the parents to the children's IQ. The strong environmental influence of the

TABLE 8.1
Correlations Between the Child's IQ X Parental
Education: Guidance Study

Age in years	N cases		Parental Education X Child's IQ	
	Boys	Girls	Boys' R	Girls' R
1¾	109	114	.00	.17
3	110	113	.12	.33**
3½	105	109	.24	.33**
4	105	107	.17	.36**
5	101	109	.41**	.34**
6	102	112	.25	.44**
7	101	107	.36**	.44**
8	94	104	.37**	.41**
9	93	102	.41**	.42**
10	95	102	.32**	.41**
12 or 13	92	100	.42**	.42**
14 or 15	83	85	.46**	.33**

**$p < .01$

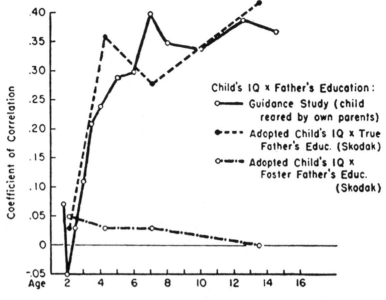

EDUCATION OF FATHER IN RELATION TO CHILD'S I.Q.

Child's IQ × Father's Education:

o—— Guidance Study (child
       reared by own parents)

●----● Adopted Child's IQ × True
       Father's Educ. (Skodak)

o—·—● Adopted Child's IQ ×
       Foster Father's Educ.
       (Skodak)

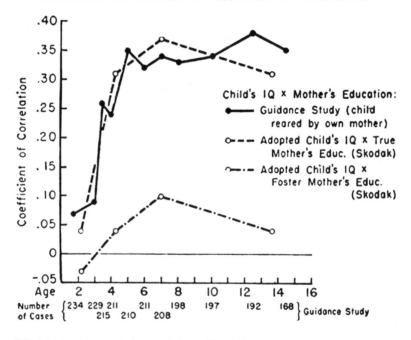

EDUCATION OF MOTHER IN RELATION TO CHILD'S I.Q.

Child's IQ × Mother's Education:

●—— Guidance Study (child
       reared by own mother)

o——— Adopted Child's IQ × True
       Mother's Educ. (Skodak)

o—·— Adopted Child's IQ ×
       Foster Mother's Educ.
       (Skodak)

Number of Cases { 234 229 211   211   198   197   192   168 } Guidance Study
               215   210   208

FIG. 8.3 Age changes in the correlations of the child's IQ with the level of education of both the true and foster parents in the Skodak-Skeels study of adopted children and the true parents in the Guidance Study.

adopting parents is indicated by the fact that the average IQ of the adopted children is 106 in contrast with the average of 86 of their biological mothers: These educated and concerned adopting parents had raised the average IQ of the children they had adopted by 20 IQ points. This figure indicates the effects of both heredity and the environment: The correlations showing the same increasing resemblance between the biological parents and children, regardless of whether or not the children were living with their parents, suggests a genetic effect whereas the relatively high average IQs of the adopted children is a function of the environment. Before we present the many environmental variables that are correlated with the mental test scores of the children, the sex differences noted earlier are discussed.

SEX DIFFERENCES

Is there precocity and a real sex difference in mental development during the period of the acquisition of language? The suggestion of a sex difference in Fig. 8.1, is more noticeable in Table 1. The difference in the age of onset of parent-child resemblance has also been reported by Hindley (1965) and by Moore (1968). We decided to look specifically at the sex differences in the test scores of the Guidance Study sample during the preschool years (Table 8.2). In this table the average scores of the boys and girls on their preschool tests are compared. The California Preschool Scale was given to the preschool aged children in the Berkeley studies. Many children had been tested in the standardization of this test, but the scale was never published because the standardization sample was not a random one and was not representative of preschool children all over the United States. The test forms, however, may be seen in Macfarlane's monograph (1938). The test items were divided into categories for each of which it was possible to obtain a test score: Motor Skill, Block Building, Language Facility, and so on. Table 8.2 summarizes the average sex differences that were statistically significant for each of the 10 tested categories at successive age periods. We note that at 21 months, the girls' scores are, on average, significantly higher than those of the boys on four subtests: Language Comprehension, Language Facility, Memory and Completions. On the 2-year test, the girls' scores are significantly higher than those of the boys on six of the 10 categories. At 30 months a highpoint of seven significant differences favoring the girls is reached. At age levels 3 and 3 1/2, there are five significant differences but at 4 years only two. Finally, at age 5, the boys catch up and pass the girls with three significant differences, including language facility. At 5 years, the girls excel only on motor skill and memory. Sex differences after the preschool years are modest and not statistically significant, sometimes favoring the girls and sometimes the boys. Eichorn et al (1981) report that the sex differences on the Full Scale IQ on the

TABLE 8.2
Significant Sex DIFFERENCES in Mental Test Scores During the Preschool Years
Guidance Group

California Preschool Scale Variables	Age: 1¾ N: 91 Boy	Girl	2 85 Boy	Girl	2½ 84 Boy	Girl	3 85 Boy	Girl	3½ 79 Boy	Girl	4 74 Boy	Girl	5 yrs 74 Boy	Girl
Motor Skill	—	—	—	—	—	*	—	***	—	***	—	***	—	***
Block Building	—	—	—	*	—	—	—	—	—	**	—	—	**	—
Drawing	—	—	—	*	—	—	—	—	—	—	—	—	*	—
Discriminates Forms	—	—	—	—	—	**	—	*	—	—	—	—	—	—
Discriminates Spatial Relations	—	—	—	—	—	*	—	—	—	**	—	*	—	—
Discriminates	—	—	—	**	—	*	—	*	—	—	—	—	—	—
Number and Size	—	*	—	—	—	*	—	—	—	—	—	—	—	—
Language Comprehension	—	—	—	***	—	***	—	—	—	—	—	—	—	—
Language Facility	—	***	—	***	—	*	—	***	—	**	—	—	**	—
Memory	—	***	—	—	—	—	—	**	—	**	—	—	—	—
Completions	—	***	—	***	—	—	—	**	—	**	—	—	—	—
Number, Significant Differences	—	4	—	6	—	7	—	5	—	5	—	2	3	2

*p < .10
**p < .05
***p < .01

Wechsler Adult Intelligence Scale at ages 40 to 48 years were not significant in two of the longitudinal samples (the Guidance Study and the Berkeley Growth Study). The men's scores in the third sample, the Oakland Growth Study, were significantly higher than those of the women because of an unusual number of low-scoring women.

The small sex difference in mental development favoring the girls during the preschool years may be comparable to the more marked sex difference in age of physical maturing in adolescence. The sex difference in the age of onset of the growth spurt in height in boys and girls is 2 years. The sex difference in language acquisition is minor by comparison. It has been argued that the reason for this sex difference is that mothers or caretakers are more responsive to girl than to boy babies (Kagan, 1971). Scarr's theory may have some relevance here. She believes that the genotype determines to some extent one's environment (Scarr & McCartney, 1983). In other words, she might argue that the slightly more mature and vocal baby girl evokes more responses from people than does her brother at the same age. The important point may be that she evokes more responses because she has 2 X-chromosomes.

EXPERIENCE IN RELATION TO THE CHILD'S IQ

Levy (1981) wrote recently that no aspect of an organism is wholly a function of its genes or wholly a function of its environment. There is a constant interplay between the two that governs development.

We have noted our work comparing the parent-child correlation for biological and adopted children (Honzik, 1957). Our next objective was to determine the effects of experience on mental growth by correlating certain family variables with the children's test scores at successive ages.

When the children in the Guidance Group were 21 months old, ratings of the family situation were obtained on the basis of interviews with the parents and observations of the children in their homes and at the Institute. Dr. Macfarlane, who interviewed the parents, and the social worker who made the home visits both rated each family on characteristics of the parents and aspects of the interaction between each parent and the study child. Weighted averages of these ratings are the values used in correlating aspects of the family situation with the children's mental test scores at successive ages. These correlations were higher than expected. Concerned that they were in some way spurious, I did not publish my findings (Honzik, 1967) for almost 10 years — until after Dr. Bayley wrote her monograph with Earl Schaefer revealing similar findings using a different methodology in assessing the Berkeley Growth Study sample (Bayley & Schaefer, 1964). Within a year after I had published my paper, Moore (1968) published a paper with the same title and similar findings based on the London sample.

What did we find? Again, a rather marked sex difference was seen in the parental correlates of mental growth in the Guidance Study. The parental ratings assigned before the children were 2 years often show an increasing relationship to IQs of the children over the years. The girls' IQs are increasingly correlated with aspects of the home situation: adequacy of play facilities in the home, marital compatibility and various assessments of a lack of conflict in the home (e.g., lack of conflict about relatives, religion, finances, use of leisure time and the discipline of the children; Fig. 8.4, 8.5, and 8.6). The girls' IQs are also increasingly related with age to the father's concern about health. We believe that the father who is concerned about his daughter's health is also concerned about other aspects of her development and probably interacts with her more and is more intellectually stimulating than the father who is not concerned about the health of his daughter.

The son's IQ is increasingly correlated with 21-month ratings of the energy level of the mother, and with both the father's and the mother's concern

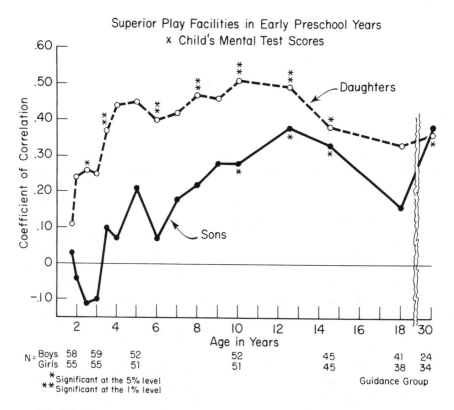

FIG. 8.4   Superior play facilities in early preschool years correlated with child's later mental test scores.

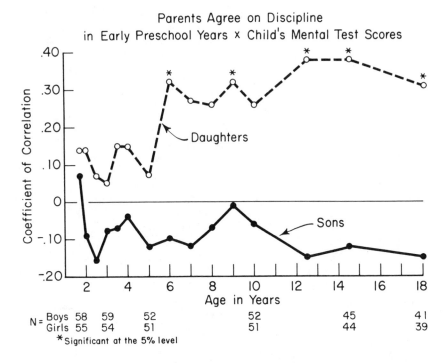

FIG. 8.5 Parents' agreement on discipline in early preschool years correlated with child's later mental test scores.

about educational achievement (Fig. 8.7, 8.8, and 8.9). The increasing correlations of the boys' IQs with parental concern about educational achievement is understandable. The correlations for the mother are higher than those for the father. Possibly the basis for the increasing correlations of the son's IQ with the energy level of the mother is that the energetic mother is probably more interactive and stimulating to her son than the mother who has little energy with which to cope and respond. The last figure in this series interests me a great deal because the closeness of the mother to her son (at age 21 months) is seen to have relatively high correlations with the son's IQ at 18 years, and we know that this early closeness of mother and son is still significantly correlated with Verbal Abilities on the WAIS at age 40 ($r = .36$). We interpret this relationship to mean that during the period of language acquisition, the close relationship of mother and son probably provides a good learning situation for the boy during at least the first 21 months of life.

In the years since these data were first analyzed, cross validation, and to some extent replication, has occurred. Yarrow, Goodwin, Manheimer, and Milowe (1973) have written about the importance of play objects for the infant and young child. And many studies have reported the relevance of

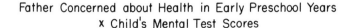

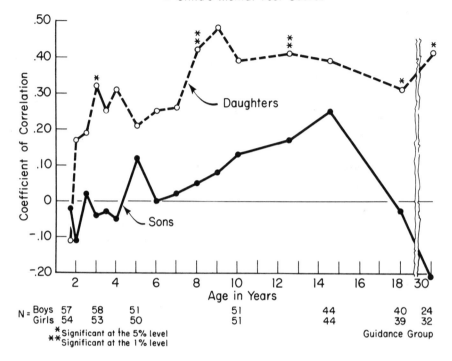

FIG. 8.6   Father concerned about child's health in early preschool years correlated with child's later mental test scores.

the parenting of the infant and young child to mental growth (Bradley & Caldwell, 1980; Thoman, 1981; Yarrow, Goodwin, Manheimer, & Milowe, 1973).

Certain of the parental correlates of mental development indicates that boys and girls are differentially affected by what seems to be the same environments. In the Guidance Study, the girls' mental development appears to be enhanced when the environment is not conflicted, that is, when the parents generally agree in many of the areas where there could be conflict. An important finding is that the closeness of the mother to her son is significantly correlated with the son's mental test scores during childhood and even correlates significantly with the son's Verbal IQ on the WAIS at age 40. The longitudinal studies reveal that boys tend to be more responsive to experiences than girls. The rating of closeness of mother and son is not related to the mother's education or intelligence, so that the ability of the mother is not a mediating factor.

Moss and Kagan (1958) wrote: "When the female child is given sufficient latitude (in terms of not being restricted) she is able to exhibit greater developmental progress as measured by the Stanford-Binet" (p. 660). Bayley and Schaefer (1964) came to a similar conclusion when they found that the mother's intrusiveness is negatively related to the daughter's test scores in the Berkeley Growth Study. In line with this finding are our correlations showing that the girls' IQs are related to an absence of conflict in the home, that is, when the parents are compatible and agree on such topics as relatives, religion, use of leisure time, and discipline of the children.

In summary, we find that certain family variables assessed before the child is 2 are predictive of mental growth. Since these family variables are unrelated to parental ability, we assume that their influence is environmental.

Subsequent to this first evaluation of the family situation when the child was aged 21 months, the family situation was assessed again at yearly intervals when the children were aged 5 through 16 years. These individual ratings

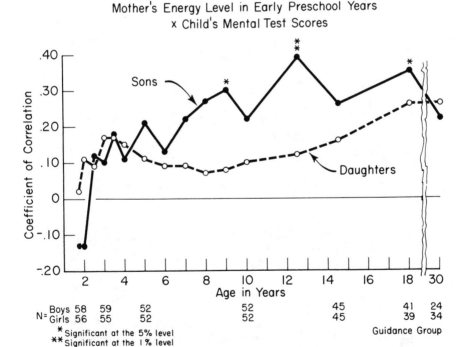

FIG. 8.7 Mother's energy level in early preschool years correlated with child's later mental test scores.

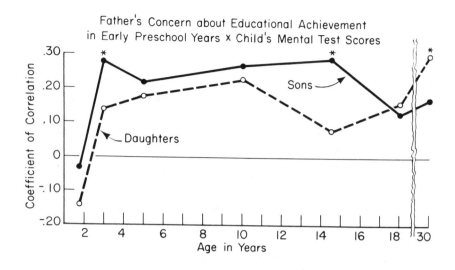

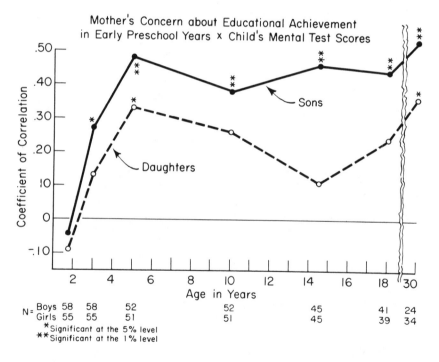

FIG. 8.8   Parents' concern about educational achievement in early preschool years correlated with child's later mental test scores.

Close Bond between Mother and Child
in Early Preschool Years x Child's Mental Test Scores

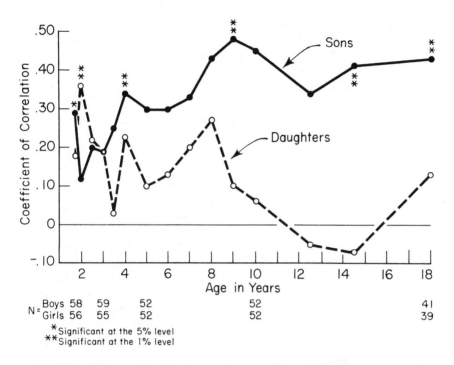

FIG. 8.9 Closeness of bond between parents and child in early preschool years correlated with child's later mental test scores.

are reasonably consistent over adjacent age periods, indicating a fair degree
of reliability. One of the issues we address in this paper is the comparative importance of the early versus the later family milieu on intellectual development. A gross count of the number of significant relationships at succeeding
ages indicates that the early family interactions have a greater impact.

EARLY ADULT YEARS

So far, we have been discussing the long-range effects of parenting on the
IQ during childhood. Our next question concerns the stability and change in
IQ that occurs during the adult years between 18 and 40. When we were giving the WAIS to 40-year-old participants in the Institute's three longitudinal
studies, they would frequently say "they had forgotten all they knew" and
that their teenaged children knew the answers to the test questions but they

did not. These middle-aged adults were wrong on both counts. They were not only earning higher scores than they had at 18 years but they were also obtaining higher scores than their adolescent children. We have tried to determine the factors in the lives of these adults that led to an average increase in IQ of about 6.5 IQ points between ages 18 and 40 (Eichorn, Hunt, & Honzik, 1981). Correlational analysis did not yield significant relationships between changes in IQ during the early adult years and such environmental variables as the quality of their educational experience, marital adjustment, or number of children. We therefore decided to look at the characteristics of the study members who showed the most marked changes in IQ between 18 years and 40. The cutoff point was the 11% who showed the greatest declines and the 11% who showed the greatest gains in IQ between 18 and 40 years. We were surprised at the clearcut results obtained. There was a disproportionate incidence of heavy alcohol consumption, debilitating illness, and depression among the IQ decreasers; and there was little evidence in the case histories that these study members had enjoyed many stimulating experiences between 18 and 40. In contrast, the increasers were more likely to be married to spouses whose adult IQs were at least 10 points higher than the study members' IQs at adolescence. Many of the increasers had traveled outside the United States, and none was a heavy consumer of alcohol. Factors that contributed to IQ increases were not always happy ones. One study member whose IQ increased quite markedly had a handicapped child, which meant she had to work with many professional persons to help her child. We believe that this deep involvement in solving multiple problems contributed to her increase in IQ. We found that the characteristics of the increasers and decreasers in IQ during early adulthood were very similar for the men and women in all three of the Institute's longitudinal studies. There has been a proliferation of studies showing the beneficial effects of a stimulating environment on the mental growth of children. Studies of the effects of an enriched experience on the mental test scores of adults are fewer in number.

THE LATER ADULT YEARS

There is one highly relevant study that Schaie (1983) has been conducting in Seattle for the past 25 years. His study (whose oldest subjects are now aged 81) supplements our findings for the early adult years. Schaie's (1983) longitudinal study of age changes in cognitive behavior is based on tests given to random samples of adults who are members of a cooperative health maintenance organization. These adults, ranging in age from 22 to 81, are tested every 7 years. To date, more than 2,000 persons have been studied over periods ranging from 7 to 21 years. Thurstone's Primary Mental Abilities are the tests used.

Comparing the average change in scores over the various age periods, Schaie (1983) reports that statistically significant age decrements are first noted during the 6th decade of life. He reports that peak ability levels are reached at 53 years for verbal meaning and at age 46 for tests of spatial orientation, inductive reasoning, number and word fluency. He found that, on average, men decline most on number and spatial orientation, and least on inductive reasoning and word fluency; women decline most on word fluency and least on spatial orientation. These are surprising findings, because they suggest that the declines are most likely to occur on those tests on which the men and women excelled respectively at earlier age periods. As Schaie says, averages can be misleading. When he looked at the percentage of increase over the various age periods, he found that there were always some individuals who showed gains in score, but the percentage showing decrements increased with age. On the other hand, there were some adults showing gains from their peak age of performance to age 81, which is the last age tested so far. Schaie also considered the predictive value of people's life style. He found that the fewest declines over 7-year periods were made by persons of high socio-economic status who were fully engaged in interactions with their environment. Persons showing the greatest declines were those with a "rather disengaged life style."

Schaie (1983) concludes: "It is apparent that those who would wish to maintain a high level of functioning in old age must be concerned with not only the efficiency of their physical selves, but also take care to maintain flexible behaviors and attitudes, to remain involved in a broad spectrum of intellectually stimulating activities and in particular to 'practice' their problem solving activities." Fortunately, Schaie says, recent research has shown that some of the observed cognitive losses can be reversed through behavioral intervention. The behavioral research he is referring to is Willis, Blieszner, and Baltes' (1981) studies at Penn State University, where older persons are being given special training in problem solving tasks. They enjoy the training, and the findings are that their cognitive skills are definitely improved.

INTERGENERATIONAL PARENTING STUDY

Our first study of environmental correlates of mental growth yielded so many significant correlations with the children's mental test scores that it seemed important that a more systematic study of parenting effects be undertaken. The idea was that a parenting scale should be devised that could be used at all age periods to measure both supportive and stressful parenting. Fortunately, Professor Mary Main also had an interest in both the long-range and intergenerational effects of parenting, so we have collaborated in an investigation based on rating the archival data in all three longitudinal studies at the Institute of Human Development on the same rating scale. Independent assessments are made by highly qualified raters at specific age periods, such as birth to 23 months, 2–5 years, 6–10 years, and early and late adolescence. Each rater sees and assigns ratings to only one age segment of the case history. Every age period is rated independently by two raters. At present, assessments by only one rater are available for study. We have determined that these first ratings are reliable, and have used them for a few preliminary analyses. In this study, we have not only the records of the parenting of the study members but also of their parenting of the next generation of children. These data thus provide an opportunity to discover whether patterns of parenting persist from one generation to the next. To the extent that we have analyzed our data, we find that parents who have experienced stressful parenting themselves are more likely to become stressful parents of their children.

The analyses performed thus far include a first look at the stability of parenting during childhood as well as the recall of parenting experiences during childhood, when the study members were aged 30 and 40 years. We have also determined the parenting variables that correlate with the IQs of the study members at ages 40 and 50 years.

Stability of the Parenting Ratings

The parenting rating scale includes not only assessments of parent-child relationships, but also variables describing the home situation such as marital compatibility, the emotional tone of the family (somber–happy), sociability of the home, coordination of the household, and child centeredness of the home.

To date we have correlated the ratings for the 2–5 age period with all later age periods. We find that the variables describing the home situation, such as marital compatibility, tend to be more stable than many of the parent-child relationships. The emotional tone of the family (somber–happy or cold–warm) is also relatively stable all through childhood, that is, from two to 18 years. Even the recall of the emotional tone of the family when the study member was 30 and 40 years of age was significantly related to the 2–5 year ratings based on the archives.

The number of significant stability correlations obtained when parenting ratings for the age period 2–5 were correlated with the later ages of childhood are similar for the boys and girls, but many more men recalled at age 30 and 40 years both the emotional support and stressful parenting of their fathers during the preschool years than was true for the women. This sex difference is so marked that a more intensive study of this difference appears warranted. This does not appear to be a chance finding, because the results are similar for ratings based on both the 30th-year and the 40th-year interviews. In other words, the study members were interviewed by different psychologists at ages 30 and 40, and different raters made the assessments. That the recall of the 30- and 40-year-old men, and (to a lesser extent) women, agrees with the observations and ratings made when these study members were preschool aged children, is of general interest, and encouraging to research workers and clinicians who often have to rely on the retrospective reports of their clients and research subjects.

Prediction of 40-Year IQs from Parenting Assessments During Childhood and Adolescence

In our earlier study we found that certain family variables assessed when the children were less than two years correlated significantly with their IQs during childhood. In the present study of parenting rated during the childhood years, we find that the home of the boy who has a high IQ as an adult was not noticeably warm, happy or child-centered during his childhood (5 to 10 years) and adolescent years. However, the mother was concerned about her son and encouraged self-control. Discipline was consistent. Intellectual and social achievements were encouraged by the parents of the high IQ boys during the preschool years and late adolescence, but apparently not during the age period 6 to 14 years.

In the first study of environmental correlates of IQ, marital compatibility was significantly related to the girls' IQ during childhood (Honzik, 1967). In the present study, the parenting variables of the girls that correlate with their 40- and 50-year IQs differ from those of the boys. Marital adjustment of the parents continues to correlate with the women's 40-year IQs, as does a variable called coordination of the household rated at all age periods from infancy to 18 years. Other parental correlates of the girls' 40-year IQs are: mother cares for the needs of her child; rules are fully enforced; parents encourage self-control but are also controlling of their daughter; discipline is consistent; intellectual and social achievements are encouraged.

Patterns of Stability and Change in Mental Test Performance

Of great interest in the study of mental growth are the individual patterns of mental test scores from infancy to middle age. Individual differences in these curves are marked, with very few children or adults maintaining the same position or score over long periods of time (Hindley, 1981).

Various methods have been used to group these curves into meaningful clusters. In the British longitudinal study, Hindley and Owen (1979) fitted polynomial equations to each subject's curve over the period six months to 17 years. These curves differed, not only in linear slopes, but also in degree and form of curvilinearity particularly over longer age periods. The investigators also used a visual method of classification that they said proved effective. Hindley and Owen concluded from their analyses that changes in IQ scores cannot be regarded as random variations but, rather, as following systematic trends that differ between subjects.

McCall, Applebaum and Hogarty (1973) reported the results of clustering the Fels longitudinal records. Sheri Berenbaum and I, assisted by Professor William Meredith, followed the same method as McCall in clustering the mental growth curves of the Guidance Study cases. The procedure involves a principal component analysis based on the table of intercorrelations of the mental test scores extending in the Guidance Study from 21 months to 40 years. Two major components were obtained, accounting for 78% of the variance in the interage matrix. In order to obtain a meaningful interpretation of these two components, a varimax rotation was performed. The two factors were named Early Mental Growth (Fig. 8.10) and Late Mental Growth (Fig. 8.11). Overall, and Klett's clustering method was used and two clusters obtained. Figure 8.12 shows the average mental test scores of the cases included in each of the two clusters. Cluster 1 is impressive in indicating that most of the gains in the mental test scores for the cases in this cluster occurred in the first 5 years. Scores for the age period 6 to 40 years are relatively stable. Cluster 2 is of interest because of the steadiness of the decline in scores. The decline is more rapid during the preschool years but continues to age 14. The average test scores of these cases are relatively stable between 14 and 40 years.

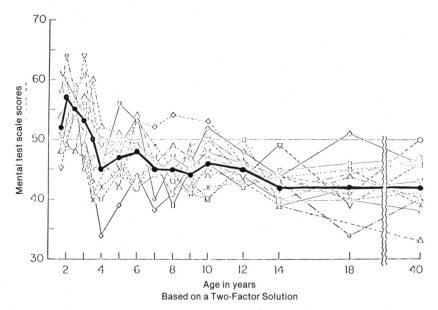

Based on a Two-Factor Solution

FIG. 8.10   Mental growth curves of individuals with high scores on the first factor of a 2-factor solution: early mental growth.

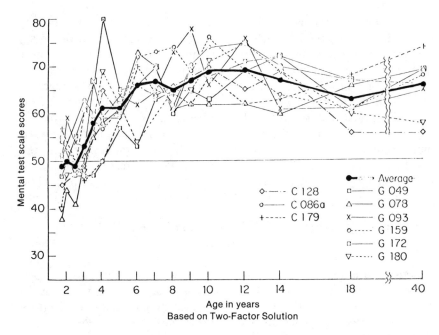

FIG. 8.11   Mental growth curves of individuals with high scores on the second factor of a 2-factor solution: late mental growth.

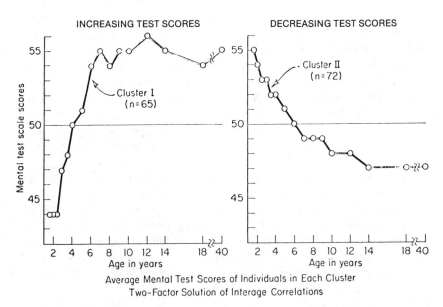

FIG. 8.12   Average mental test scores of individuals in clusters I and II based on a 2-factor solution of interage correlations.

We believe that the parenting scale that has been described will be very helpful in showing the pattern of parenting that corresponds with the age changes in test scores in the clusters of mental test curves. In fact, it was in part to relate changes in parenting to changes in mental test scores that the parenting project was undertaken. What we plan to do is to find average parenting patterns for the different clusters of subjects. We might expect from the correlational analyses greater changes in the pattern of parenting for boys for whom the correlates of a high adult IQ change from a relatively warm mother-child interaction in infancy to relatively authoritative parenting during the preschool and school years. The father's indifference and seeming lack of interest in his highly intelligent son may in some ways be helpful because it leaves the boy freer to solve his own problems.

MENTAL GROWTH CURVES OF TWO GIRLS AND TWO BOYS

The great variation in the mental growth patterns of individuals is clearly shown when relatively extreme cases of stability and change in mental test performance are compared. Figure 8.13 presents the mental test records of four individuals who were studied over a period of 50 years.

Case 534 is unusual, in fact unique, in the stability of test scores from age 21 months to 50 years. At all ages, her scores are approximately two standard deviations above the means of the group. Stability of test performance in the later years of childhood is to be expected, but prediction from a test given at 21 months is seldom accurate. On the first test at 21 months, case 534 came in with her mother, who was supportive but not intrusive during the test session. Case 534 was extremely interested in all the test material and the challenge of the problems to be solved. She would lean forward as each test item was completed and say, "More, more." Case 534's interest has continued through the years. Even at age 50, she was pleased when the time came for her test. All members of the family have superior mental abilities and are graduates of prestigious universities. Case 534's parents were always supportive but never exploitive. The children of this women have earned similarly high scores on all tests.

In contrast to case 534, case 567's score at 21 months was two standard deviations below the mean, but by age 40 her score was two standard deviations above the mean. On the 21-month test, she was uncooperative and her mother's responses to the irritable behavior were not helpful. Case 567's life experiences have not been as supportive and stable as those of 534, and she refused to come in for the 50-year followup of interviews and tests. One wonders if this woman would have shown greater stability in test performance if she had been reared in a more supportive and stable environment. It seems probable that the volatile temperaments of the members of this family are important determinants of their reactions to all situations, including test taking.

Case 557 is the much loved son of a very affectionate and happy family. His above average test scores at 21 months possibly reflect the warmth of the responses of the family to this boy. His later test scores are in line with the family pattern of abilities. This boy has good mechanical ability and is perhaps the friendliest man in the study. He knows and cares a great deal about all his former classmates in high school and looks forward to class reunions. He has made a good living, and his outgoing, friendly manner has probably contributed to his success. He cares a great deal about his family and they hold him in high regard, as evidenced by his 6-year-old son's drawing of the family. His father was placed not only in the middle of the family group but

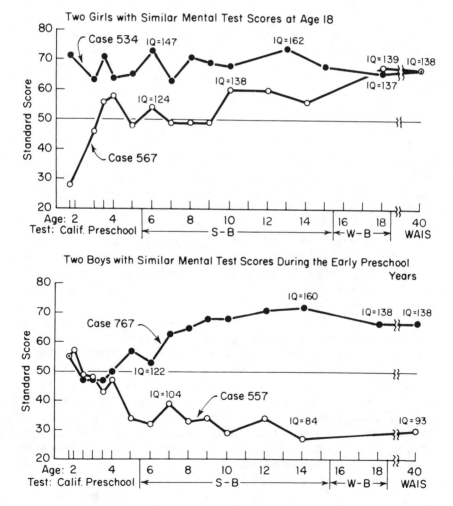

FIG. 8.13   Mental growth curves of two boys and two girls.

standing higher than the rest on a little mound. The boy positioned himself next to his father.

Case 767 is in many ways the most interesting of the four. He was the first son in the family and had a close relationship to his mother in his early years. Life for him became more difficult as he grew older. He had a low energy level, and his mother became somewhat overbearing and intrusive. She encouraged self-control but was restrictive and critical of him, as she was of his father. Both father and son withdrew but did not interact with each other. Case 767 was not physically robust and would often be observed to be idle, (e.g., sitting on the sidewalk). Clearly, there was enough stimulation from school, church and the family so that his mental development was superior. High test scores are in line with the parents' IQs. It was always thought that this young man would marry a quiet young woman who would not threaten him unduly, but instead he married a very vigorous, outgoing woman who is deeply fond and considerate of him. They have many children, to whom both parents are devoted. All the children have superior mental abilities, and have been unusually successful as young adults.

SUMMARY

The longitudinal studies provide the opportunity to observe not only the changes that occur in the development of mental abilities over a lifetime, but also the relation of certain factors to these changes. We note that children increasingly resemble their parents during the first 6 or 7 years of life. Since adopted children show the same changes in relation to their biological parents, we assume that genetic factors determine these changes.

The findings of a number of longitudinal studies suggest a modest sex difference in the early development of mental abilities. The girls are somewhat more precocious than the boys during the early preschool years. We believe that this difference is sufficiently great so that a slight difference in the age of entry to what the children call real school (in contrast to nursery school) should be considered. Let the girls go first!

We also observe differences in the environmental correlates of mental growth. The boy's IQ will likely be higher in later childhood and adulthood if during the first years he lives in a family where he has a close relationship to the mother or other caretaker who will listen and respond to him while his verbal skills are being learned. In contrast, girls' mental abilities appear to flourish in a family atmosphere that is nonintrusive (Bayley & Schaefer, 1964) and if she is given sufficient latitude (in terms of not being restricted) according to Moss and Kagan (1958). In the Guidance Study, a similar phenomenon was noted: the women's IQs at age 40 are correlated with parental capability and a relative absence of conflict between the parents in early childhood. In other words, a serene, well-ordered home where independence and intellectual interests are encouraged are the family variables observed in early childhood that are related to girls' adult IQ. Aspects of parenting during childhood that are related to high IQ in adulthood for both males and females include parental control, encouragement of self-control and self-reliance, firm enforcement of rules in the home and consistent discipline. Parental encouragement of both intellectual and social achievement during childhood is also significantly related to high IQ in the adult years.

Those are the group findings. What about the individuals? We believe that new insights about mental growth will be obtained from a more extensive study of the relation of the total trajectory of parenting to the children's test records. Although mental abilities are important, we note in studying individual cases that other attributes such as social skills, creativity or empathy may be even more important in the lives of these middle-aged people.

REFERENCES

Bayley, N. (1949). Consistency and variability in the growth of intelligence from birth to eighteen years. *Journal of Genetic Psychology, 75,* 165–196.

Bayley, N., & Schaefer, E. S. (1964). Correlations of maternal and child behaviors with the development of mental abilities: Data from the Berkeley Growth Study. *Monographs of the Society for Research in Child Development, 29*(6, Whole No. 97).

Bradley, R. H., & Caldwell, B. M. (1980). The relation of home environment, cognitive competence, and IQ among males and females. *Child Development, 51,* 1140–1148.

Eichorn, D. H., Hunt, J. V., & Honzik, M. P. (1981). Experience, personality and IQ: Adolescence to middle age. In D. H. Eichorn, J. A. Clausen, N. Haan, M. P. Honzik, & P. Mussen (Eds.). *Present and past in middle life.* New York: Academic Press.

Falkner, F. (Ed.). (1955). *Une base commune de recherches pour les études longitudinales sur les croissance de l'enfant.* (A baseline for longitudinal investigations of growth studies in the child). Published in English and French. Paris: Centre International de l'Enfance.

Hindley, C. B. (1965). Stability and change in abilities up to five years: Group trends. *Journal of Child Psychology and Psychiatry, 6,* 85–100.

Hindley, C. B. (1981). Individual differences in the patterning of curves of D.Q. and I.Q. scores from 6 months to 17 years. In M. P. Friedman, J. P. Das, & W. O'Connor (Eds.), *Intelligence and learning.* New York: Plenum Press.

Hindley, C. B., & Owen, C. F. (1979). An analysis of individual changes in IQ for ages between 6 months and seventeen years. *British Journal of Psychology, 70,* 273–293.

Honzik, M. P. (1957). Developmental studies of parent-child resemblance in intelligence. *Child Development, 28,* 215–228.

Honzik, M. P. (1967). Environmental correlates of mental growth: Prediction from the family setting at 21 months. *Child Development, 38,* 337–363.

Honzik, M. P. (1983). Measuring mental abilities in infancy: The value and limitations. In M. Lewis (Ed.), *Origins of intelligence: Infancy and early childhood* (2nd ed.). New York: Plenum Press.

Kagan, J. (1971). *Change and continuity in infancy.* New York: Wiley.

Klackenberg-Larsson, I., & Stensson, J. (1968). The development of children in a Swedish urban community. A prospective longitudinal study. IV. Data on the mental development during the first five years of life. *Acta Paediatricia Scandinavica* (Suppl. 187), 28–47.

Levy, J. (1981). Lateralization and its implications for variation in development. In E. S. Gollin (Ed.), *Developmental plasticity and biological aspects of variations in development.* New York: Academic Press.

Macfarlane, J. W. (1938). Studies in child guidance methodology of data collection and organization. *Monographs of the Society for Research in Child Development, 3*(6).

McCall, R. B., Applebaum, M., & Hogarty, P. S. (1973). Developmental changes in mental performance. *Monographs of the Society for Research in Child Development. 150.*

Moore, T. (1967). Language and intelligence: A longitudinal study of the first eight years. Part I: Developmental patterns of boys and girls. *Human Development, 10,* 88–106.

Moore, T. (1968). Language and intelligence: A longitudinal study of the first eight years. Part II: Environmental correlates of mental growth. *Human Development, 11,* 1–24.

Moss, H. A., & Kagan, J. (1958). Maternal influences on early IQ scores. *Psychological Reports, 4,* 655–661.

Scarr, S. & McCartney, K. (1983). How people make their own environments: A theory of genotype-environment effects. *Child Development, 54:* 424–35.

Schaie, K. W. (1983). *Midlife influences upon intellectual functions in old age.* Paper presented at the biennial meeting of the International Society for the Study of Behavioral Development. Munich, Federal Republic of Germany.

Skodak, M., & Skeels, H. M. (1949). A final follow-up of one hundred adopted children. *Journal of Genetic Psychology, 75,* 85–125.

Terman, L. M. (1919). *The intelligence of school children: How children differ in ability, the use of mental tests in school grading, and the proper education of exceptional children.* Boston: Houghton-Mifflin.

Thoman, E. B. (1981). Early communication as the prelude to later adaptive behavior. In M. J. Begab, H. Garber, & H. C. Haywood (Eds.), *Psychosocial influence in retarded performance.* Baltimore: University Park Press.

Willis, S. L., Blieszner, R., & Baltes, P. B. (1981). Intellectual training research in aging: Modification of performance on the fluid ability of figural relations. *Journal of Educational Psychology, 73,* 41–50.

Yarrow, I. J., Goodwin, M. S., Manheimer, H., & Milowe, I. D. (1973). Infancy experiences and personality development at ten years. In I. J. Stone, H. T. Smith, & L. B. Murphy (Eds.), *The competent infant.* New York: Basic Books.

III SALUTOGENIC AND PATHOGENIC PROCESSES

9 Intergenerational Networks and Transmitting the Sense of Coherence

Aaron Antonovsky
Ben-Gurion University of the Negev

THE SENSE OF COHERENCE

For many years, I studied the role of social and psychological factors in the etiology of diseases. My work started with multiple sclerosis and later moved to cancer and coronary disease. The independent variables of major concern to me were social class, poverty, and immigration, which led me into the field of life events and stress research.

A significant change occurred in the late 1960s when I realized that I was really interested in disease — or, as I called it in a 1972 paper, breakdown (Antonovsky, 1972) — rather than any specific disease. "Why do people break down?" I began to ask. It does not matter in which particular disease category this breakdown is expressed. The mystery is defined as the disruption of homeostasis and my thinking, like that of all my colleagues, reflected the medical model dichotomy of healthy-diseased. It is amusing to think that had I worked in a different area of sociology (being a committed adherent of conflict theory), I would probably have sought to understand how social systems manage to hold together. But, evidently, assuming that the natural course of social systems is to break down is less anxiety provoking and more easily admitted than making the same assumption with regard to the human organism.

The focus on overall vulnerability, then, was not yet a paradigmatic shift of perspective. But I had begun to move toward a decline of interest in stressors and to move toward a focus on resistance resources. My studies of concentration camp survivors and poor people suggested that some (fewer than in comparison groups, but, nonetheless, some), had the wherewithal to make it. A variety of epidemiological and sociological studies had suggestive leads. Our own study of subcultural variations in adaptation to menopause (Datan, Antonovsky, & Maoz, 1981), for example, pointed to cultural stability as a valuable generalized resistance resource. The idea of social supports was just beginning to come into vogue. But these were seen largely as buffers, which, when the relatively rare disruptions of homeostasis occasioned by stressors occurred, could ward off deleterious health consequences. It was not easy to break out of this mold of thought. It took several more years to formulate a "salutogenic" orientation that might provide a valuable new perspective to take as a starting point that the human organism, in a very well-defined and clearly delimited long run at the most (see Fries & Crapo, 1981), is subject to increasing entropy by the inevitable, endemic stressors from both the internal and the external environments that bombard us all incessantly.

THE QUESTION OF SALUTOGENESIS

The first systematic formulation of the salutogenic orientation appeared in my book *Health, Stress and Coping* (Antonovsky, 1979). Since then I have become increasingly convinced that adoption of this orientation, instead of the traditional pathogenic paradigm, leads to radically different thinking and research. It would take us much too far afield to spell this out here, and it has been done elsewhere (Antonovsky, 1984). Let me just note in brief that salutogenesis liberates one from being trapped in the dichotomous study of specific diseases. One focuses on coping resources rather than on stressors as the key to adaptation; stressors are not automatically viewed as distressors but as possible eustressors. It allows one to distinguish between tension and stress as stages in the coping process; it leads one to study the mystery of the deviant case, the person who makes it despite a high stressor load.

The first tentative answer to the salutogenic question was the generalized resistance resources concept. But there were nagging questions: How do social supports, cultural stability, money, and so on work? What do they have in common? A brilliant paper by Cassel (1974) suggested a direction. Kohn's work on schizophrenia pointed in the same direction (1973). One of the spinoffs of working salutogenically is that one reads the epidemiologist Cassel and the sociologist Kohn, whereas the pathogenecist is much more likely to concentrate on "his" or "her" disease. The answer was finally formulated as the *sense of coherence* (SOC). The meaning of a generalized resistance resource, I proposed, is that one undergoes life situations or experiences with specifiable characteristics. These experiences generate, over time, a way of seeing one's world. It is this generalized, perceptual-emotional way of viewing one's internal and external environments that I called the SOC. I viewed it as a decisive variable in coping with the inexorable stressors of existence or, if one wills, as a determinant of negative entropy.

What are the characteristics of the life experiences involved in social supports, cultural stability, money and so on? Please note these carefully, for they point to the central question I ask in this paper, namely, to what extent do intergenerational network patterns provide such experiences? First, the experiences are consistent, continuous, and developmentally harmonious with previous experiences. Second, they pose demands that fit the given person, demands that neither overload nor underload. And third, they define one as a participant in decision making, as being socially valued, as having something significant to contribute.

These experiences are coordinate with the three components of the SOC, which I can now define as follows: One has a strong-to-weak SOC to the extent to which: (a) the demands confronting one in the course of living are cognitively perceived as structured-to-disordered (i.e., *comprehensibility*); (b) one feels that very adequate-to-very-inadequate resources are available to one to meet these demands (i.e., *manageability*); and (c) one emotionally-motivationally feels that these demands are challenges-to-tribulations (i.e., *meaningfulness*). A detailed discussion of the concept and its components, as well as of the operationalized definition (in a 29-item questionnaire), is found in Antonovsky (1983). But let this suffice for the moment.

The SOC as a Dependent Variable

Heretofore, I have largely devoted my work on the SOC to its consideration as an independent variable that affects movement on the health-illness continuum. I have not considered its possible consequences for such favorites of laboratory psychology as frustration tolerance, attentiveness to others' needs or task performance, or other aspects of well being. Beyond a few pages in the book on a general level, I have not given systematic, detailed attention to the SOC as a dependent variable. Clinicians who have heard me speak, evidently impressed by the seemingly substantial explanatory power of the construct, often have been disturbed by my suggestion that, for most people, location on the SOC continuum is more or less fixed during young adulthood. They would like to be able to modify it. To do so requires understanding of how the SOC comes into being and how it endures or changes.

To begin to confront that question in a systematic way, let us assume that the strength of one's SOC has important consequences for one's physical and possible other aspects of well being. The general question, then, is how do socially structured and culturally patterned relations, occurring in a historical context, facilitate or impede the development and maintenance of one's location on the SOC continuum? We cannot give full attention to all of society, culture, and history. Hence, let us focus on one of the two major life areas (the other being one's work) that shape one's SOC: the status role set one occupies in one's intergenerational network. It would have been interesting to trace this issue throughout the life cycle, but even if I had the time to do so, I do not have the competence and knowledge. I can only suggest a way of dealing with the question at two life cycle stages and hope that others, finding the approach cogent, will take it from there.

THE SENSE OF COHERENCE IN OLD AGE

It is not accidental that I chose to focus first on the last stage of life. It is not only because I have recently been immersed in the retirement literature. My sensitivity to this stage was sharpened in the very days this paper was being drafted; the days before, during, and after the celebration of Passover. For the first time in 23 years, my son (recently married and living in Jerusalem while we are on sabbatical in Berkeley, California) was not with us at the *seder* (ritual home celebration of Passover, most often conducted in the extended family). But we thought of him and his wife, now living in the house into which we had moved when he was 6 months old, unusual in the western world, even more unusual for Jews. At the same time, my parents, 93 and 88 respectively — in remarkable cognitive and emotional well being and physically creaking not much more than Oliver Wendell Holmes' (1859/1884) wonderful one hoss shay at the same age — came from New York to be with us. Though present as a 4-month-old infant, I do not remember the first seder my mother prepared and my father conducted just 60 years ago. But there is continuity from 1924 to the other night, when he again conducted the seder. Seated around the table were members of four generations who had gathered in Berkeley from San Francisco, Redwood City, Sante Fe, New York, and Israel. Let me exploit this personal situation to analyze how intergenerational networks transmit, to a greater or lesser extent, the SOC.

In starting with old age, I follow Erikson's precedent in his last "re-view of the *completed* life cycle" (1982). Reading his monograph, I was surprised and pleased to come across the following sentence in his discussion of integrity, which he saw as the dominant ego syntonic trait in the last stage of life.

> This in its simplest meaning is, of course, a sense of *coherence* and *wholeness* that is, no doubt, at supreme risk under such terminal conditions as include a *loss of linkages* in all three organizing processes: in the Soma...in the Psyche . . . and in the Ethos, the threat of a sudden and nearly total loss of responsible function in generative interplay. (pp. 64–65)

What helps one withstand this risk? It is unlikely that Erikson borrowed the sense of coherence phrase from me. Yet his discussion of integrity, in which he uses phrases like "a tendency to keep things together . . . a comrade-ship with the ordering ways of distant times" surely has much in common with my formulation, including the similarity between what I called an "inauthentic SOC" and what Erikson calls "pseudointegration as a defense against lurking despair."

Intergenerational Contexts and the SOC

What, then, is the intergenerational context that facilitates or impedes the maintenance of a strong SOC in one generation and the transactional trans-mission to another, keeping as an index focus an old man or woman? Note that I have said "transactional," for I would make a crucial point right at the outset: the SOC of the index person, at any life cycle stage, is always influencing, and is always being influenced by, the structure and content of relations with the other generations in his or her family.

The first and least problematic context characteristic that maintains a strong SOC is *continuity*. Holmes' shay was driven by deacon after deacon in succeeding generations, each, as he reached old age, undoubtedly recalling the drives with his father and grandfather and speaking of them to his grand-children. The roads were better paved, and alongside them ran telegraph wires and railroad tracks. (For a remarkably contemporaneous-sounding de-scription of the rapidity of social change, see Holmes' introduction to the 1884 revised edition of the volume, which contains "The Deacon's Master-piece"). Day after day, the deacon was reminded, despite these changes, of family and historical continuity.

In 1984, my parents could recall their own parents, over 8 decades ago, conducting a seder. California is not the Ukraine of 1900; we are not Ortho-dox Jews; the Hagada is now recited in the Sephardic Hebrew accent; our standard of living is immeasurably higher. But the seder was, for my parents (no less than for me), what I have called developmentally harmonious with previous experiences. I stress that it is not only a matter of four generations being present that matters to them, important as this is. It is the link to the past and to the future, through the family to a specific culture and history, which is crucial. In this specific case, then, the seder provided a structured ex-perience that contributed to the comprehensibility component of my parents' SOC.

Consistent experiences, however, are not enough to maintain the SOC. Ritual can become frozen, viewed as archaic, not genuinely legitimated by succeeding generations. If participation by later generations becomes me-chanical, the older person will sense the devaluation, the end of his or her having something significant to contribute. Rosow's (1976) incisive analytic distinction between status and role concepts is of help here. His typology dis-tinguishes among the familiar Institutional status role, the Tenuous case, which consists of "definite social positions *without* roles," (p. 463), and the Informal type, which "represents role behavior that is *not* connected with any particular status or position, but which *serves significant group functions*" (p. 467). Clearly, the younger generations, responding to ritual as archaic, by physically or emotionally absenting themselves from involvement, convey the message to the older persons that the elders are superfluous. Presiding at a seder in such a case places one in the formal status but role emptiness of the Tenuous type, perhaps even more inimical to the SOC than the total disappearance of role and status. On the other hand, the experience of an intergenerationally confirmed Institutional status role contributes to the meaningfulness component of the SOC. In simple words, that succeeding generations are genuinely delighted and respectful because Grandma can still make delicious gefilte fish and movingly bless the candles; and Grandpa can still recite the Hagada at breakneck speed, occasionally breaking into familiar chanting, enhances meaningfullness.

It is the delight and respect of significant others that conveys the experience of social valuation. Yet there is the third element of crucial experiences for the SOC, hinted at by the words "still make" and "still recite." For Grandma no longer has the energy to go shopping for the fish, and Grandpa's eyesight is failing, so that his reading of the Hagada is no longer letter perfect. What happens when objective competence is reduced, as it invariably is with the elderly? Are they then relegated by younger generations to the ranks of the senile and dependent, perhaps to be cared for generously, but with no room for receiving from the young? This becomes the classic underload situation. How can ties with the younger generation make it possible for the manageability component to be maintained? Let me give two examples.

Social scientists dealing with old age have long noted the disappearance of the transmission of wisdom and knowledge from old to young in rapidly changing technological societies. But they have failed to take note of a far more mundane matter of significant import — conveying to the older generation that what they do still matters very much and providing them with experiences that fit their remaining capacities. I refer to the simple matter of giving money. The elderly are no longer disproportionately poor. Without denying the dire straits that many still find themselves in and the consequent dependence on the state and their children, in the present context we must ask: How many of the elderly continue to provide substantial sums, going far beyond birthday presents, to their children and grandchildren? Trust funds are set up; down payments on homes are provided; college tuition for grandchildren is paid. I know of no data to document these transactions. But for the elderly, they are repeated experiences demonstrating that they have something significant to contribute, that there are demands they can meet, and that, having brought up children to adulthood, they continue to maintain a one-way gift relationship. Such relationships, of course, vary greatly between different subcultures and social classes, and we might well infer the hypothesis that the level of the SOC of the elderly, shaped in part by the monetary relationships of dependence, independence, and reverse dependence, will vary considerably between different subgroups.

Money, of course, is only one medium of power. In contemporary society, only infrequently can the elderly exercise direct power over the lives of their children. They cannot determine their marriages, their work, or their styles of life except in rare cases. But the influence of childhood is never totally dissipated. For the old person, the child is still, at some profound level, a child. Who of us has not, at the same profound level, responded to our parent with the love and ambivalence and anger, or rebellion and guilt and desire for approval, of the child and adolescent? I am not suggesting that there cannot be mature, adult relations between adult child and parent on the whole. I am saying that there can never be either a total severance or an egalitarian friendship between parent and child. The involvement, which remains even with little overt contact, is a source of power for the elderly: They know their children can never be free of them. How power is used, to exploit and destroy or to sustain and support, remains germane throughout the life cycle, if not at the same level of intensity as in infancy and childhood. The extent to which it exists and is used in a way that elicits a grateful response from succeeding generations contributes to shaping the older person's SOC.

In speaking of ritualized occasions, social valuation, the gift relationship and power, I have suggested a number of different channels through which the SOC of older persons can be sustained through intergenerational networks. At this point it is worth recalling that the salutogenic orientation posits that conflict and tension are endemic in all social existence. This is no less true in family relations than in any other area. Homeostatic mechanisms may abound, containing conflict, channeling it into less devastating modes, perhaps even sublimating it. But underlying ambivalences remain, and new sources arise throughout the life cycle. Family life is forever volcanic. Having said this, I have tried to point out how it might not be destructive. For the elderly in contemporary society, where so many other webbed relationships unravel, it might well be decisive.

Summary

To allow a systematic summary, I again turn to Rosow's (1976) typology. In one sentence, he puts the matter clearly, when he speaks of "people who . . . are *not* assimilated in those coherent [see my comprehensibility] subcultures that afford them significant group support [see my meaningfulness] and clear behavioral expectations [see my manageability]" (p. 464). The most devastating sociological situation is that of classification of the old person by the family in the empty, amorphous social category of the old, having neither status nor role. He or she is then a stick of furniture, socially invisible, having no social consequences. We may well think of such old persons, as Zola (1982) noted in his moving book on severely disabled persons, as in-valid. Scarcely distinguishable from this type is the Tenuous. One retains one's formal status as mother or grandmother, but no social role expectations are attached to the status. Or, rather, in our welfare culture, we maintain certain responsibilities toward them, such as providing physical care (polishing the furniture), but they have no duties or responsibilities toward us. Their lives are consequential for us only in the sense that we feel called upon to allocate resources for their sustenance. But they are defined as performing no functions upon which the intergenerational network depends. Only by indicating suffering, pain, and helplessness can they still elicit response, a response that inevitably is ambivalent. And thus the destruction of the SOC proceeds apace.

Given the inevitable physical concomitants of aging, the emergence of new bases of power and independence, and the confrontation of rapidly changing social and technological environments, there is little likelihood that institutional family status roles will continue to be preeminent in old age and will continue to provide experiences that maintain the SOC. More and more, informal family roles become the only fruitful alternative. I have pointed out how these can indeed provide such experiences. Though I am reasonably familiar with the gerontological literature, I am not aware of any systematic study of the structural conditions that foster the emergence of such roles within the family system, though there is some work referring to informal roles outside the family (Unruh, 1983).

THE SENSE OF COHERENCE IN ADOLESCENCE

My concern has not been primarily to analyze the situation of the elderly, but to suggest a model that can clarify the role of intergenerational networks in strengthening or weakening the SOC. Can this model be applied to another stage of the life cycle? The question that remains central is: How does the interaction between the index case—I now turn to that of an adolescent girl—and previous generations shape the SOC?

Before doing so, the contrast immediately points to the need for an important corrective to what I have said till now. The adolescent girl can hardly be said to have crystallized a stable, deeply rooted location on the SOC continuum. A person entering old age has long had such a location. Older persons characterized by a strong SOC or, in Erikson's terms, having successfully resolved earlier psychosocial crises, are likely to successfully withstand the decline of institutional status roles and take initiative in finding new informal status roles and in rejecting tenuous ones. They not only react to, but also act upon, the members of other generations, utilize and even generate negative entropy. On the other hand, weak SOC older persons, if indeed they have survived, are not likely to be the beneficiary of experiences offered by intergenerational networks.

Family Functioning and the SOC in Adolescence

In considering the case of the adolescent girl, I have been influenced by the work of Reiss (1981). His psychological approach, when combined with Rosow's (1976) sociological analyses, can give us a powerful tool for understanding how the family shapes the girl's SOC. The core of adolescence is the need to face, in Reiss' words, an ambiguous, often chaotic world of an inner and outer environment (p. 302). What she has at her disposal, and has had since her birth, is her family's "construction of social reality." Families differ, he wrote, "in whether they conceive the world as governed by an underlying and stable set of discoverable principles or whether the world is shaped by invisible capricious forces capable of moving on their own" (p. 249). "The family has come to play a central role in providing understanding and meaning of the stimulus universe for each of its members . . . a set of explanations . . . that serve as the primary organizer of internal and external experience" (p. 155).

Reiss (1981) proposed that the family processes information, meets problems, and lives its life by systematically behaving along three central dimensions: coordination, closure, and configuration. He identified three types of families. The *environment-sensitive* family is high on configuration, (i.e., perceives and organizes experiences into structured patterns); it is high on coordination, which involves a sharing process and belief in the importance of worked-out consensus; and it delays reaching closure, though not indefinitely, in order to utilize a wide variety of information, with high sensitivity to the extrafamily environment. The *consensus-sensitive* family also is high on coordination, but with a closed-in hyperresponsiveness, disregarding information from without. This is what is crucial, and, to this end, closure is rapid and little demand is made for configuration. The *interpersonal-distance* family places a premium on everyone going his or her own way; there is not only no configuration, but also no coordination, and closure is rapid lest complications arise.

Let us now consider the adolescent girl in each of these three types of families in Rosow's status role terms. What status roles are offered her by each of the families? And what experiences does she encounter as a result that affect her SOC? The interpersonal-distance family says, in essence: Go your own way, we won't interfere. You occupy a tenuous status, which carries no role expectations in either direction. Neither institutional status roles nor informal roles are offered or demanded. Thus, over and over again, her experiences in the family—and the picture she gets from her family of what the world is like—is devoid of continuity; of social valuation; of involvement; of tasks that are proportionate in some way to her capacities and limitations, for they are arbitrary. With great fortune, she may find a family substitute in a peer group, though after 16 years of her family experiences, the likelihood of her being open to any considerable modification of the tentative world view, which is all that she has had to work with till now, is small.

The consensus-sensitive family is most likely to place the highest premium on institutional status roles. The lines are laid down clearly; the rules are spelled out. Ritual is high; continuity specified. Achievement expectations are unambiguous and most often moderate, though the culture context will determine whether these are to be in the form of the dutiful daughter, of high school grades, or of marrying the right spouse. She is shut off not only from the outside world, except through formally approved channels screened in advance, but from any individual, inner world. There is little room for informal roles, for these derive from interaction between individual and group and provide for spontaneity. The experiences of the girl living in a consensus-sensitive family, then, are partially conducive to a strong SOC. Surprises are few and quickly explained, and life is routinized and ritualized; the demands made on her are generally appropriate, for they are not tailored for extremes, but for the average. Difficulty arises in particular for the girl who, because of temperament, unique experience outside the family, or some other reason, manifests deviant individuality, dreams her own dreams, chafes at being a good girl and fitting in. She will never be socially valued, rewarded for her own sake.

The environment-sensitive family allows, and perhaps even revels in, precisely the girl who dreams and encourages her to test these dreams in engaging a world which is broad, novel, and discoverable. This family encourages the informal role, not derived from any defined social status. It reassures the spontaneities, the uniqueness. The institutional status roles are flexible, with much room for individual interpretation. The potential, then, for the girl to be socially valued, to feel a sense of deep engagement and challenge, is great. Yet there are, especially in this light, immanent dangers in terms of the experiences which foster the SOC. The values are applied not just to the girl alone; others enjoy the same freedoms. Hence, conflict and clash are frequent. Even though delayed closure is acceptable, interminable openness is maddening. Coordination and profound consensus are not easily achievable. The comfort of routine and ritual, the warmth of nonnovelty can easily be sacrificed to the excitement of innovation. For the adolescent girl, no stranger to inner turmoil, what can often and easily become family turmoil hardly contributes to a sense of comprehensibility and may well not always facilitate a sense of managability.[1]

Neither I nor Reiss (1981) suggests that these are the only three types of family. (In fact, in the course of his research, Reiss identified an "achievement-sensitive" family.) In analyzing two stages in the life cycle, my intention has been to do no more than suggest the utility of looking systematically at the way intergenerational networks create environments that affect a person's SOC. The crucial question has always been: Do certain types of families and/or certain structural arrangements provide experiences that are ordered–chaotic, that are demand–balanced or under–overloaded, and that are participatory–externally imposed?

CONCLUSIONS

The further we move away from infancy through the life cycle, the less crucial do intergenerational networks become in having an impact on one's SOC. We always carry our families with us, but as time goes by, other life elements, particularly the work we do, become more important. I have in this chapter, for the sake of analysis, ignored these elements, which operate directly as well as through their influence on family structure. Second, I have tried to point up the potentials for devastating damage as well as magnificent contribution of the family, which I wish neither to deify nor demonize. Third, even though here and there I have specified some cultural content, I should like to emphasize that the experiences that shape the SOC, for better or for worse, can be found in a wide variety of cultures. And, finally, I hope I have made it clear that there is not necessarily one good answer that is both scientifically accurate and consonant with our values. I mean this in two senses. First, I am the last to claim that a strong SOC is good in and of itself—a Nazi may have a strong SOC. Second, whichever path one takes, somehow there always seems to be a price to pay. Multiply experiences that enhance comprehensibility, and you may damage manageability.

REFERENCES

Antonovsky, A. (1972). A needed fourth step in the conceptual armamentarium of modern medicine. *Social Science and Medicine, 6,* 537–544.
Antonovsky, A. (1979). *Health, stress and coping.* San Francisco: Jossey-Bass.

---

[1]Had I selected for detailed consideration younger children, I would have called attention to the work of Boyce (1983), who focuses on "behavioral rhythmicity" in the family, continuity, and what he calls "the sense of permanence."

Antonovsky, A. (1983). The sense of coherence: Development of a research instrument. *W. S. Schwartz Research Center for Behavioral Medicine, Tel Aviv University Newsletter and Research Reports, 1,* 1-11.

Antonovsky, A. (1984). The sense of coherence as a determinant of health. In J. Matarazzo, S. M. Weiss, J. A. Herd, N. E. Miller, S. E. Weiss (Eds.), *Behavioral health: A handbook of health enhancement and disease prevention* (pp. 114-129). New York: Wiley.

Boyce, W. T. et al. (1983). The family routines inventory: Theoretical origins. *Social Science and Medicine, 17,* 193-200.

Cassel, J. (1974). Psychosocial processes and "stress": Theoretical formulation. *International Journal of Health Services, 4,* 471-482.

Datan, N., Antonovsky, A., & Maoz, B. (1981). *A time to reap: The middle age of women in five Israeli subcultures.* Baltimore: Johns Hopkins University Press.

Erikson, E. H. (1982). *The life cycle completed: A review.* New York: Norton.

Fries, J. F., & Crapo, L. M. (1981). *Vitality and aging: Implications of the rectangular curve.* San Francisco: Freeman.

Holmes, O. W. (1884). *The autocrat of the breakfast table* (rev. ed.). Boston: Houghton Mifflin. (Original work published 1859)

Kohn, M. L. (1973). Social class and schizophrenia: A critical review and a reformulation. *Schizophrenia Bulletin, 7,* 60-79.

Mannheim, K. (1952). The problem of generations. In P. Kecskemeti (Ed.), *Essays on the sociology of knowledge.* London: Routledge & Kegan Paul.

Reiss, D. (1981). *The family's construction of reality.* Cambridge, MA: Harvard University Press.

Rosow, I. (1976). Status and role change through the life span. In R. H. Binstock & E. Shanas (Eds.), *Handbook of aging and the social sciences* (pp. 457-482). New York: Van Nostrand.

Unruh, D. R. (1983). *Social worlds of the aged.* Beverly Hills: Sage.

Zola, I. K. (1982). *Missing pieces: A chronicle of living with a disability.* Philadelphia: Temple University Press.

10 Reciprocal Socialization and the Care of Offspring with Cancer and with Schizophrenia

Judith A. Cook
Bertram J. Cohler
The University of Chicago and Michael Reese Hospital

Socialization within the family involves the induction of members into new roles. Most often, this socialization has been studied in terms of the beliefs and norms taught by parents to offspring, referred to as "forward" socialization. To date, much of the concern with forward socialization has focused on role transitions that are expectable and orderly in terms of the timetable of life (Neugarten & Hagestad, 1976), such as entry into anticipated, on-time marriage or advent of the parental role. There has been little recognition of the extent to which this forward socialization is important, not just during childhood and early adolescence, but across the adult years as well. With parents living into very old age, it is fairly common for the elderly to teach their middle-aged children about retirement, the physical decline that occurs in the later years, and, ultimately, ways of confronting death itself.

Not only do parents socialize children in a forward manner but, children reciprocally socialize parents in a reverse direction. Over the past decade, as a result of increased interest in the "generation gap" (Bengtson & Black, 1973; Hagestad, 1981), together with findings from a number of longitudinal studies of family relations (Klein, 1983), there has been renewed appreciation of the extent to which children influence their parents, including the induction of parents into new conceptions of major adult roles. To date, much of this study of reciprocal socialization has concerned parents and young adult offspring and has focused on orderly (rather than disordered) role transitions, such as efforts by university students to socialize their parents into more flexible definitions of sex roles.

The present chapter focuses on reciprocal socialization in two contexts: children with terminal cancer and young adults with remitting, recurrent

223

schizophrenia, where role transition are disordered or "off time" in the expectable course of life. Although the two categories of illness may appear to be different, they show similar characteristics within the context of reciprocal socialization. Each illness demands that parents confront disappointment and loss. Particularly in the case of childhood cancer, children are in the position of socializing their parents into the bereavement status rather than, as is more characteristic in our society, parents expecting to die first and preparing their offspring for dealing with death. Both cancer and schizophrenia are illnesses that display an unpredictable course and require that parents learn to live with uncertainty. Finally, each illness forces parents to confront lowered expectations of what offspring are able to accomplish, and ill offspring may teach their parents to accept these diminished expectations.

PARENTHOOD AND ROLE STRAIN: THE PROBLEM OF SICK OFFSPRING, SOCIAL TIMING, AND THE EXPERIENCE OF PARENTHOOD

Socialization within the family is possible only as a result of shared understandings of relationship, person, and time (Berger & Kellner, 1964). In particular, a shared sense of the expectable course of lives enables family members to compare their present place in the social timetable with what is expected. Two aspects of social timing are particularly important. First, feelings of positive morale are generally determined by a sense of congruence between anticipated and realized status attainments (Cohler & Boxer, 1984) and role transitions occurring at socially expected points in the life course (Neugarten & Hagestad, 1976).

Characteristically, role transitions or life events taking place earlier in the life course than is expectable have a more adverse impact than those taking place late. Since there is little opportunity for role rehearsal, unpleasant events, such as widowhood, that take place early off-time are felt as even more adverse than when they occur at expectable times (Lopata, 1975). Teenage pregnancy has the same character of affecting morale because of the off-time transition to parenthood (Gershenson, 1983).

Second, timing of entrance and exit from major adult roles has an impact on the morale of a wide circle of family members. As Cohler (1983) has noted, lives are interdependent, and events affecting particular family members also affect significant others within the family. For example, when an older parent suffers illness such as Alzheimer's disease, the spouse, adult offspring, and their wives and husbands all are drawn into caretaking. Other relatives (grandchildren and older brothers and sisters of both the ill older parent and his or her spouse) also are affected, since these relatives often have important relationships with the ill older person and feel an obligation to participate in caretaking.

Because women in this society are particularly involved in relationships with others in the family and with kin keeping (Cook, 1983b), and are more "context sensitive" and involved with interdependent family ties than men (Chodorow, 1978; Cohler & Grunebaum, 1981; Gilligan, 1982), adverse off-time events particularly affect women and create additional caretaking burdens for them. As Elder and Rockwell (1978) note, with the onset of family problems, men are more likely to withdraw into work or to develop asocial problems and leave the family, while the wife and mother, feeling burdened and conflicted, remains to hold the family together.

Stressful Events, Parenthood, and Family Relations

The morale of family members may be affected not only by stressful life events but by strain and overload in the performance of such expectable adult roles as that of parent. It should be noted that, following Pearlin (1975), the present discussion distinguishes between *stressful life-events* or changes, which are usually unexpected, adverse, and potentially disruptive for personal adjustment, and *role strain,* referring to the everyday hassles associated with ongoing performance of major life roles, such as problems at work, marital conflict, or difficulties in caring for offspring.

Beginning with the transition to parenthood (Rossi, 1968) and continuing through the years when there are young children at home (Cohler, 1983) into the time when offspring are grown but continue to be involved with their parents in the family of adulthood (Cohler & Boxer, 1984; Cohler & Grunebaum, 1981; Rossi, 1980), parents report continuing role strain and overload, characterized by feelings of "chronic emergency" (Gutmann, 1975) in resolving inevitable conflicts betwen parenthood and other adult roles, as well as in dealing with strains intrinsic to the parental role itself. Consistent with this view of parenthood, Pearlin (1975) notes that disenchantment with the parental role increases with the number of children in the household, and Glenn (1975) reports finding greater happiness among middle-aged mothers whose offspring are no longer living at home than among mothers with at least one child still in residence.

Benedek (1973) has observed that parenthood is a lifelong role. Although there is certainly transition into this role, there is little opportunity for exit as long as parents retain the memory of their offspring. Even when offspring die, the reality of having once been a parent sustains this role. The continuous nature of parenthood also is a source of strain: few other adult roles are maintained over such a long period of time and require such continual role redefinition (Cohler, 1982). Moreover, much of this redefinition of the parental role occurs as a response to role changes in the lives of offspring, such as the decision of offspring to marry or the advent of grandparenthood (Rosow, 1976).

Particular strain is encountered when the attainments of offspring fail to conform to parental expectations or when limitations are imposed on possible attainments because of physical illness or a psychiatric disorder. Most often, these failures are experienced by parents as reflecting their own failure in performing the parental role (Rapoport, Rapoport, Strelitz, & Kew, 1977). Requests by teachers to discuss school difficulties, a child's delinquency, early school leaving, and failure to establish a satisfactory marriage are among the disappointments leading to increased feelings of self doubt and distress among parents.

To date, there has been little consideration of the joint effects of life-event changes and role strain as they affect the family unit across the life course. Much of the discussion of stress and strain has been focused on individuals, although more recent study in this area has adopted a life course perspective (Brim & Ryff, 1980; Hultsch & Plemons, 1979; Reese & Smyer, 1983). Since Hill's (1949) landmark study of the adjustment of the wife/mother to her husband's wartime absence from the family, there has been further research reevaluating the classic, three-stage pattern of visible disorganization, recovery from crisis, and reorganization of the family system (Burr, 1973).

This more recent research (Doyle, Gold & Moskovitz, 1984; Klein, 1983; McCubbin & patterson, 1983) also has explored the manner in which family members cope with the press of adverse events. For example, in families where cystic fibrosis had been diagnosed in young children, life changes sparked by this initial adverse event lead to a "pileup" of interconnected adverse events and increased role strain within the entire modified extended family. The child with cystic fibrosis requires constant care, not only imposing strain on performance of that parental role but also affecting the nature of the parents' relationships with other children in the family. Further, because grandparents and aunts and uncles are often called upon for childcare during periods of crisis when the ill child is hospitalized, feelings of role strain extend both laterally and horizontally within the family unit.

RESEARCH ON ILL OFFSPRING

The study of ill offspring and their parents is important both for increased understanding of reciprocal socialization and for assisting the family to respond more effectively to adverse life events. Indeed, one of the earliest statements of reciprocal socialization (Klebanoff, 1959) concerned the impact of a psychotic youngster on family interaction. This perspective was later elaborated in Bell's (1964, 1968) discussion of parents and their handicapped children and by Bell and Harper (1977) in the formulation of a more general model of reciprocal socialization.

Much of the attention in studies of reciprocal socialization and the impact of the ill offspring on the family has been limited to younger children and their parents (Lerner & Spanier, 1978), and much of that has focused on physical illness rather than psychiatric disturbance. Comparative study of physically ill offspring and those with psychiatric impairment, including both adolescents and adult offspring, offers an opportunity to examine the interplay of stressful life events, strain in performance of the parental role, and reciprocal socialization processes within the family as determinants of the family's capacity to cope with the illness and its effects.

Particularly striking in the study of children with cancer is the reverse socialization carried out by children who shape their parents' understanding of the dying process. Families with schizophrenic offspring also display dramatic reverse socialization as schizophrenic offspring induct their parents into recognition of disappointment and a kind of mourning for lost opportunities. To an even greater extent than among families with a fatally ill child, schizophrenic offspring teach their parents new but often maladaptive modes of dealing with the real world, as parents increasingly are drawn into the troubled offspring's idiosyncratic mode of processing information.

Each of these changes in the lives of offspring also leads to increased strain in parents' performance of adult roles, as well as strain for other family members. Childhood cancer and schizophrenia both involve terrifying diagnoses for patient and family, and each illness involves repeated hospitalizations and the necessity of dealing with numerous health care professionals regarding treatment and rehabilitation. Characteristic modes of relating to the world outside the family and to using community institutions (Cohler & Grunebaum, 1981; Cook & Wimberley, 1983) may add to role strain of parents in coping with the illness, generally involving complex relationships with a spectrum of doctors, nurses, social workers, and other professionals.

PARENTS AND DYING CHILDREN: CANCER DURING CHILDHOOD AND ADOLESCENCE

Medical Intervention in Childhood Cancer

Over the past several decades, impressive advances in biophysical technology have improved treatment methods and extended the lives of pediatric oncology patients. Throughout the 1920s, 1930s and 1940s, most children who developed cancer lived for 5 months or less (Bozeman, Orbach, & Sutherland, 1955). From the 1950s through the 1970s, survival time increased from about a year (Natterson & Knudson, 1960) to as many as 3 years in the case of treatment for leukemia (Share, 1972). Today, due largely to the development of new chemotherapeutic agents and a better understanding of how to use them in combination with other drugs, radiation, and surgery, remissions of 5 or more years are obtained for up to 50% of leukemic children (Comaroff & Maquire, 1981). Indeed, children with some types of cancer (such as Wilms tumor or Ewing's sarcoma) can now expect lengthy remissions and anticipate a normal life span, leading to the first generation of pediatric oncologic survivors to reach adulthood. (See, for example, Obetz, Swenson, McCarthy, Gilchrist, & Burgert, 1980.) Unfortunately, progress in treatment of other forms of childhood cancer has been less dramatic, so that most children who develop cancer do not survive.

Treatment of pediatric cancer patients invariably involves interaction with the child's family members. Earlier discussions of work with parents generally portrayed them as behaving in a somewhat irrational, hysterical manner, characterized by hostility toward medical and nursing staff (Knudson & Natterson, 1960; Toch, 1972). Intrapsychic processes were given precedence in understanding parents' emotional reactions to the illness (Bozeman et al., 1955), and little attention was paid to the treatment parents received from hospital staff, or to parental perceptions of hospital policies in understanding why mothers and fathers reacted as they did. At this time, parents typically were allowed to visit a hospitalized child only twice a week or (in institutions with liberal policies) every other day. Starting in the 1950s, hospitals began to reverse this exclusionary policy and to encourage parent participation in the child's hospital care, including sleeping overnight in the child's room. This change was a result of research indicating that parental interaction in the hospital facilitated the child's treatment by providing parents with a means for reassuring their child, relieving the child's pain, and dealing with parental feelings of guilt (Hamovitch, 1964; Richmond & Waisman, 1955).

Another influence on parents' experiences of their child's fatal illness was the prevailing norm concerning how much information should be given to the child. Until the 1970s, most professionals advised hiding the diagnosis and prognosis from the child (Share, 1972). This policy was supported by research showing that hospitalized terminally ill children exhibited extreme passivity and withdrawal from hospital staff, other patients, parents, and extended family (Bozeman et al., 1955; Knudson & Natterson, 1960). This behavior was interpreted as indicating that the children were using denial as a coping mechanism and preferred to remain ignorant of their condition. Adults were willing to oblige, even though a few investigators admitted suspecting that their deception did not really reassure sick children (Futterman & Hoffman, 1970; Lascari, 1969).

This attitude began to change with the publication of a 1965 article by Vernick and Karon entitled "Who's Afraid of Death on a Leukemia Ward?" By interviewing 51 leukemic 9- to 12-year-olds, the authors discovered that *everyone* was afraid of dying, but that children would not express their fears unless given a safe, supportive environment in which to do so. When parents were evasive, falsely cheerful, and deceptive, children interpreted this as a sign that something was seriously wrong, but "off limits" for discussion. As a result, children felt abandoned and were forced to devise their own — often inaccurate — definitions of the situation. Typical staff responses to children's questions about other children who had died ("Oh, he went home"; "He went to another hospital"; "He went to another floor") did not fool these children, as in the case of one 9-year-old boy (Vernick & Karon, 1965):

> This lad had frequently received the answer that certain children "had gone to the thirteenth floor" (another ward of the National Cancer Institute clinical center). It even appeared that Tommy accepted these statements as true until, as a result of space shortages on the pediatric floor, it became necessary to transfer him to the thirteenth floor. This child suddenly became completely unmanageable and displayed such panic and anger that he had to be literally held to protect him and others. It took over an hour to learn that he did not want to go to the thirteenth floor because "that's where kids go to die." He went on to explain that "when kids get sent to the thirteenth floor I never see them again" (p. 394).

This trend toward increased honesty was supported by a research study conducted in the early 1970s by Eugenia Waechter (1971) involving interviews with 48 hospitalized children between the ages of 6 and 10. Analysis of results on the General Anxiety Scale revealed that the scores of fatally ill children were twice as high as those of other hospitalized children, despite the fact that only two of the 16 terminal patients had been told of their prognosis. Moreover, 63% of the stories told in response to TAT cards involved the theme of death, as in the case of one 8-year-old girl with a malignant tumor whose mother was adamant that the diagnosis be hidden from her daughter. This child revealed a preoccupation with death in all eight stories; she angrily concluded most accounts with the death of the main character, remarking, "And nobody cared — not even her mother!" Waechter also found that children who had been given an opportunity to discuss their illness openly showed no higher level of anxiety than did patients who were shielded.

An interesting implication of these studies concerns the process of reverse socialization (Klebanoff, 1959), in which children act as socializing agents for their parents. This research led to a recognition of the phenomenon of children shielding their parents from the knowledge that they were aware of their fatal prognosis. The maintainence of this mutual pretense between parents and children was examined by Bluebond-Langner (1978) in her participant-observation study of a children's cancer ward. She found that children sought to protect their parents by going to great lengths to appear ignorant of approaching death. "When a seven-year-old boy's Christmas presents arrived three weeks early and Santa came to visit him, suggesting that the boy would not live to Christmas, he turned to his choked-up family and the staff members around his bed, saying, 'Santa has lots of children to see, he just came here first' " (1978, p. 204).

Around this time, the death and dying movement initiated by Elizabeth Kübler-Ross (1969) began to promote the notion that professionals, patients, and laypersons should employ honesty, openness, and expressiveness as coping mechanisms for dealing with death. Accompanying this was a dramatic increase in self-help groups for parents of dying children (Videka-Sherman, 1982). Literature on these groups (more than fifteen published articles) began to focus attention on the parental perspective including shared definitions of the child's illness, familial responses, and role changes. This added a new dimension to the study of familial reactions and led to the development of the following research on parental experiences, useful for exploring the nature of reciprocal socialization.

Parental Role Strain and Care of Children with Cancer

As long as the life expectancy of children with cancer was very brief, with the last months managed largely by hospital staff with whom parents had limited contact, and as long as parents and children were not expected to be honest with each other in discussing the illness and its outcome, the major task confronting parents was psychological preparation for the child's death. However, with the possibility of extended periods of remission from illness and the corresponding need for greater honesty in communication between parents and children, increased demands were placed on parents for the care of their offspring. Ironically, parent support groups may have added to parental role strain, as these groups often emphasized closeness between generations that was previously absent from the family. Most important, these changes in the care of children with cancer led to increasingly divergent demands for mothers and fathers.

From the first psychosocial studies of childhood cancer, most research concerning parental reactions actually analyzed *mothers'* experiences. Repeatedly, the maternal bond was emphasized as the major or crucial relationship influencing the child's adjustment, and effects of the illness on the father were seldom discussed.

Gradually, however, investigators began to notice and point out maternal–paternal differences. With the advent of parental participation in illness management both inside and outside the hospital, it became clear that mothers were much more involved in the child's care than fathers. Chodoff, Friedman, and Hamburg (1964) suggested that men did not handle the hospital environment as well as women, because women were better at adopting required nursing and mothering roles (p. 744). In two studies of families of childhood leukemia victims (Binger et al., 1969; Heffron, Bommelaere, & Masters, 1973), fathers were observed to withdraw from interaction with their child, wife, and other family members, often by retreating into work or hobbies. In other cases, men appear to be pushed away from the family and excluded consciously or unconsciously from the child's care because of their emotional and/or physical absence from day-to-day decision making (Cook, 1984; Gyulay, 1978).

These findings raise interesting questions regarding whether the father's exclusion from care of his ill child is a result of a deliberate decision among other caretakers to exclude him, job pressures confronted uniquely by men, socialization that leads women to become nurses and nurturers and men to avoid the illness because they are unable to deal with their own feelings of guilt and grief, or the interaction of these multiple effects. The father who feels uncomfortable in the hospital or has difficulty being with a child in severe pain may be only too willing to respond to cues that his "awkward" presence is not welcome at the hospital. It is likely that a tradeoff occurs, in which fathers' lesser involvement provides short-term advantages of avoiding the illness but long-term disadvantages stemming from lack of father-child reciprocal socialization, resulting in men's poorer emotional preparation for the child's death (Cook, 1983a; Pearse, 1977).

The mother's experience with childhood cancer is radically different from the father's. Expected to provide nursing care and emotional support for the ill child, she is also expected to help her husband accept the meaning of the illness and to deal with the complex feelings of the child's brothers and sisters (Gyulay, 1978). In addition, women often carry an extra load of guilt because they feel responsible for causing the illness and for managing the painful treatment process (Coddington, 1976; Fromufod, 1980). Furthermore, the task of parenting a dying child involves adherence to a philosophy or ideology of the illness acquired from hospital staff, other parents, and experiences with one's own child. This includes learning a new set of definitions to accompany ambiguous and unpredictable illness situations (Chodoff et al., 1964; Comaroff & Maguire, 1981), and also how to establish a delicate balance between emotional investment in the child and acceptance of the disease's terminal nature (Hoffman & Futterman, 1971). Parents, usually mothers, seek out other mothers of dying children to help them interpret their ill child's behavior, especially in later stages of the illness (Bluebond-Langner, 1978). Through this interaction, they are socialized into the role of "mother of a dying child" and begin to define behavioral expectations by observing the reactions of ill children and of other mothers (Heffron et al., 1973).

The present trend of centralizing cancer care in large cities away from many families' communities has created a series of problems that have influenced how parents relate to their children. Having to travel long distances to the hospital often means that one parent remains there, isolating him or (usually) her from the siblings at home (Johnson, Rudolph, & Hartmann, 1979). Mothers and fathers often schedule their visiting so that one "relieves" the other, especially on weekends, when fathers may stay at the hospital and give mothers a chance to spend time at home (Cook, 1982). This "sequential parenting" pattern can lead to problems between spouses in coordinating ways of dealing with the child and each other, while the lack of consistency may be manipulated by children who sense this shifting and feel insecure. This is especially likely when children fear the male parent's unfamiliarity with managing the illness and cling to their mothers both inside and outside the hospital (Gyulay, 1978).

To summarize, issues of reciprocal socialization have arisen as successive cohorts of children with cancer have begun to live longer, and the cultural illness management philosophy has increasingly promoted honesty in dealing with death. Moreover, two features of the social context of childhood cancer are important influences on the interaction between children and parents. These two features are gender differences between mothers and fathers, and the tendency to shield children by attempting to deceive or evade them. Even with the barriers these features create, children do socialize their parents into ways of managing the illness, as when offspring feign ignorance to protect parents' feelings or view their mothers as superior nursing caregivers. The stress of negotiating a comparatively new social role relationship (parent and childhood cancer survivor) forces each party to attend closely to the feelings of the other, and this may be a source of strain in and of itself.

PARENTS OF SCHIOZOPHRENIC OFFSPRING: PROBLEMS OF GRIEF AND DISAPPOINTMENT

Over the past quarter century, dramatic advances have been made both in understanding the origins of schizophrenia and in controlling many of the troubling and socially disruptive symptoms associated with this disturbance. Although the precise biochemical pathways leading to the appearance of symptoms have not been determined, available evidence suggests that these symptoms result from disruption of information transmitted across the synapse between neurons, possibly as a result of an excess of the neurotransmitter dopamine, leading to the disordered cognition characteristic of schizophrenic psychosis (Haracz, 1983; Kety, 1982; Snyder, 1978). This unusual sensitivity to dopamine appears to be genetically determined, and much research has shown a strong relationship in appearance of symptoms among patients and their first degree relatives (Gottesman & Shields, 1982).

Genetically inherited vulnerability to schizophrenic symptoms appears to interact in complex ways with environmental factors in the onset of symptoms. Persons already genetically predisposed to symptoms appear to experience a psychotic break following the pileup of life events (for example, graduating from high school, getting married, changing jobs). Often these events have an idiosyncratic meaning, leading to a sense of stress in the predisposed patient that cannot be easily appreciated by others (Beck & Worthen, 1972). Although many patients succumb to a first episode in the late teen or early adult years, persons appear to be vulnerable across the lifecourse (Zubin & Steinhauer, 1981). Recently developed neuroleptic medications provide some relief from psychotic symptoms such as hallucinations and delusions. However, these psychotropic drugs also have a number of serious side effects, such as uncontrollable gestures and repetitive nervous tremors. These side effects, typically irreversible and more serious when resulting from medication begun earlier in life, intensify the "stigma" and labelling as "crazy" which contributes to problems in maintaining a satisfactory post-hospital adjustment.

Family Process and the Origins of Schizophrenia

It has been proposed that, allowing for the influence of biological factors, the expression of psychotic symptoms may reflect deviant patterns of socialization and communication within the family. Three such major family approaches have been formulated (Mishler & Waxler, 1968): (a) the "double-bind" concept of Bateson, Jackson, Haley, and Weakland (1956); (b) the "communication of irrationality" concept of Lidz, Fleck, Cornelison, and associates (1965); and (c) the "communication deviance" approach of Wynne and his colleagues (1981). Even prior to formulation of these approaches, investigators had noted within families of schizophrenic adolescents and young adults patterns of conflict and disorganization that were believed to be responsible for the appearance of psychotic symptoms. Most of these family studies maintained a model of forward socialization from parent to offspring in which it was assumed that the parents' styles of communication, and their orientation to reality, provided the basis for the offspring's psychotic disorder.

Recently, several investigators have questioned the causal attribution of the forward model of parental socialization. Comparing schizophrenics interacting with parents of well offspring and well offspring interacting with parents of schizophrenics in an experimental communication situation, Waxler (1974) found that whereas the effective communication of well offspring was not adversely affected when interacting with the parents of schizophrenic offspring, the presence of a schizophrenic patient interacting with parents of well offspring led to a deterioration in communicative performance. This finding suggests that reverse socialization may be at least as significant as forward socialization, and that offspring with disorders of communication and attention may "teach" these faulty transactional modes to their parents. Over longer periods of time, parents may also adopt faulty modes of transacting with others, leading to the development of a shared family pathology (Waxler, 1974).

A related formulation suggests that vulnerable offspring show increased genetic loading for schizophrenia and that life events experienced over many months as particularly troublesome lead to increasingly idiosyncratic modes of processing information and interacting with the external environment. During this period of time, parents attempting to maintain contact with their disturbed offspring, gradually learn to talk in the language of the prospective patient. Expression of florid psychotic symptoms occurs relatively late in the prehospital period, by which time deviant patterns of communication experienced within the family context may have already become well established for both parents and offspring.

Parental Response to Schizophrenic Offspring

It is possible that family process may be less significant in understanding the origins of schizophrenia than in determining the subsequent course of the illness. In particular, the constant role strain and feelings of hassle on the part of parents, including marked feelings of hostility and resentment, may be particularly significant in determining the prognosis of this disturbance. Not just the initial hospitalization, but each subsequent admission evokes a renewed sense of crisis within the family. Urgent phone calls and frequent family conferences, discussions of reported breakthroughs in therapy, and the search for better means of treatment are familiar to those who work with families of patients with other chronic illnesses.

The impact of the schizophrenic disturbance on the coping ability of the family, together with the degree of parental role strain induced by the disturbance, has been dramatically illustrated in Sheehan's (1982) account of a recurrently schizophrenic young woman with more than ten hospitalizations in private and public psychiatric hospitals, and numerous admissions to community mental health facilities. The patient's increasingly unpredictable, violent behavior in the weeks just prior to admission; parental efforts to forestall the inevitable increase in symptoms and to ensure their own personal safety, together with feelings of guilt and disappointment over their daughter's lack of compliance with medication and problems managing side effects; all further compound the family's sense of dismay. In one particularly poignant moment, the parents are too exhausted from coping with the disruptions of their daughter's illness to celebrate their fortieth wedding anniversary.

Sheehan's (1982) moving portrait, the most detailed account to date of a family's life experiences with a schizophrenic offspring, increases our understanding of a phenomenon known as *Expressed Emotion,* or EE. Early observations reported by Brown, Carstairs, and Topping (1958) suggested that familial expression of criticism and hostility towards schizophrenic offspring discharged from psychiatric hospitals had an adverse impact upon the posthospital adjustment of these former patients. Since schizophrenics are particularly susceptible to the emotional nuances of their social environment (Leff, 1976), the experience of parental hostility leads to deterioration in the first year following discharge and is associated with increased symptomatology and rehospitalization. It is for this reason that formerly hospitalized patients living at home show less satisfactory posthospital adjustment than patients living in board-and-care facilities.

To date, discussion of EE has focused on the implications of parental frustration for the offspring's posthospital adjustment. What is often overlooked in this concern for understanding determinants of posthospital adjustment is the information provided regarding reciprocal socialization. Consistent with Sheehan's (1982) portrayal, parental feelings of frustration are the inevitable outcome of years of struggle to accept the offspring's limitations in coping (Bell, 1964) and their resentment of being forced to adopt the role of caretaker for a recurrently symptomatic offspring.

As both Kreisman and Joy (1976) and Sheehan (1982) have observed, no matter how disruptive the patient's psychopathology or how intense the parents' feelings of rage and hostility, patients and parents both seek to reunite the family rather than to have the ill offspring live apart. Although this effort to maintain the family intact might be seen as a sign of family symbiosis, more likely it reflects the interdependent nature of family life, based on continued ties of care and concern as well as of anger and despair (Cohler, 1983). Indeed, the tension between these feelings of concern and despair is the source of much strain felt by parents in continuing to care for their schizophrenic offspring.

Finally, in view of earlier theories regarding the emotional life of families of schizophrenic patients, it is interesting that high levels of EE did not characterize families as a whole, or even in relation to all offspring, but were restricted to the particular constellation of parents and troubled offspring. Further, findings reported by Valone, Norton, Goldstein, and Doane (1983) suggest that EE is not uniquely characteristic of one or the other parent, but of the parents together when relating to their schizophrenic offspring. Leff (1976) also reports that EE is charactersistic of marital pairs when one spouse is a former psychiatric patient. This finding suggests that feelings of hostility and disappointment may be reactive to the role strains associated with a spouse's disturbance and disruption of major social roles, rather than causal in determining psychosis.

While it is possible that continued parental criticism reflects a process of conflict in parenting that contributes to the initial illness, it is equally possible that the strain evoked by appearance of psychotic symptoms, together with the effects upon the family of dealing with these symptoms, leads parents to feel loss of control. Parental hostility and criticism may be responses to the situation, rather than evidence of causality attributed to faulty forms of forward parental socialization. Feelings of disappointment and despair among parents of schizophrenic patients are similar in some respects to those in cases of relapse after a period of remission from childhood cancer, reminding family members that the patient is not well after all. Concern for the patient's future well being are mingled with anger at socially disruptive actions requiring rehospitalization, leading to further familial disorganization.

As schizophrenic offspring are recurrently hospitalized, unable to sustain relationships or to realize personal goals, parents begin to mourn the psychological death of their offspring. Further, since both suicide and other paradoxical, often fatal, outcomes are prevalent among schizophrenics, parents are confronted with losses equivalent in many respects to those faced by parents of offspring with cancer. Although there has been little study of parents of chronic schizophrenics, clinical impression suggests that the nature of grief confronted in this situation may be similar to that of other illnesses having a tragic outcome.

Just as with childhood cancer, schizophrenia among offspring presents parents with feelings of profound disappointment and sadness. Initial diagnosis of each disorder still carries stigma, which further adds to the burdens of caretakers; yet the salience of this illness for parents has not been fully explored. Consideration of schizophrenia in light of family life course social science may provide important findings for those who work with schizophrenic patients and their families, including the impact on definitions of the situation that result from having a psychotic family member, as well as the strain engendered in the parental role.

Much of present information on the relationship between parents and their schizophrenic offspring assumes that the two generations remain frozen in time. There has been little continuing study of the relationship between the generations over longer periods following hospitalization in young adulthood. Indeed, there has been little study of the adult life course of recurrently schizophrenic patients as compared with that of their well counterparts. Findings reviewed by Cohler and Ferrono (in press) suggest that many characteristic, schizophrenic symptoms such as hallucinations and delusions "burn out" by midlife. Further, there appear to be a number of different adult schizophrenic careers, with some patients only infrequently re-hospitalized, functioning effectively in major adult roles.

Little is known about changes in the expression of symptoms or regarding differences in posthospital adjustment as these factors are related to the continuing parent-offspring relationship. It is possible that as these offspring enter middle age and their parents become elderly, much of the earlier conflict between the generations will disappear. As primary symptoms disappear over middle and later life, much of the communication deviance said to characterize families with schizophrenic offspring may also disappear. Comparative study of the adult life-course of so-called schizogenic and well families is much needed.

FAMILIAL STRAIN AND RECIPROCAL SOCIALIZATION: COMPARISON OF THE TWO ILLNESS PATTERNS

Consideration of the literature on parents of offspring with cancer and with schizophrenia reveals some interesting parallels between the two disorders. Moreover, results from family studies in oncology may be useful in understanding the parental role strain encountered by parents of schizophrenic offspring. Problems in each area may best be understood in terms of the reciprocal socialization that occurs among parents and their progeny. While this model of forward and reverse socialization can be said to characterize all familial interaction, reciprocal effects may be especially important, given the unpredictable nature of each illness and modes of treatment, which are complex and difficult for patient and family.

The assumption that socialization effects are reciprocal implies that stress also is shared reciprocally between parents and ill offspring. To some extent, this leads to a shared "stake" in management of role strain and life stress, which may help to cement bonds across generations. This is manifested in the frequent efforts of schizophrenic offspring to return home, even to highly critical and hostile parents. In cancer, this bond is evident in the efforts of ill children to protect their parents by feigning ignorance regarding impending death and hiding their anxiety. Despite normatively governed developmental needs for independence, separation, and individuation, seriously ill children know that they depend on their parents to a greater degree than well offspring. Victims of each kind of disorder often view themselves as a burden to their parents, a definition that may be reinforced by the attitudes and behavior of other siblings.

The highly dependent nature of the parent-child bond, both in cancer and schizophrenia, runs counter to the typical life course pattern of increasing autonomy between parents and children during adolescence and young adulthood. Serious illness among offspring presents parents with demands for continued provision of primary care, and the passage of time does not bring relief from these obligations. In fact, in the case of each illness, continued responsibilities for skilled nursing care extend primary parental caretaking long after the early childhood years. Often, the required skills are highly emotional, such as cajoling a daughter with cancer to eat even when nauseous from chemotherapy or persuading a paranoid son to take his Thorazine or to voluntarily sign himself into a hospital. Generally, this continued provision of primary care is off-time, in the sense that such care is more often expected for much younger children.

Each illness has been addressed through major improvements in treatment methods over the past three decades. Today, offspring with both disorders are likely to experience remission; during these healthy periods each generation may come to hope that the illness will end. This factor is important, because other chronic childhood illnesses such as mental retardation and spina bifida do not display dormant phases in which symptoms recede.

To some extent, these rapid medical advances in treatment have created a cultural lag (Ogburn, 1946) or lacuna of normative guidelines for parental behavior. The re-entry of cancer and mental patients into the community has presented parents with a new set of parenting imperatives accompanied by a lack of historical tradition or normative consensus. As a result, parents of offspring with cancer and schizophrenia must deal with the effects of social stigma and serious role ambiguity as they struggle with strains in realization of the parental role.

In the allocation of responsibility for parenting, mothers experience disproportionate obligations and are generally charged with managing the child's illness in cases of both cancer and schizophrenia. In addition to greater responsibility, women are also likely to feel greater guilt than men. The mother of a cancer patient may blame herself for physical harm to her unborn child during pregnancy through smoking, diet, or exposure to carcinogens. Similarly, the mother of a schizophrenic is likely to fault herself for inadequate socialization, given our cultural tendency to hold women responsible for their offspring's emotional development. Mothers of children with either illness blame themselves for being unable to relieve their child's suffering, making helplessness a prominent feature of mothering under these circumstances.

Fathers of offspring with cancer are vulnerable because of their lack of involvement in the child's illness. Social definitions of the father's role support his reluctance to become involved with the ill child and encourage his withdrawal into work. Those fathers who do try to become involved may encounter exclusion or simple lack of encouragement to parent their offspring. To date, it is not clear whether fathers of offspring with psychotic disorders experience responses similar to fathers of children with cancer.

Fathers and mothers also differ in the extensiveness of their support networks. In both illnesses, fathers are less likely to attend meetings of support groups while mothers tend to gravitate toward each other, sharing stories about each child's behavior and status (Heffron et al., 1973; Sheehan, 1982). Within their own families, women are more likely than men to turn to their parents, particularly their mothers. At the same time, there are some aspects of caring for the child that are too difficult for parents to share, even with other family members. In the terminal stages of cancer, when seriously disfigured children need basic physical care, or in profound schizophrenic episodes, when offspring are violent and abusive, parents—particularly mothers—feel it necessary to bear the burden of care alone. The sense that no one except medical and psychiatric professionals understands how difficult it is to parent such an ill child increases feelings of loneliness and lack of social consensus regarding how to define appropriate responses. The deleterious effects of treatment for each illness (severe nausea, baldness, and organ damage in cancer, and permanent, Parkinsonian side effects in schizophrenia) injects an additional element of uncertainty into parental decision making regarding the most appropriate way to proceed. The ambiguity of the child's medical management, then, creates more parental role strain.

Even during periods of remission, parents both anticipate and dread the return of symptoms; in fact, the strain of waiting and watching takes an emotional toll on all family members. Parents of children with cancer may resent their offspring's attempts to act as socializing agents. In schizophrenia, parental pessimism can become self-fulfilling as offspring respond to their parents' feelings of disappointment and anger with increased expression of psychotic symptoms.

CONCLUSION

The experiences of parents of severely ill children suggest that an appropriate model of familial socialization must include both forward and reverse processes so that the direction of effects is viewed as reciprocal rather than one-way. Additional research regarding the experience of parenting schizophrenic offspring is needed in a framework similar to that used in studies of parents whose children have cancer. For too long, the study of schizophrenia and the family has been concerned with issues of origins rather than with the impact of the illness on family relationships. It is now necessary to move beyond the earlier focus on parental contribution to the determination of psychiatric symptoms. Exploring the influence of reciprocal socialization and role strain on parents' definitions of familial bonds may lead to a better understanding of the effects of mental illness upon the larger family unit.

REFERENCES

Bateson, G., Jackson, D., Haley, J., & Weakland, J. (1956). Toward a theory of schizophrenia. *Behavioral Science, 1,* 351–164.

Beck, J., & Worthen, K. (1972). Precipitating stress, crisis theory, and hospitalization in schizophrenia and depression. *Archives of General Psychiatry, 26,* 123–129.

Bell, R. Q. (1964). The effect on the family of a limitation in coping ability of the child: A research approach and a finding. *Merrill-Palmer Quarterly, 10,* 129–142.

Bell, R. Q. (1968). A reinterpretation of the direction of effects in studies of socialization. *Psychological Review, 75,* 81–95.

Bell, R. Q., & Harper, L. (1977). *Child effects on adults.* Hillsdale, NJ: Lawrence Erlbaum Associates.

Benedek, T. (1973). Discussion of parenthood as a developmental phase. In T. Benedek, *Psychoanalytic investigations: Selected papers.* New York: Quadrangle Books.

Bengtson, V., & Black, K. (1973). Intergenerational relations and continuities in socialization. In P. Baltes & K. Schaie (Eds.), *Life-span developmental psychology: Personality and socialization* (pp. 208–234). New York: Academic Press.

Berger, P., & Kellner, H. (1964). Marriage and the construction of reality. *Diogenes, 45,* 1–25.

Binger, C. M., Albin, A. R., Feuerstein, R. C., Kushner, J. H., Zoger, S., & Mikkelsen, C. (1969). Childhood leukemia: Emotional impact on patient and family. *The New England Journal of Medicine, 280,* 414–418.

Bluebond-Langner, M. (1978). *The private worlds of dying children.* Princeton, NJ: Princeton University Press.

Bozeman, M., Orbach, C., & Sutherland, A. (1955). Psychological impact of cancer and its treatment. III: The adaptation of mothers to the threatened loss of their children through leukemia. *Cancer, 8,* 1–19.

Brim, O. G., Jr., & Ryff, C. (1980). On the properties of life events. In P. Baltes & O. G. Brim, Jr. (Eds.), *Life-Span Development and Behavior, 3* (pp. 368–388). New York: Academic Press.

Brown, G., Carstairs, G., & Topping, G. (1958). Post-hospital adjustment of chronic mental patients. *Lancet, 2,* 685–689.

Burr, W. (1973). *Theory construction and the sociology of the family.* New York: Wiley.

Chodoff, P., Friedman, S., & Hamburg, D. (1964). Stress, defenses and coping behavior: Observations in parents of children with malignant disease. *American Journal of Psychiatry, 120,* 743–749.

Chodrow, N. (1978). *The reproduction of mothering: Psychoanalysis and the sociology of gender.* Berkeley: University of California Press.

Coddington, M. (1976). A mother's struggles to cope with her child's deteriorating illness. *Maternal-Child Nursing Journal, 5,* 39–44.

Cohler, B. (1982). Personal narrative and life course. In P. B. Baltes & O. G. Brim, Jr. (Eds.), *Life-Span Development and Behavior, Volume 4* (pp. 206–243). New York: Academic Press.

Cohler, B. (1983). Autonomy and interdependence in the family of adulthood: A psychological perspective. *The Gerontologist, 23,* 33–39.

Cohler, B., & Boxer, A. (1984). Middle adulthood: Settling into the world—person, time and context. In D. Offer & M. Sabshin (Eds.), *Normality and the life cycle: A critical integration* (pp. 145–203). New York: Basic Books.

Cohler, B., & Ferrono, C. (in press.) Schizophrenia and the life-course. In N. Miller & G. Cohen (Eds.), *Schizophrenia and aging.* New York: Guilford.

Cohler, B., & Grunebaum, H. (1981). *Mothers, grandmothers, and daughters: Personality and child-care in three generation families.* New York: Wiley.

Comaroff, J., & Maguire, P. (1981). Ambiguity and the search for meaning: Childhood leukemia in the modern clinical context. *Social Science and Medicine, 15,* 115–123.

Cook, J. A. (1982). *The adjustment of parents following the death of a child from terminal illness.* Unpublished doctoral dissertation, The Ohio State University, Columbus.

Cook, J. A. (1983a). A death in the family: Parental bereavement in the first year. *Suicide and Life-Threatening Behavior, 13,* 42–61.

Cook, J. A. (1983b). An interdisciplinary look at feminist methodology: Ideas and practice in sociology, history, and anthropology. *Humboldt Journal of Social Relations, 10,* 127–152.

Cook, J. A. (1984). Influence of gender on the problems of parents of fatally ill children. *Journal of Psychosocial Oncology, 2,* 71–91.

Cook, J. A., & Wimberley, D. (1983). If I should die before I wake: Religious commitment and adjustment to the death of a child. *Journal for the Scientific Study of Religion, 22,* 222–238.

Doyle, A., Gold, D., & Moskovitz, D. (1984). *Children in Families under Stress.* San Francisco: Jossey-Bass.

Elder, G., & Rockwell, R. (1978). Economic depression and post-war opportunity: A study of life-patterns and health. In R. Simmons (Ed.), *Research in community and mental health* (pp. 249–304). Greenwich, CT: JAI Press.

Fromufod, A. (1980). Chronically ill institutionalized children: Psychosocial effects of prolonged hospitalization of the terminally sick child. *Social Science and Medicine, 14,* 239–242.

Futterman, E., & Hoffman, I. (1970). Shielding from awareness: An aspect of family adaptation to fatal illness in children. *Archives of the Foundation of Thanatology, 2,* 23–34.

Gershenson, H. (1983). *The ecology of childrearing in white families with adolescent mothers.* Unpublished doctoral dissertation, The University of Chicago.

Gilligan, C. (1982). *In a different voice: Psychosocial theory of women's development.* Cambridge, MA: Harvard University Press.

Glenn, N. (1975). Psycho-social well being in the post-parental stage: Some evidence from national surveys. *Journal of Marriage and the Family, 37,* 105–110.

Gottesman, I., & Shields, J. (1982). *Schizophrenia: The epigenetic puzzle.* New York: Cambridge University Press.

Gutmann, D. (1975). Parenthood: A key to the comparative study of the life-cycle. In N. Datan & L. Ginsberg (Eds.), *Life-span developmental psychology: Normative life crises* (pp. 167–184). New York: Academic Press.

Gyulay, J. (1978). *The dying child.* New York: McGraw-Hill.

Hagestad, G. (1981). Problems and promises in the social psychology of intergenerational relations. In R. Fogel, E. Hatfield, S. Kiesler, & E. Shanas (Eds.), *Aging: Stability and change in the family* (pp. 11–46). New York: Academic Press.

Hamovitch, M. B. (1964). *The parent and the fatally ill child: A demonstration of parent participation in a hosital pediatrics department.* Los Angeles: Delmare.

Haracz, J. L. (1982). The dopamine hypothesis: An overview of studies with schizophrenic patients. *Schizophrenia Bulletin, 8,* 438–469.

Heffron, W., Bommelaere, K., & Masters, R. (1973). Group discussions with parents of leukemic children. *Pediatrics, 52,* 831–840.

Hill, R. (1949). *Families under stress: Adjustment to the crises of war separation and reunion.* New York: Harper/Harper & Row.

Hoffman, I., Futterman, E. (1971). Coping with waiting: Psychiatric intervention and study in the waiting room of a pediatric oncology clinic. *Comprehensive Psychiatry, 12,* 67–81.

Hultsch, D., & Plemons, J. (1979). Life events and life-span development. In P. Baltes & O. G.

Brim, Jr. (Eds.), *Life-span development and behavior, Vol. 2* (pp. 1-36). New York: Academic Press.

Johnson, F., Rudolph, L., & Hartmann, J. (1979). Helping the family cope with childhood cancer. *Childhood Cancer, 20,* 241-251.

Kety, S. (1982). Neurochemical and genetic bases of psychopathology. *Behavior Genetics, 12,* 93-100.

Klebanoff, L. (1959). Parents of schizophrenic children. *American Journal of Orthopsychiatry, 29,* 445-454.

Klein, D. (1983). Family problem solving and family stress. In H. McCubbin, M. B. Sussman, & J. Patterson (Eds.), *Social stress and the family: Advances and developments in family stress theory and research* (Marriage and Family Review Series, Vol. 6, No. 1 & 2) (pp. 85-112).

Knudson, A. & Natterson, J. (1960). Participation of parents in the hospital care of their fatally ill children. *Pediatrics, 26,* 482-490.

Kreisman, D., & Joy, V. (1976). The family as reactor to the mental illness of a relative. In M. Guttentag & E. Struening (Eds.), *Handbook of evaluation research, volume 2* (pp. 483-516). Beverly Hills, CA: Sage.

Kübler-Ross, E. (1969). *On death and dying.* New York: Macmillan.

Lascari, A. (1969). The family and the dying child: A compassionate approach. *Medical Times, 97,* 207-215.

Leff, J. (1976). Schizophrenia and sensitivity to the family environment. *Schizophrenia Bulletin, 2,* 566-574.

Lerner, R., & Spanier, R. (1978). *Child influences on marital and family interaction.* New York: Academic Press.

Lidz, T., Fleck, S., Cornelison, A. & Associates. (1965). *Schizophrenia and the Family.* New York: International Universities Press.

Lopata, H. (1975). Widowhood: Social factors in life-span disruptions and alternatives. In N. Datan & L. H. Ginsberg (Eds.), *Life-span developmental psychology: Normative life crises* (pp. 218-236). New York: Academic Press.

McCubbin, H., & Patterson, J. (1983). The family stress process: The double ABCX model of adjustment and adaptation. In H. McCubbin, M. B. Sussman, & J. Patterson (Eds.), *Social stress and the family: Advances and developments in family stress theory and research* (Marriage and Family Review Series, Vol. 6, No. 1 & 2) (pp. 7-38). New York: Haworth Press.

Mishler, E., & Waxler, N. (Eds.). (1968). *Family processes and schizophrenia.* New York: Science House/Aronson.

Natterson, J., & Knudson, A. (1960). Observations concerning fear of death in fatally ill children and their mothers. *Psychosomatic Medicine, 22,* 456-465.

Neugarten, B., & Hagestad, G. (1976). Age and the life-course. In R. H. Binstock & E. Shanas (Eds.), *Handbook of aging and the social sciences* (pp. 35-55). New York: Van Nostrand Reinhold.

Obetz, S., Swenson, W., McCarthy, C., Gilchrist, G., & Burgert, E. (1980). Children who survive malignant disease: Emotional adaptation of the children and their families. In J. Schulman & M. Kupet (Eds.), *The child with cancer.* Springfield, IL: Charles Thomas.

Ogburn, W. F. (1946). *The social effects of aviation.* Boston: Houghton-Mifflin.

Pearlin, L. (1975). Sex roles and depression. In N. Datan & L. Ginsberg (Eds.), *Life-span developmental psychology: Normative life crises.* New York: Academic Press.

Pearse, M. (1977). The child with cancer: Impact on the family. *Journal of School Health,* March, 174-179.

Rapoport, R., Rapoport, R., Strelitz, Z., & Kew, S. (1977). *Fathers, mothers, and society: Towards new alliances.* New York: Basic Books.

Reese, H., & Smyer, M. (1983). The dimensionalization of life events. In E. Callahan & K. McCluskey (Eds.), *Life-span developmental psychology: Non-normative life events* (pp. 1-34). New York: Academic Press.

Richmond, J., & Waisman, H. (1955). Psychologic aspects of management of children with malignant diseases. *AMA Journal of Diseases of Children, 89,* 42–47.

Rosow, I. (1976). Status and role change through the life span. In R. Binstock & E. Shanas (Eds.), *Handbook of aging and the social sciences* (pp. 457–482). New York: Van Nostrand Reinhold.

Rossi, A. (1968). Transition to parenthood. *Journal of Marriage and the Family, 30,* 26–39.

Rossi, A. (1980). Aging and parenthood in the middle years. In P. Baltes & O. G. Brim, Jr. (Eds.), *Life-span development and behavior,* Volume 3 (pp. 137–205). New York: Academic Press.

Roth, J. (1963). *Timetables: Structuring the passage of time in hospital treatment and other careers.* Indianapolis: Bobbs-Merrill.

Share, L. (1972). Family communication in the crisis of a child's fatal illness: A literature review and analysis. *Omega, 3,* 187–201.

Sheehan, G. (1982). *Is there no place on earth for me?* New York: Houghton-Mifflin.

Snyder, S. N. (1978). Dopamine and Schizophrenia. In L. C. Wynne, R. Cromwell, & S. Matthysse (Eds.), *The nature of schizophrenia: New approaches to research and treatment* (pp. 87–94). New York: Wiley.

Toch, R. (1972). Too young to die. In B. Schroenberger, A. C. Carr, D. Peretz, & A. Kutscher (Eds.), *Psychosocial aspects of terminal care.* New York: Columbia University Press.

Valone, K., Norton, J., Goldstein, M., & Doane, J. (1983). Parental expressed emotion and affective style in an adolescent sample at risk for schizophrenia spectrum disorders. *Journal of Abnormal Psychology, 92,* 399–407.

Vernick, J., & Karon, M. (1965). Who's afraid of death on a leukemia ward? *American Journal of Diseases of Children, 109,* 393–397.

Videka-Sherman, L. (1982). Coping with the death of a child: A study over time. *American Journal of Orthopsychiatry, 52,* 688–698.

Waechter, E. (1971). Childrens' awareness of fatal illness. *American Journal of Nursing, 71,* 1168–1172.

Waxler, N. (1974). Parent and child effects on cognitive performance: An experimental approach to the etiological and responsive theories in schizophrenia. *Family Process, 13,* 1–22.

Wynne, L. (1981). Current concepts about schizophrenia and family relationships. *Journal of Nervous and Mental Disease, 169,* 82–89.

Zubin, J., & Steinhauer, S. (1981). How to break the logjam in schizophrenia: A look beyond genetics. *Journal of Nervous and Mental Disease, 169,* 447–492.

11

Elder Abuse Resulting From Caregiving Overload in Older Families

Eloise Rathbone-McCuan
University of Vermont
Social Work Program

Elder abuse is a seriously neglected topic. Efforts to raise the issue often reveal that experienced professionals find the problem too threatening to discuss. They prefer less controversial gerontological topics such as retirement and bereavement, which as normative events carry minimal social stigma. Many dimensions of the problem of elder abuse are centered in the structure and function of family life where violence is generated, tolerated, and transferred within and across generations.

Socialization patterns among generations of family members, especially the elderly and their grown children, can best be understood through a lifespan approach. The shifts in family decision making and control, expectations about dependency and meeting needs, and family member priorities are part of life cycle changes. When generational lines move to give authority once held by the oldest family members to younger generations, there is the possibility of either smooth progression in developmental tasks or tension and conflict in the transitions.

That adult children abuse their elderly parents challenges the traditional assumption that aggressive behavior moves only downward in the generational system. Cycles of violence spread in numerous directions. Seemingly, no subsystem in the family is immune to being abusive or suffering from abuse. The adult child and aged parent subsystem is clearly no exception.

This chapter provides an analysis of how older family members, especially adult children and aged parents, experience disruption in caregiving to impaired elders as the result of complex factors producing "caregiver overload." It links intergenerational conflict and dysfunctional relationships to a particular subset of caregiving outcomes categorized as elder abuse and neglect. A summary of the present state of knowledge about multiple types of elder victimization provides a context for understanding the specific type of abuse resulting from family actions or inactions.

A critical review of current research suggests that the limitations of these studies are the partial explanation for the limited knowledge base from which to plan intervention and prevention services. Two preliminary causal theories are discussed. Both attempt to clarify how behavioral patterns and social conditions surrounding family-provided care may result in elder abuse. These theories suggest a direction for practitioner activities.

The theories also offer a basis for linking theories of family violence, life cycle shifts in older families, and clinical practice theory into a comprehensive framework. At present, practitioners are required to intervene in cases of elder abuse without knowing why the problem occurred or how to treat what they perceive to be a new form of family pathology. Although the convergence of different theoretical areas would by itself be no panacea easing the difficult task of intervention, such a convergence might suggest ideas or even verify the importance of interpersonal and situational variables accessible to change.

The process of practitioner assessment and intervention is considered from the standpoint of family behavior and the larger service environment where resources are available. From this discussion of detection and case evaluation, a range of alternative interventions is suggested. Two family-directed therapies have been selected for consideration. They represent a cluster of therapies that are potentially applicable to cases of elder abuse. The Task-Centered Practice approach, which I employed in a recent study, is discussed in light of its field-tested outcome. The second approach is the Child-Abusive Family Intervention method now being applied in the Medical Center at the University of Mississippi. That treatment scheme is derived from social learning and behavior change principles.

VICTIMIZATION OF THE ELDERLY

Victimization describes many conditions that result in maltreatment of the elderly (Kosberg, 1983a). Victimology, as a broad social science theory, provides an organizing framework to understand more about the dynamics of maltreatment (Viano, 1983). Three broad categories of risk dominate the theme of elder maltreatment: (a) institutionalization; (b) community life; and (c) family systems. The maltreatment that takes place in each category has an individual and environmental domain, and the specific problems within each are frequently the result of interactions among the domains.

The theme of the elderly as victims of specific and generic losses has long characterized gerontological research. Victimization has a psychological impact on the individual who encounters some combination of social, emotional, economic and health changes that translate into personal loss. Minor and major transitions are required if the person is to adapt successfully and continue to grow and develop in later life (Schlossberg, 1984). Losses occur in a broader sociological context, since America is an aging society. Large numbers of elders can be at risk by such factors as:

1. RETIREMENT INCOME
   Inadequate Social Security benefits
   Reduced employee pensions
   Diminished assets
   Employment discrimination
   Partial welfare income assistance

2. HEALTH
   Insufficient health services
   Inappropriate health services
   Substandard institutional care
   Poorly trained health providers
   Uncoordinated service resources

These factors delineate some of the conditions that can victimize thousands of the older cohort (age 55 to 60), the elderly cohort (ages 65 to 74), the aged cohort (ages 75 to 84) and the very old (85 years and over). The victimizing impact of these trends becomes greater, perhaps increasing a million cases per year, as large numbers of the current population reach very advanced stages in the aging process.

Health Care Environments and Elder Victimization

Institutional environments (hospitals and nursing homes) play a major role in the lives of the elderly. For most elderly people, institutionalization is experienced as a short stay in the hospital. Rates of hospitalization increased 55% between 1965 and 1981. For a smaller proportion of elders, largely from very old cohorts, contacts with institutional environments include both hospitals and nursing homes. On a given day, seven out of every 100 persons 75 to 84 years of age and one out of every five persons 85 and older are in nursing homes.

Too little attention has been given to the maltreatment elders experience in the context of receiving health services and in the settings where they receive short or longterm care. Health care workers victimize elderly patients through stereotypical attitudes that get translated into interactions with the aged patient (Solomon, 1983). In the hospital, preferential treatment is sometimes given to the younger patient whose acute problems can be resolved, compared with older patients who have irreversible chronic conditions. This differential treatment can begin in the emergency room admission, where the younger acute patient is given priority care over the aged person, whose symptoms are often of a chronic nature in an acute phase. While in hospital, younger patients continue to receive priority for surgical and rehabilitative procedures as well as in use of diagnostic medical technology. Under these circumstances the elderly patient can withdraw, regress, and become depressed and isolated.

No part of the acute hospital experience is more victimizing than the discharge phase. Reimbursement pressure for quick discharge, needed bed space, limited personnel to handle hospital departure, and general indifference about the aftermath of acute care produces forms of maltreatment. Sometimes no time is spent interacting with the patient, explaining discharge as a process or considering the choice of alternatives to be used after leaving hospital.

During the discharge process an elderly person frequently makes a transition from acute to long-term environments such as nursing homes. Significantly greater attention has been given to the victimization of elders who are nursing home patients. Fraud and abuse operate in these settings (Halamandaris, 1983). Stathopoulos (1983) pointed out the typical types of elderly abuse: (a) financial abuse where personal funds are stolen or misused; (b) civil rights abuse that violates privacy and provision of information; (c) neglect that includes inattention to the patient and environmental conditions; and (d) physical and psychological abuse. Sometimes treatment regimes are modified, or prescribed medications are reduced to cut costs. A pervasive practice that reflects multiple forms of maltreatment is promotion of learned helplessness among nursing home patients (Mercer, 1983).

These hospital and institutional settings can also play a very positive function in the treatment of abused elders. The acute hospital environment can offer a place to detect, report, and treat injuries from direct abuse or neglect. In numerous cases, nursing homes become a safe and comfortable haven for aged persons who would otherwise be maltreated by their caregivers or endangered if left alone in the community. The experiences of individual elders within these environments can either promote or reduce victimization experiences, depending on the overall quality of the long-term care facility.

Community Environments and Elder Victimization

Fraud, fear of crime, and other dimensions of community-based problems have meaning for understanding in-home and family-connected elder abuse. It is sometimes assumed that the elderly are better protected against maltreatment and victimization if they live with or very close to family. This is a false assumption if generalized to all the aged. Abuse and neglect occur in the home environment within the context of multigenerational family interactions. The fear of negative outcomes of family care is present among the elderly, especially for the group that contemplates future dependency with great uncertainity. The themes that are part of this fear, often not verbalized, are connected to both their own fate and those of their children. Feeling like a burden is not more or less comforting than considering what the future holds if the family does not provide the care and there is no known option.

This broad category of community-based victimization can be divided into illegal activities and crimes that make elderly people victims, and broader community conditions that increase risk. Consequences of victimization involve injuries, need for medical care, loss of routine activity performance, and destruction of property and valuables. These possibilities can create fears that disrupt the elderly's associational patterns (Liang & Sengstock, 1983). The rates of personal victimization may vary with socio-demographic characteristics.

Frauds against the elderly are numerous and diverse. They include fradulent in-home work schemes, sales securities and franchises, distributorships, and commodities, land and home improvements, funeral plans, medical aids and devices, pensions and insurances and medical quackery. Intimates as well as strangers may perpetuate these frauds. Consumer education would protect the elderly from strangers, but it might not alter situations where trusted family members or friends are privately manipulating the elder's resources.

Of all the variables associated with criminal victimization, fear of crime is the most perplexing and disruptive to the routines of elders. No single variable can explain the fear, but the results foster isolation (Rathbone-McCuan and Hashimi, 1982). The degree varies with the individual and community environment. Finley (1983) suggested that research into the fear of criminal victimization should take three directions:

1. information on the personality and affective correlates of very fearful and less fearful persons in similar environments and demographic circumstances
2. experimental testing of the causal theories of fear
3. general methodological refinements to improve conceptual and scientific quality of the research.

In this section, victimology and specific types of maltreatment were discussed. Family life and the home environment, despite our cultural belief in the home as sanctuary, are part of the spectrum of endangering situations the elderly face. The remainder of this chapter explores the problem of elder abuse in the context of the family system. Major attention is given to linking research and theory with potential treatment strategies for family care givers at risk of, or actually engaged in, elder abuse.

ELDER ABUSE AS A FAMILY DYNAMIC

Elder abuse within the intergenerational network context represents family dysfunction. If the problem is detected and intervention provided, there can be improvement in the family dynamics whether or not the elder continues to live in the same household with the abusive member. This section reviews studies of elder abuse in the broader context of research on older families.

Studies that explore the general dynamics of older two and three generational family units tend to indicate strong bondings and mutual regard among the generations. The capacity to deal with the problems of caregiving are managable so that informal care continues to be the major assistance given the frail, noninstitutionalized aged living alone or with younger family members. The first studies on elder abuse were a deviation from the general research on older families. Practitioners were seeing cases of abuse in the community but did not trust their suspicion of family abuse or neglect. Interest in this problem resulted from recognition that some families were deviating from the positive norm of elder care giving.

Potential stress from overload was suggested by some of the researchers as the cause for many types of family dysfunction. They hypothesized limits to what could be expected from families in helping aged members. Kuypers and Bengtson (1983) reflected this caution. "Given the data and personal observations of the intensive ambivalence encountered by family members as they adapt to their aging family, we must caution against the notion that more equals better and closer equals happier" (p. 220).

An extensive survey of adult children's care giving tasks and their attitudes toward these responsibilities was framed as a study of the younger generation carrying the responsibility of elder care. Cicirelli (1983) noted the following:

> When there is a mismatch between the kind of behavior an elderly person expects of a child and the way adult children interpret and carry out the filial role in middle age, there is likely to be conflict . . . interpersonal conflicts between parent and child can interfere with help to the parent when the conflict has been long standing . . . however, positive and negative feelings can coexist in the relationship — the existence of conflict would not necessarily interfere with the helping behavior (pp. 36-37).

An unknown proportion of families experience conflict in the process of elder care giving. Physical abuse and intentional failure to provide care are extreme expressions of conflict found in a very small number of family care giving efforts. But it is abuse and the possibility of willful neglect that lead domestic violence specialists and gerontologists to attempt to investigate this as a syndrome falling into the continuum of family violence. In its most extreme form, elder abuse consists of the active physical abuse of an elderly dependent person in the home of a relative, often an adult child. In its most common and less dramatic form, elder abuse includes exploitation, neglect, and psychological mistreatment (Giordano & Giordano, 1984).

Douglass and Hickey (1983) reviewed recent research on elder abuse and neglect. Table 11.1 presents a summary of the methods employed in these studies. The mailed surveys conducted by O'Malley, Segars, Perez, and Associates (1979) and Block and Sinnott (1979) provide a measure of the extent to which practitioners in the field actually report cases of elder abuse. The study conducted by Douglass, Hickey, and Noël (1980) in Michigan produced a significant advance on the data base of the problem. They provided information about where and how to identify cases, suggested alternative exploratory hypotheses, and raised many questions for future research.

Table 11.2 demonstrates the variation in the definition of elder abuse and neglect. Douglass and Hickey (1983) discussed the conceptual overlap between concepts of abuse and neglect and what was an active or inactive response by the care givers. Intentionality on the part of the abuser is another dimension of abuse, however, it is the most difficult factor to measure. Pedrick-Cornell and Gelles (1982) indicate that there is conceptual justification for including a diversity of acts and behaviors as part of the phenomenon because research is still in the exploratory phase. Giordano and Giordano (1984) suggest using the broad categories of physical abuse, negligence, financial exploitation, psychological abuse, violation of rights, and self-neglect as a preliminary categorical continuum of abuse. Each of these problems were identified as part of the larger elder abuse issue by the Select Committee on Aging (1980).

Hickey and Douglass (1981a, 1981b) have argued against providing prevalence and incidence statistics about elder abuse. They caution that current data is methodologically limited by isolated, respective, and nonrandom samples. All researchers conducting survey or case studies on this topic question their own prevalence estimates. Many problems complicate the collection of statistics. Since there is no uniform reporting procedure that operates in each state or a national unit charged with the collection of annual data, the commonly cited range of 500,000 to 2.5 million cases a year cannot be considered an accurate enough basis for forming national social policies on elder protective services (Giordano & Giordano, 1984).

Exploration of Some Reasons for Elder Abuse

Rathbone-McCuan and Hashimi (1982) provided a summary of the various hypothesized reasons for elder abuse. These include:

1. *The Revenge Framework*: based on the assumption that the abusers actually were or perceived themselves to have been mistreated in the past and thus ill treat the parent in the present.

TABLE 11.1

Characteristics of Elder Abuse Studies

Principal Author(s)	Release Date	Design(s)	Method(s) of Data Retrieval	Study Site(s)
Steinmetz	1978	Case studies	—	Delaware
Rathbone-McCuan	1978	Case studies	Hospital, emergency room, police	Greater St. Louis, MO
Lau, Kosberg	1978	Case studies	Case review	The Cleveland, Ohio Chronic Illness Center
O'Malley, Segars, Perez, Mitchell, Kneupfel	1979	Mail survey to general lists and selected individuals of health, human service, police and voluntary agencies and staff	Respondent—completed questionnaire 34% response rate	Massachusetts
Block, Sinnott	1979	Soliciting cases from selected agencies. Direct mail to elderly. Mail survey of medical, nursing social work and aging services personnel in Greater Washington, DC	Case solicitation. Direct mail survey to elderly-0.7% response rate. Direct mail survey of professionals, 31.4% response rate	Greater Washington, DC-Maryland Members of American Psychological Association, emergency room physicians and gerontological society
Douglass, Hickey, Noël	1980	Personal interviews with practitioners, providers; Police data analysis; Nursing home admission data analysis: 238 interviews + 15 anecdotal interviews	Personal interviews in field. 97% sample response rate. Secondary analyses of Detroit criminal data; Oakland County Michigan Medicare nursing home admission data	State of Michigan: City of Detroit Kent County (Grand Rapids) Lake County Marquette County (Marquette) Oakland County (Pontiac)

Note. From Douglass & Hickey (1983), p. 117.

TABLE 11.2
Operational Definitions of Elder Abuse

Lau, Kosberg (1979)	Block, Sinnott (1979)	O'Malley, et al (1979)	Douglass, Hickey, Noël (1980)
Physical Abuse	Physical Abuse	Physical Trauma	Physical Abuse
Direct beatings (hit frequently)	Bruises, welts	Bruises, welts, wounds, cuts,	Verbal-Emotional Abuse
Lack of personal care	Sprains, dislocations	punctures, bone fractures	Active Neglect
Lack of food	Malnutrition, lacerations, cuts,	abrasions, lacerations,	Passive Neglect
Lack of medical care	punctures	sprains, burns, scaldings	(Financial Abuse or Exploitation)
Lack of supervision	Direct Beating	Debilitating Mental Anguish	
Psychological Abuse	Lack of personal care	Malnutrition	
Verbal assault	Lack of food	Sexual Abuse	
Threat	Lack of supervision	Freezing	
Fear	Tied to bed		
Isolation	Tied to chair		
Material Abuse	Psychological Abuse		
Theft of money or property	Verbal assault		
Misuse of money or property	Threat		
Violation of Rights	Fear		
Forced from home	Isolation		
Forced from nursing home	Material Abuse		
	Theft of money or property		
	Misuse of money or property		
	Poor Residential Environment		

Note. From Douglass & Hickey (1983), p. 123.

2. *The Pathological Personality Framework*: based on a variety of psychoanalytic and psychodynamic theories of personality disorders that might explain aggressive behaviors that can be played out in intimate relationships.

3. *The Generational Transmission Framework*: assumes that violent behavior is transmitted from generation to generation as a learned behavior related to chronic stress management.

4. *Absence of Community Resource*: the assumption is that there is a lack of community resource to help carry the burden of care and the burden gets expressed in frustration through violent behavior.

5. *Functional Incompetency of Care Giver*: the responsible person is seriously functionally impaired, incapable of actually performing the care tasks.

6. *Economic Exploitation Framework*: a cluster of motivators operate to lead the care giver to misuse economic and material resources of an elderly person in order to preserve assets or gain control over them (pp. 179–182).

Each of these theories has been applied in some studies, but no single theory appears to explain elder abuse. A combination of them may, in fact, be more useful in explaining the phenomenon. Some further conceptual analysis is needed to order and integrate these hypotheses.

The description of the "typical" abused and/or neglected elder set forth by Douglass and Hickey (1983) continues to be confirmed by case descriptions given by practitioners in the field:

> The population at risk for domestic abuse or neglect can be identified as those elderly who are most vulnerable because of advanced age, frailty, chronic disease or physical or mental impairment . . . least capable of independent living and most dependent on others. They are less conscious of alternative living arrangements or means of support than others in their age cohort, and they are more likely to be aged women than men. On the average, victims will have two or more physical disabilities. . . . With the aged, unlike children who survive abuse, vulnerability increases over time. It is relatively uncommon for incidents of neglect or abuse to be isolated. . . . Episodes of abusive behavior can be expected to continue and increase in a specific family as a dependent older person ages, unless some form of intervention changes the family's circumstances. Racial, socioeconomic or other social criteria have not been found to identify population segments at higher risk (p. 122).

Specialists in domestic violence and social gerontology continue to approach the problem of causation at many levels. There is some agreement on the importance of the care giving relationship of family members, their coping patterns, stress levels, and isolation. The concept of "generationally inverse families" has been proposed to explain the dependence of the elderly person on children and the coping abilities of the care giver in the younger generation. When abuse or neglect is present in the context of elder care giving, it is associated with dependency, stress, and the tendency to use abusive conflict resolution techniques (Steinmetz, 1983; Steinmetz & Amsden, 1983). The dependency may be due to the elder's frail condition or related to social and behavior dependency of the adult child. Sometimes dependency needs in both generations feed into destructive interactions.

These issues were incorporated into a study of the problem of isolation, which is frequently present in families where there is elder abuse (Rathbone-McCuan & Hashimi, 1982). Several factors were identified that combined stress and isolation in the context of elder victimization. The daily life circumstances of the care giver were so burdening that, separate from the elder, these individuals had emotional and physical problems. Whatever the specific combinations of limitations of the adult care givers, they were incapable of providing care. Many should never have assumed the task of caring for the frail aged they eventually maltreated.

The search to explain the behaviors of the care giver should not be separated from consideration of the behaviors of the aged. The growth and developmental expectations of normal family life cycle behaviors may not be present in elder abusing families, possibly because of a failure of adult children to complete emotional tasks that prepare them to manage elder parent dependency. Steinmetz and Amsden (1983), reporting on the behaviors of elderly victims, indicated that they were seeking control in an out-of-control situation. Sixty percent of their sample of aged cases used pouting or withdrawal as a means of dealing with the conflict. Other psychological methods included manipulation, pitting one family member against another, and imposing guilt on the care giver for some inadequacy. These behaviors have a provoking influence on the care giver. Many elderly people may respond with some of these behaviors, but fortunately most care givers do not react with maltreatment.

Protective laws and services will not be enacted until a compelling body of research persuades policy makers of the widespread incidence of the problem. Fortunately many practitioners already are aware of a crisis and their own need to respond to it. Their service responsibilities include case detection, clinical assessment, service advocacy for the aged person, and sometimes clinical intervention with the family.

The next section deals with the complex issue of case assessment. It looks at effective directions to improve assessment activities. Some suggestions are adapted from new clinical work in the area of child abuse that seems relevant to the dynamics of older abusing families. Other models are mentioned in relation to intake and case planning.

ASSESSMENT OF ELDER ABUSE CASES

One way to approach the problem of elder abuse is through analysis of case dynamics. This method in no way substitutes for analysis of larger data bases provided by community surveys; however, it provides knowledge useful for intervention by contributing to an understanding of the causal dynamics.

When a suspected case is reported, detection is often completed by an investigator who gathers facts about the case that will be the bases for decisions about next steps. These steps could include referral for clinical treatment. With that referral should come case information that orients the practitioner to the general background of the case. From that point, the clinical expert conducts an assessment.

Case assessment takes place after a situation of abuse or neglect has been verified. Practitioners complete assessments for the purpose of providing specific treatment and monitoring its progress. Variations in format are required, depending on the location of the elder, for example, whether the elder is in the hospital or community. In the former setting, it is possible to utilize more health directed evaluation procedures to determine what medical risks are present. If the elder is in the community, in-home interviews can be conducted to evaluate the physical environment and its deficiencies for in-home care provision.

Adapting Approaches From Child Abuse Services

Practitioners have found it necessary to look outside the gerontology field for intervention models. If part of intervention is directed toward multigenerational problem solving, family therapies that apply a systems approach can be useful to an understanding of sources of conflict and communication breakdowns. These more generic family therapy approaches also highlight some of the historical patterns of family behavior. Some of the developmental gaps in the relationship between elder and adult child may be better understood and addressed in future counseling. One of the more promising intervention approaches is to offer one-to-one counseling to the care giver, to help the care giver learn alternative ways to manage stress, develop an alternative plan for care giving, and generally learn how to live effectively with an elder. Some of these issues have been important in treating child abusing parents (Kelly, 1984). They extend into the arena of older family life as well as in earlier stages, where child care management is a major family function.

Physically abusive behaviors toward the elderly must be conceptualized along a continuum of family interactions. Given the central role that care giving appears to play in elder abuse, it is that behavior, in all its complexities, that becomes the starting point for assessment. It may be assumed that at one end of the care-giving continuum are individuals who are never abusive, who rarely experience stress, and who utilize effective coping techniques to handle elder care giving. At the other end are care givers who are frequently abusive, continually experiencing stress, and having no ability to manage frustration other than through aggressive or harmful means (including passive neglect). Distributed between the extremes are care givers who may sometimes exhibit aggressive patterns and frustration and employ a variety of coping mechanisms of mixed effectiveness. For these care givers, abuse is a potential component of the care giving process.

This continuum of care giving is similar to the idea of a child management continuum that allows practitioners to make some estimates of management capabilities relative to child care. To clarify patterns, practitioners must gather detailed information about how the care provider gives assistance to the elder, what needs are being met through that care, the perceptions of the care giver about the need for assistance, the environment where care is given, and information about frustrations associated with the tasks.

Abusive care givers will respond aggressively to the elder if they have difficulty in finding other ways to cope with what they perceive as the demands of the situation. Aggressive behaviors may have a punitive aspect that ranges from very mild to very aggressive. Both for very young children and for frail elders, the slightly aggressive act has potential for causing serious damage. Assessments consider the severity of consequences individually because the consequences of harm differ according to the target of abuse.

A social learning approach to care giver assessment takes into account the style of care giving and the responsible person's manner of stress and anger management. A practitioner would want to learn how the care giver has gained information about performing tasks. Part of what is unknown about elder abuse is the extent to which care giving is performed by highly incompetent persons who are not equipped to fulfill care giving tasks.

Incorrect information, physical and psychological incompetencies, and actual physical tasks requiring more than one person are all common conditions that further burden the care giver (Rathbone-McCuan & Hashimi, 1982). In effective care giving situations, those providing care have been taught by persons qualified to teach them correct procedures. Part of that instruction becomes a matter of preparing family members for frustrations and alerting them to the importance of knowing when tasks become too difficult. The demand level of care could encompass the knowledge about procedures, physical strength and/or skill and mechanisms of coping with the elder's response.

Part of the assessment must extend to the behavioral responses of the elder. Assumptions about the elder's behavior should be avoided if possible. It is important not to "blame the victims" for causing their own plight but to consider the possibility that they may be making routine daily family functioning a crisis for all members. Practitioners should make direct observations in the care giving environment. Many elders do not easily accept care if they are in pain or mentally disoriented. Their attitudes toward the care-giving family member, feelings about being dependent, and perceptions of the situation may all influence their responses. They may be in a state of constant conflict with the care giver as a way of seeking some personal control. The life stage issues of control and interdependency start to manifest in the phases of early adulthood and continue as adult children and older parents deal with the balance of authority and responsibility between the generations.

If care givers rely on aggressive behaviors to manage elders, physical and verbal conflicts may be making the situation worse. As an elderly person's condition weakens, which is likely if he or she is frail, levels of aggressiveness increase to control a more tense episode. The assessment should be a way to understand intrapersonal dynamics of the care giver, the elder, and their interpersonal interactions. The next step of assessment moves into an environmental context.

Data from elderly protective service programs indicate how essential it is to draw on the full range of resources, both formal and informal, as part of the intervention. The next step in assessment moves into a community service environmental context. Many of the most difficult bases are beyond the point where informal resources can alter the situation. Case assessment needs to include determination of which agencies and services should and can aid the client and family. Austin (1981) has conceptualized the allocation of services into three distinct phases: screening, assessment, and care planning. These are activities that need to be performed with elder abuse cases. They are proposed in the service delivery model by Douglass and Hickey (1983).

An agency charged with elder protective service authority may serve only the aged or a diverse set of clients. The agency must be in a position to receive case referrals from all possible sources in the community. The key linkage agencies will vary with the community service structure. The reporting components are the first source of screening.

Kosberg (1983b) listed a number of factors that inhibit case reporting and found them explainable in view of the social stigma and dynamics of the problem. First, the elder may believe the problem is a family affair and should remain within its domain. Second, there is often a sense of stigma and fear of reprisal about further maltreatment if the victim makes a report. Third, the elderly person may feel guilty, as though the culprit (Lau & Kosberg, 1979). Most states have found that hot lines that keep the reporting person's name confidential and mandatory reporting laws are two ways to stimulate increased reports. Once the case is reported, preliminary judgments are made in the screening phase.

Gathering valid and reliable case data continues to be a major service priority. Who performs the intake and screening and when it occurs are two significant variables in the initial phase of all forms of domestic violence interventions. The individuals performing the screening need to have standardized procedures that afford them legal protection and a reliable strategy for assessment. These conditions are met in only a few of the agencies that handle elder abuse. Some programs lack funding to complete in-depth assessments involving multiple trips to the household, tracking down people who may be able to give information about the situation, and close supervision to guide the worker. Only 26 states have developed some form of elder abuse protection service law. In 1981, a survey was completed to determine the extent to which these states had responded through the creation of legal service supports. Of the 26 states with such laws, many have very limited statutory authority. Only 16 states had mandatory reporting Oakar & Miller, 1983). Effective case reporting and assessment depend upon an organizational service structure. New models for organizing resources for abused elders are needed to assist communities in service planning. Unless there is a system with resources for reporting, screening, and assessment, intervention effectiveness is lowered.

CASE INTERVENTION PLANNING AND IMPLEMENTATION

A case plan must be developed as a requirement for effective service. It is the guide for clinical treatment and service decisions. Because elder abuse services are often connected to public welfare agencies, there is a wide difference in the training of people who complete care planning. Interdisciplinary care planning is a luxury in many of these agencies. The provision of services to victims is rendered difficult when resources are controlled by different organizations, poorly linked together and seriously understaffed. Workers must contend with shortages of qualified clinicians to whom they can refer their clients for the provision of family counseling.

Many workers define family members, even those not directly involved in abuse, as part of the problem. Clinical intervention with the family system around the issues of elder abuse is at a primitive level of therapeutic development. Counseling involving the family is often excluded as a treatment recommendation because clinicians assume families won't be willing to enter counseling because of low motivation. This oversight has serious consequences because many elders will not leave the home situation, and the caregiver relationship and the abuse will continue. Leaving even an abusive situation is difficult for the elder, and court authority to make an involuntary relocation is frequently impossible to obtain. For better or worse, the care giver and elder may remain locked together, and the only possibility of change is to provide counseling involving the family network. Finding a counselor proves difficult. Family therapists may not want to deal with "old" families, who are viewed as less interesting than younger families. This attitude may be reinforced by their stereotypes about the aging process within the family system. Many clinicians do not want to deal with family abuse problems of any type. Families may not have the economic resources for counseling, and third party reimbursement often does not cover such expenses. Economics resources is a major problem if intervention requires paying for a homemaker, respite care, or day care. Combining supportive services with family counseling costs may be too expensive, even though these are all vital to changing the situation (Rathbone-McCuan, Travis, & Voyles, 1983).

It is useful to conceive broad intervention possibilities with older abusive families. To date, there has been no major effort to develop an intervention scheme that is especially or exclusively for elder abuse. Such an effort could have many starting points, depending on the orientation of the developer. A framework for starting to build an intervention paradigm might be the Family Support Cycle Framework. It conceptualizes intergenerational dynamics relevant to the give-and-take process of support and indicates some of the complex dynamics of role exchange and communication. The framework specifies theoretical issues that show breakdown in the intergenerational relationships (Kuypers & Bengtson, 1983). Elder abuse is one extreme example of breakdown in the support cycle, but the types of conditions leading to abuse can be found in many conflictual older families. A social science framework such as this one can be supplemented with specific clinical intervention models that direct treatment.

The family histories of older families are connected to present abuse. These need to be understood and selectively addressed in the intervention. One approach to treating these families emerged from an effort to combine social work practice theory and social gerontology. In the Task-Centered Approach, an intervention model developed from clinical social work research to sharpen the effective of short-term counseling is combined with the Family Support Cycle framework. For example, a practitioner would have the conceptual base for assessing causal factors and a specific treatment approach to follow. Rathbone-McCuan, Travis, and Voyles (1983) summarize the clinical field experience using the Task-Centered Approach with an elder abuse caseload:

> Given the diverse caseload, the intervention model must have relevance to either very rapid intervention approximating crisis intervention and/*or problems that are ongoing and chronic*. . . . Elders and care givers may need to learn new skills, especially if they wish to continue to live together and/or be independent. We would apply more care-giving skills training as a specific intervention...if time and resources permitted. (p. 366).

The Task-Centered model provides a way of organizing the clinical intervention. For the care giver, an important goal might be to improve the elder care management skills and, over time, change the care-giving style by reducing the stress associated with the performance of care tasks. Some aspects of the intervention may be directed toward the elder victim, however, work with the abusive care giver would come first (Fortune & Rathbone-McCuan, 1981).

While some care givers attempt to hide their frustrations, eventually the problem gets identified in the assessment. Cases treated in the Task-Centered field project showed that care givers experienced very high levels of frustration and reported being in constant conflict when they were attempting to manage the elder. Techniques for helping increase the coping capacity of the care giver and providing alternative skills has not been the focus of most elder abuse intervention. As with assessment, practitioners may find that some valuable ideas for treatment are emerging from child abuse research.

Kelley (1984) outlined several areas of child-abusive family therapy that seem to be transferable. Table 11.3 shows an adaptation of these methods as they would fit goals of elder management skills training. An assumption is made here that for some care givers, learning more effective ways of providing care and coping with giving care can reduce the level of conflict between the elder and the care giver. In addition to these two approaches, anger control skills training seems to be another applicable technique, especially as it regards prevention. These techniques have the potential of being useful to any adult child or other family member who has yet to face the demands of long-term home care. With the growing numbers of families that may be facing this situation, prevention of family overload is a first step to prevent elder abuse.

CONCLUSION

Extending some of the theoretical principles of life span development into an analysis of elder abuse could prove valuable to advance the status of causal and clinical research. The ability of each adult child to perform elder care giving tasks is connected to the dynamic of aged parent-adult child interactions. Complex behavioral and emotional factors associated with intergenerational interdependency and relationship management in elder abuse are life span concerns.

It is difficult to predict the future. It is hoped that society will begin to take a more serious look at this problem as citizens become more aware of the prevalence, variety, and severity of domestic violence in America. Abusing elderly dependent people has a variety of possible causes, but a large proportion of this violence is connected to care giving. As the social policies controlling resources for long-term care become more restrictive and less available to support costly community and in-home care, more informal care giving will result. Currently we see elder abuse operating in a society that does

TABLE 11.3
Training Approaches for the Abusing Care Giver

Training Abusing Care Givers to Use Non Aggressive Strategies	*Training Abusing Care Givers to Use Attention Withdrawal*
Goal: To increase care giver awareness of alternative care giving techniques leading to more effective elder management	Goal: To promote care giver awareness of their influence on key elder behaviors
Reviewing the appropriate approach to care tasks	Determining when the care giver should use attention withdrawal procedures
Giving information on the dysadvantages of inappropriate approaches	Teaching care giver to use the procedure correctly
Giving care giver a chance to express their view about appropriateness	Reviewing the rationale for using this approach
Teaching care giver when to use "time out" (a technique that has multiple steps involving selecting specific elder behaviors as target where frustrations need to be reduced, selecting the space for time out, linking the time out to the targeted behavior, setting up the time intervals)	Teaching how to apply it selectively and consistently
	Discussing the results produced by application of the procedures
Familiarize care givers with the need to be consistent and utilize a strategy to reinforce desired elder behaviors	

not usually mandate relatives to care for elderly family members. This may be changing as the result of increasing numbers of states begin to propose "filial support laws." The content of such laws implies financial responsibility for adult children to contribute to the cost of elder parent care. Families could eventually be mandated to provide care even in situations where the care is provided at great risk. Older families are part of the growing problem of domestic violence, which includes wife battering and child abuse. It is not a myth or a declining phenomenon; it is a fact, and changes in demographics and declining formal social service supports suggest that the problem is likely to increase among older families. Continued apathy about the problem and failure to develop national prevention efforts will contribute to increased prevalence of elder abuse.

REFERENCES

Austin, C. D. (1981). Client assessment in context. *Social Work Research and Abstracts, 17,* 4–12.

Block, M. R., & Sinnott, J. D. (1979). *The battered elder syndrome: An exploratory study.* (Final Report to the U.S. Administration on Aging). College Park: University of Maryland, Center on Aging.

Cicirelli, V. G. (1983). Adult children and their elderly parents. In T. H. Brubaker (Ed.), *Family relationships in later life* (pp. 31–46). Beverly Hills, Sage.

Douglass, R. L., & Hickey, T. (1983). Domestic neglect and abuse of the elderly: Research findings and a systems perspective for service delivery planning. In J. I. Kosberg (Ed.), *Abuse and maltreatment of the elderly: Causes and interventions* (pp. 115–133). Boston: John Wright.

Douglass, R. L., Hickey, T., & Noël, C. (1980). *A study of maltreatment of the elderly and other vulnerable adults.* (Final Report to the U.S. Administration on Aging and the Michigan Department of Social Services.) Ann Arbor: University of Michigan, Institute on Aging.

Finley, G. E. (1983). Fear of crime in the elderly. In J. I. Kosberg (Ed.), *Abuse and maltreatment of the elderly: Causes and interventions* (pp. 21–39). Boston: John Wright.

Fortune, A. E. & Rathbone-McCuan, E. (1981). Education in gerontological social work: Application of the task-centered model. *Journal of Education for Social Work, 17,* 98–105.

Giordano, N. H. & Giordano, J. A. (1984). Elder abuse: A review of the literature. *Social Work, 29,* 232–236.

Halamandaris, V. J. (1983). Fraud and abuse in nursing homes. In J. I. Kosberg (Ed.), *Abuse and maltreatment of the elderly: Causes and interventions* (pp. 104–114). Boston: John Wright.

Hickey, T. & Douglass, R. L. (1981a). Neglect and abuse of older family members: Professionals' perspectives and case experiences. *Gerontologist, 21,* 171–176.

Hickey, T. & Douglass, R. L. (1981b). Mistreatment of the elderly in the domestic setting. *American Journal of Public Health, 71,* 500–507.

Kelly, J. A. (1984). *Treating child abusive families: Intervention based on skills-training principles.* New York: Plenum Press.

Kosberg, J. I. (Ed.) (1983a). *Abuse and maltreatment of the elderly: Causes and interventions.* Boston: John Wright.

Kosberg, J. I. (1983b). The special vulnerability of elderly parents. In J. I. Kosberg (Ed.), *Abuse and maltreatment of the elderly: Causes and Interventions* (pp. 263–276). Boston: John Wright.

Kuypers, J. A. & Bengston, V. L. (1983). Toward competence in the older family. In T. H. Brubaker (Ed.), *Family relationships in later life* (pp. 211–228). Beverly Hills: Sage.

Lau, E. & Kosberg, J. I. (1979). Abuse of the elderly by informal care providers. *Aging,* pp. *299–300,* 10–15.

Liang, J. & Sengstock, M. C. (1983). Personal crimes against the elderly. In J. I. Kosberg (Ed.), *Abuse and maltreatment of the elderly: Causes and interventions* (pp. 40–67). Boston: John Wright.

Mercer, S. O. (1983). Consequences of institutionalization of the aged. In J. I. Kosberg (Ed.), *Abuse and maltreatment of the elderly: Causes and interventions* (pp. 84–103). Boston: John Wright.

Oakar, M. R. & Miller, C. A. (1983). Federal legislation to protect the elderly. In J. I. Kosberg (Ed.), *Abuse and maltreatment of the elderly: Causes and interventions* (pp. 422–436). Boston: John Wright.

O'Malley, H., Segars, H., Perez, R., & Associates (1979). *Elder abuse in Massachusetts* (a report). Boston, MA: Legal Research and Services for the Elderly.

Pedrick-Cornell, C. & Gelles, R. J. (1982). Elderly abuse: The status of current knowledge. *Family Relations 31,* 457–467.

Rathbone-McCuan, E. & Hashimi, J. (1982). *Isolated elders: Health and social interventions.* Rockville: Aspen Systems.

Rathbone-McCuan, E., Travis, A. & Voyles, B. (1983). Family intervention: Applying the task-centered approach. In J. I. Kosberg (Ed.), *Abuse and maltreatment of the elderly: Causes and interventions* (pp. 355–375). Boston: John Wright.

Schlossberg, N. K. (1984). *Counseling adults in transition: Linking practice with theory.* New York: Springer.

Select Committee on Aging, U.S. House of Representatives (1980). *Elder abuse: The hidden problem* (Committee Publication 96–220). Washington: U.S. Printing Office.

Solomon, K. (1983). Victimization by health professionals and the psychologic response to the elderly. In J. I. Kosberg (Ed.), *Abuse and maltreatment of the elderly: Causes and interventions* (pp. 150–171). Boston: John Wright.

Stathopoulos, P. A. (1983). Consumer advocacy and abuse of elders in nursing homes. In J. I. Kosberg (Ed.), *Abuse and maltreatment of the elderly: Causes and interventions* (pp. 335–354). Boston: John Wright.

Steinmetz, S. K. (1983). Dependency, stress, and violence between middle-aged caregivers and their elderly parents. In J. I. Kosberg (Ed.), *Abuse and maltreatment of the elderly: Causes and interventions* (pp. 134–149). Boston: John Wright.

Steinmetz, S. K. and Amsden, D. G. (1983). Dependent elders, family stress and abusive. In T. H. Brubaker (Ed.), *Family relationships in later life* (pp. 173–192). Beverly Hills: Sage.

Viano, E. C. (1983). Victimology: An overview. In J. I. Kosberg (Ed.), *Abuse and maltreatment of the elderly: Causes and interventions* (pp. 1–18). Boston: John Wright.

Author Index

Subject Index

t